To my sweet, Ms. Jones,

TAKE THE LEAD

*How every woman can take the lead in her life,
her community, and her world.*

ALICEANNE LOFTUS

*You are such a
positive light in my life.
I truly appreciate
you! xoxo,*

Aliceanne

Hardcover: 979-8-9851360-0-5

Paperback: 979-8-9851360-1-2

Ebook: 979-8-9851360-2-9

First paperback edition March 2022.

Edited by Jeni Chapelle

Cover art by Cutting Edge Studio

LoftHouse
PUBLISHING

Annapolis, Maryland

www.lofthousepublishing.com

To my daughter, Marissa. Shine bright, take up space, and lead your own way! Please know you are more than enough. The choices I have made in the present were built from the lessons of my past and for the dreams of your future.

TABLE OF CONTENTS

FOREWARD
By Jennifer Klepper

Remastered footage of the Beatles creating what became their final album went viral in 2021 with a clip of Paul McCartney composing the iconic "Get Back" in real time. At the tune's birth, it's a riff, a jaunty chord progression played out on a bass guitar. McCartney experiments, sometimes crescendoing into promising territory, other times hitting an odd note or a word babble that trails to nowhere. McCartney reverts, takes what worked, adds to it, and spins it in a different direction. He continues to iterate. Some discarded notes find their way back as he builds the chorus, structures the bridge, and adds words. Along the way, a tune, a song, *a classic* is revealed. The world watched in awe as McCartney and then the Beatles crafted this work in progress from inception to the masterpiece that made it onto millions of circles of pressed vinyl.

Why am I talking about a rock band in the foreword of AliceAnne Loftus's leadership memoir? To be fair, AliceAnne is a beautiful singer, and even by non-musical standards, she can be considered a rock star in her own right. But more importantly, AliceAnne exemplifies and celebrates the wealth and opportunity of a work in progress—its potential to be a masterpiece.

My life intersects with AliceAnne's in triplicate. Lifelong learners, we share a love of books, though her ability to consume words far-outpaces my own. As friends, we share the value of family (biological and chosen, immediate and generational) as a foundational force. And as women in business, we share a passion for community and the synergies of collaboration.

Every one of these intersections ties to *growth*: personal growth, growth of our loved ones, growth of our peers, and—always—living (and loving) ourselves as a work in progress.

Any creative and any businessperson knows the drill of a work in progress, whether it's a song, a new product, or a new storefront. And they may recognize that a work in progress is like life. You riff. You live a verse—whether that means a decade, a year, a week, or even a day. You see how that verse plays out. You take what worked, and you live your next verse revised, always iterating and learning from the past.

Some may say the Beatles achieved perfection with "Get Back," but the fact the Beatles themselves performed three versions of it in their famous rooftop concert proves that even a masterpiece can continue to be a work in progress. As AliceAnne relates in this book, perfection is a façade. What's real is resilience and living a life of self-reflection and purpose. What's real is being dedicated to discovering your truths and living them openly in all facets of life.

In the pages that follow, AliceAnne gives us a view into her own life's riffs, raw and unfiltered. Her past, her future, her triumphs, her failures, her mistakes, her epiphanies—each verse of her life as it rises or falls. The stories in this book demonstrate how those iterations formed the version of the work in progress (or masterpiece, depending on how you look at things) AliceAnne brings to the table as a leader and as a peer among leaders today.

AliceAnne shows us that a leader is more than what she is in the moment, more than what she is in the office, in the boardroom, in the family room at home. A leader is the sum total of everything she's lived and experienced, including those early riffs and the trailing sequences that didn't *really* go nowhere, because, in fact, they informed a new direction. It's all these things and—possibly most importantly—it's *what she does with those things.*

When McCartney composed his song on film, he proved that the record we hear on the radio isn't a masterpiece only in its pressed vinyl stage. It was a masterpiece from the very beginning, because that record wouldn't exist but for every moment along the way. As AliceAnne shows us in *Take the Lead*, every note of our lives, whether flat, sharp, or in perfect pitch, is an opportunity to iterate and compose ourselves so we can be the leaders we want to be.

PROLOGUE

I can't stop looking at my hands.

Picture me, driving down River Road in Crownsville, Maryland, catching a glimpse of my nails and having to do a double take to make sure they're mine.

If you're laughing at that, don't worry. It *is* pretty funny.

For those of you who have never taken a drive down River Road, please know that no description I write could ever do it justice. This is the road I drive every day, multiple times a day, to get everywhere I need to go—my office, my preschools, my kids' schools, Trader Joe's...

If I need it, it's probably at the other end of River Road.

By now, the twists and turns are familiar, which allows me to look around as I follow the winding path. The road follows the graceful dips and turns of the Severn River, rolling gently along fields and forests resplendent in their seasonal colors. For me, that's the real draw of Maryland. Every season is so lush, so different as it flows between colors, textures, and scenes. From the vibrant, emerald greens of the spring to the muted pastels of the wintertime, pulling onto River Road each day is like stepping into a brand-new world.

It's the kind of place you can see the seasons play out before you, a place where nature moves with or without your regard.

Maybe this is what makes my hands so funny. Amidst all this natural splendor, I can't help but notice them as I glance over the steering wheel. I look at my hands—invariably manicured, nails shaped and perfectly painted—and laugh because I just can't believe they're mine. As I drive down this beautiful, picturesque road, the thought hits me hard and fast.

Is this my real life?

If you had told eight-year-old AliceAnne Loftus about these River Road drives, she would have laughed at you. She probably wouldn't have even recognized my hands as her own. People say eyes are the window to the soul, but if you really want to know where someone's been, where they are, and where they're going, check out their hands.

I guess I keep going back to hands because they tell you so much about another human without any interpersonal interaction. You can see what a person's been up to if their hands are dirty, stained, or calloused. Even though a preschooler may hesitate to admit they've been sneaking into the fingerpaints, you can unravel the evidence pretty quickly with a glance at their grubby fingers. A mechanic is more likely to have rough, coarser hands, while an office worker is probably able to maintain a professional manicure much more easily. Someone with blue hands has either been working with some sort of paint or needs serious medical attention, and if a toddler waddles up to you with dirty, dripping hands…

Well, you might want to keep your distance.

As a Filipino immigrant, my mother was *very* intentional about keeping up her manicure. She never went to a salon, but I remember her sitting on the couch, radiating her quiet, calm beauty as she lacquered her nails with expert precision. My mother's hands were (and continue to be) lovely. As the only Filipino woman in our small, midwestern town, it was important to her to take care of them, no matter how hard she worked. Now that I'm older, I recognize that this was her way of keeping things together—to ensure that *something* stayed beautiful, no matter what the circumstance.

My hands, however, were a completely different story. I chewed my nails. I cracked my knuckles. I had paper cuts, hangnails, and calluses, and nothing made me more aware of how hideous they looked than the sight of my mother sitting on the couch, faithfully caring for that one simple feature.

That's why I always have a manicure. It's a strange kind of vanity, a symbolic connection to those days in small-town Kansas. From the top looking down, my hands are clean, polished, and ready for preconceived notions about my lifestyle, my income, my marriage, or whatever else people want to assume. If you saw me driving down River Road, gripping my steering wheel with my pretty, polished nails, you probably wouldn't believe half of what it took to end up in the driver's seat of that car.

At least, not until you turn my hands over.

Manicured hands are like the end of a fairytale—and everyone loves the ending to a good fairytale. Who doesn't want to go to Disney World to wave at Cinderella in the high towers of her castle, radiant in her magical gown with her handsome prince at her side? Who doesn't want an image (even a fabricated one) of kindness, goodness, and beauty reaping some sort of karmic reward?

But that's the strangest part, isn't it? Everyone wants to celebrate with the princess, basking in her fortunes and successes, but have you ever heard of anyone who wanted to visit Cinderella's bed of ashes? Get in line for the "I'm Newly Orphaned, and My Stepmother Is Emotionally and Physically Abusive, Thereby Forcing Me to Marry a Rich Stranger to Escape My Desperate Circumstances" flume ride? Skip the Bibbidi Bobbidi Boutique for the "Years of Backbreaking, Unpaid Labor Galleria?"

I can practically hear the crickets chirping.

When we think of a "fairytale ending," we don't think about the pain, strife, and growth it took to get there. And when Cinderella is safe in her castle—when the crowds leave, the cheering dies, and those adoring villagers trudge back to their cottages—I can't help but think...

Now what?

The deeper truth is that our fairytale endings are illusions. You can't have happy endings without great struggle, and "endings" themselves aren't really endings—just the point when the crowd stops watching. Cinderella's story keeps popping up in my mind because I can't help but feel like she's misunderstood, and that's something I relate to. Deeply.

It's easy for people to look at my hands and make assumptions about my family, my businesses, and Leading Ladies as a whole. And who could blame them? When our culture sees authenticity as a buzzword rather than a value, it's hard *not* to look at all of this without a healthy dose of skepticism. Between the Leading Lady Facebook Group, podcast, masterclasses, live events, and workshops, it wouldn't be a stretch to dismiss this book as another seminar—maybe even a gimmick or a tell-all personal memoir.

If that's the image you want to take away, you're more than welcome to it. But that's not the point of this book.

•••

If this is your first interaction with the Leading Ladies, I want to welcome you from the bottom of my heart. The Leading Lady brand is dedicated to helping women lean into their power, recognize their unique gifts and talents, and gain confidence to live with authenticity. Our community is now worldwide, over six thousand strong, and made up of women from every walk of life—old and young, outgoing and reserved, entrepreneurs, CEOs, mothers, plumbers, Antarctic explorers…

We're women in the lead, and that's all there is to it.

When I started professionally coaching from a place of passion and purpose, I never imagined Leading Ladies would take off like it did. Our group is still growing by the day, and I have to pinch myself whenever I think about that. It's one thing to *say* empowered women empower other women. It's another thing entirely to see thousands of women from around the world coming together to truly make that happen.

There are many reasons I wanted to write this book, but the unbelievable growth I've seen over the last five years is definitely one of them. As our group grows (and, with dedication to our values, we *will* continue to grow), I find it's just as important to look behind as it is to look ahead—to acknowledge, validate, and learn from the places we've been in order to blaze a path into the future.

To be completely honest, this book has been the most difficult project I've ever undertaken. I've wanted to write something like this for years, but only in the last two could I even *fathom* trying to start. There are so many facets of my life, so many cracks, crevasses, and dark places I'm not particularly proud of. I've lived one hundred lives and been one hundred different people. Where do I begin? What do I even say? How can I take all *this*—the pain, the beauty, this *life*—and distill it into something that makes a modicum of sense?

When the answer came to me, it slapped me upside the head.

L.E.A.D.E.R. The guiding acronym and foundational core of the Leading Ladies: listening and learning, engagement, authenticity, dedication, emotional intelligence, and resilience.

That's it. That's the point.

You can take the superficial fairytale image if you want, but it's what's beneath that's valuable. Each and every woman has the inherent power to be the leader in her own life, and as we connect with one another—genuinely and authentically pull up seats at the table to speak, listen, and learn—something incredible happens. When we make space to show up as our best selves, we *give* space for others to do the same.

Here's what this book is, and here's what it isn't.

When I say, *Take the lead; the rest will follow*, it's not just a motto. It's an ethos. This isn't just my story, my experience, or my business. The tapestry of these lives, lessons, and circumstances may be coming from my own perspective (frankly, it's the only one I've got), but this isn't about *me* teaching *you* how to do anything.

In other words, this isn't a self-help book. If you're looking for someone to give you a best-selling, nine-step method for lifetime success and fulfillment, I'm sure there are plenty of those on the shelves at your local bookstore. This isn't about me telling you to lean in, buck up, eat, pray, or love. My story isn't a guide to any sort of fairytale ending, and it certainly isn't over. I'm still living my life, still figuring things out day by day.

Instead of offering answers, I'd like to show you my scars—every beautiful, tragic crack that taught me how to show up as a Leading Lady. There's a lot of worth in scars, and as I walk the shadowed corridors of my past, I can begin to puzzle out the value of what I was learning, whether I recognized that value in the moment or missed it completely.

And I'm *still* learning, each and every day. Time after time, I have to pull out my trusty ol' L.E.A.D.E.R. acronym to remind myself what that word truly means.

Here's how I break it down:

L—A Leading Lady is a *learner*, constantly discovering more about herself and open to learning from others. In order to do that, she also needs to be a *listener*. She knows she doesn't have all the answers, but that's a good thing. No experience is ever a waste.

E—She's *engaged*. She lives at the cause rather than the effect and takes back her power rather than being a victim of circumstance. She actively chooses how she wants to show up, and she taps into her strengths to uplift herself and others.

A—She's *authentic*. She knows what she values and puts those values first when making decisions. Instead of letting the outside pressures of fear and insecurity define her actions, she stands strong and secure, knowing that her true self is her best self. By being honest and setting real intent, she can consistently show up as that best self.

D—She's *dedicated*. No matter how risky and uncomfortable it may feel to be vulnerable, she's determined to stay dedicated to her authenticity. No matter how she falters or how tumultuous life gets, she knows that circling back to her values will bring her into balance.

E—She's *emotionally intelligent*. She recognizes, validates, and actualizes her own emotions while being aware of and respecting others'. She's able to discern how others react to her emotional responses and seeks to understand how these emotions impact the relationship.

R—She recognizes *resiliency* as a process rather than an action. Every failure and setback can be seen as an opportunity, and when things fall apart, she's able to give herself space to rest, heal, learn, and then return as the leader she wants to be.

•••

Before you get excited and write these down in your daily planner, know that this acronym is *not* a checklist. These letters aren't a step-by-step program, a to-do list, or a scavenger hunt. They're always interconnected, always working together, and always flowing in sync. For instance, in order to be dedicated, you have to know what you value, which means you need to be authentic to discover those values, emotionally intelligent to recognize them, actively engaged in that authenticity with a learner's mindset, resilient for when those lessons get hard…

I'm sure you get the point.

Just because you're feeling particularly vulnerable or inauthentic one day doesn't mean you're magically zapped out of your "leader" powers, and it's completely possible to be engaged while lacking in the emotional intelligence department. As a leader, you can't look at this acronym as some sort of marker or achievement. There's no possible way to show up as your best self *every second* of your life.

This book isn't a recipe for a "perfect, do-it-all woman." If I had that kind of formula, this would be a very different book. *You* have to take the lead for yourself, and you can only do so by *actively making the choice* to show up in your own life.

Self-help is telling someone what to do. Leadership is showing them it can be done.

That's why this leadership book is made up of stories.

Stories connect us. They draw us in, paint pictures in our minds, and show us the truth beyond what we can see. Sure, I could have written *How to Be a Leader with AliceAnne Loftus* featuring planners, vision boards, and your very own Leading Lady Coloring Book.

But, again, that's not the point.

In order to break things down, it's helpful to have both context and illustration. These lofty leadership concepts didn't magically appear in my dreams one dark and stormy night. No one wakes up one random day and is suddenly a Leading Lady. Still waters run deep, and what may appear to be simple on the surface is most likely a bloody, grueling battle of a lesson. Delving into these stories and translating them into something readable—nay, *intelligible*—has been quite the process, but it's given me incredible perspective and clarity.

Think of these stories as lenses rather than personal anecdotes or cure-all solutions. We're not machines to be coded. We're humans who actualize and thrive from experiences.

Stories are a huge part of that.

With that being said, I have to sneak in a caveat.

Every story in this book is an authentic experience from my life— but that doesn't mean these stories are mine and mine alone. For this reason, certain names and personal details may be changed and/or omitted out of respect for others' privacy.

How is that consistent with authenticity? I'm so glad you asked.

Authenticity does *not* mean spilling everything for the sake of shock and publicity. Authenticity doesn't mean putting everything up on social media for the world to see. True authenticity is staying dedicated to your values, and just as I respect my own boundaries for myself and my family, I also respect others' privacy. While every word of this book comes from my personal experience, it's neither my place nor within my abilities to speak for anyone else.

If you're looking for salacious gossip or a juicy, lurid tell-all, you've got the wrong book. I'll be the first to warn you that these stories contain all sorts of tidbits from every corner of my life—masks, chickens, capes, and even dental floss bikinis—but if you want anything less than the real thing, you should put this book down right now. At this point, I can't afford to be anything less than authentic.

Life lessons are hard. They're messy, even painful at times. Gleaning the truth of those lessons doesn't mean wallowing in that pain or reopening wounds. No one exists in a vacuum; my journey is directly enmeshed with others. In writing this book, I've had to recognize that I play roles in others' stories, just as they play roles in mine.

The people mentioned in these stories are so much greater than my reflections and experiences. While combing through these memories, I've tried to focus more on the *what* rather than the *who*— the lesson someone taught me rather than the person themselves.

Trust me. You'll get much more out of this if you try and do the same.

•••

If there's one thing that keeps coming back to me during my long drives down River Road, it's this: Real leaders don't collect followers. They empower other leaders.

As I sit in my front seat, marveling at my hands, my journey—the sheer, wonderful *ridiculousness* of it all—I can't help but laugh. I laugh at judgment. I laugh at assumptions. I laugh at how many tears it took to wear these scars with pride, and I laugh because I know that while this "fairytale" is a warzone, it's certainly far from over.

When I offer you my hand, it's not to drag you down any particular path. It's an invitation to see the underside of the manicure—the wrinkles, the grit, the grime, and what I've learned in earning every scar. The eyes may grant a window into the soul, but if you really take the time to examine someone's hands, you're sure to find evidence of all the things they've carried.

This book isn't an answer. It's an invitation to take a real look at these hands—every beautiful, scarred part of them.

L is for learning.

CHAPTER 1: VALUE GROWS UP

Here are two things most people don't know about me:

1. I have an inexplicable phobia of chickens.

2. I wasn't born in the United States.

Before you start judging, let's talk about the chicken thing. Maybe *inexplicable* isn't the right word. In fact, a fear of chickens is both rational and practical. Chickens are cunning. Neurotic. As the closest living relative to the Tyrannosaurus rex, it's not hard to imagine that under all those grubby feathers, deep beneath the dry, scaly skin is a predatory lizard brain—a savage strain of prehistoric genes just waiting to unleash chaos on the civilized world.

Chickens are both territorial and cannibalistic. Enough said.

As for my childhood, it's a bit more complicated than evil poultry and lizard brains. I hesitate to talk about my early years because I'm not exactly sure how to portray this period of my life. Some of it's dark, and most of it's lonely, but I know, deep in my heart, that these years were invaluable. Why? Because if I had the opportunity to go back and change my past—to "magic" things away or craft myself a completely different life—I wouldn't do it.

This isn't a story about how horrible my life was. I'm not going to sit here and spin yarns about how I triumphantly overcame every obstacle the world threw at me. There was a lot of happiness in my childhood and a lot of love and joy that came along with that.

Instead of a tragic tale, let me offer you a story about cycles—the good, the bad, and the ugly—and how learning who we've been shows us the full potential of who we can become.

L is for learner, and for me, that started at birth.

I'm an American citizen, but I was actually born in the Philippines in November 1981. I spent my early years on the island of Luzon in a small village outside of Mabalacat. I don't remember much about this time in my life, but I know for a fact that those early years of my childhood were blissful. The Filipino culture treasures the concept of a large family. My mom was one of eleven children, and she was eager to nestle me into all the love, comfort, and goodness her heritage had to offer.

My dad hailed from Kansas and was stationed in the Philippines with the Air Force (for the life of me, I can't remember what exactly he did), which added another dynamic to the situation. Not only was I born with extremely light skin in a westernized hospital on the U.S. military base; I *was* American. And in a country where girls left home at the age of twelve to work and support their families, that meant something most people don't understand. I remember my aunts doting on me, dressing me up like a doll as they cooed and fawned. Before I could even put words to this feeling, I became the symbol of something—a linchpin between two worlds I hadn't even begun to comprehend.

My mom was magical. She still is. As one of the "older" generation of siblings in her family, she didn't even get to finish high school before she started working to put her younger brothers and sisters through the lower grades. She got housekeeping and nannying jobs, and years later, she still sent money back to her parents. For her, marrying my dad didn't just mean a future in America. It meant starting a whole new life for her family. Not only did she start having children in her twenties—she uprooted her entire existence in the hope of something better.

Having been a young mother myself, that's something I just can't imagine.

As a military man, my dad was always on the move. Before we settled in the States, we spent a stint in Panama where my mom became pregnant with my little brother, Michael. At the same time, my family adopted one of my mom's younger brothers, Charles (technically, my uncle), who was a full eight years older than me. And—just like that—I went from being an only child to a middle child.

These are the years I really start remembering. There's one scene in particular I've never been able to get out of my head.

Mom is cleaning the house. She wanders into the nursery to check on the baby. I follow. I peek through the bars of his crib, only to find that my new baby brother is blue.

Mom sweeps him up and swaddles him. The baby is so very blue—as blue as my parent's blue bedspread where she lays him down. She's screaming and crying. There's shouting and sobbing and chaos. Mom makes him breathe again, but what now? What do you do with a blue baby?

I was five years old.

At the time, I didn't understand that little baby Michael had brushed hands with death. SIDS—sudden infant death syndrome—was rampant in the eighties, and the fact that he survived was nothing short of a miracle. The military whisked both him and my mom away to the United States for more comprehensive medical care, and my dad followed them shortly after. Charles and I were left behind with family friends.

All of a sudden, I was alone, abandoned with a brother I didn't know in a country where I didn't belong. My five-year-old mind immediately concluded that my mom must have died. The memories are shallow, painful, and blurry, but I can vividly recall feeling lost and so, *so* scared.

I distinctly remember when the anxieties of survival came crashing down.

Will I ever see my mom again? Does this new family even want me here? And what happens if they don't?

This was the moment I became a student of emotions. Even at that young age, I understood that, in order to stay safe, I needed to have some sort of control—no matter how weak or pitiful that control may be—over my environment. I had to be *likeable*. I had to keep people *happy*. I knew our temporary foster family was burdened by two more unexpected mouths to feed, and no amount of charity could ease that strain. I learned to recognize the tightness in their voices, the curt, measured looks, and the shadows of exasperation. They certainly weren't *bad* people for taking in two kids out of the goodness of their hearts. Just stressed, and rightfully so.

"Don't cry," one of them told me—gently but with stern undertones.

Crying was inconvenient. *Crying* was just another burden on top of every other factor in this impossible situation.

"If you're a good girl," came the promise, "you'll be back with your mommy."

I remember sitting on the steps, clutching the balustrade for dear life.

Don't cry, I kept telling myself, over and over as I twisted my toes into knots. *Whatever you do, just don't cry.*

That singular moment left a lasting impression on me. No matter what I saw, felt, or experienced, I had to be strong. I had to be *good*. I had no idea what the heck was going on, but I knew I had to act a certain way to keep myself safe. And, of course, this begged a powerful question.

If Mommy comes back for me when I'm a good girl, did she leave me for being a bad one?

It's easy to look at five-year-old AliceAnne and judge her for that. Of course, my mom didn't *abandon* me in Panama. She did what she had to do to save my brother's life. As a mother, I can't even begin to imagine the anguish of stepping onto a plane, holding your dying baby in your arms while knowing you'll be separated from your other children by thousands of miles. But in the moment, I truly *felt* abandoned. I didn't understand what was going on. I could only observe the turmoil around me and try to make sense of it as best I could.

It wasn't my fault. It wasn't anyone's fault. It just *was*.

Unfortunately, I didn't have that kind of perspective at the time. For many years, I harbored anger and resentment against my mom for leaving us behind. Whenever I told this story, I spoke of the incident as being abandoned, and viewing the situation through a five-year-old's eyes, that's a pretty fair assessment.

I was doing my best. My mom was doing her best. We were *all* doing our best.

Changing that narrative took time and the mindful ability to zoom out and view the situation with empathy. No one is born knowing how to look at the world from someone else's perspective. In fact, empathy is the *opposite* of our instincts. When you're a child—especially a child in a vulnerable situation—you scramble to learn how the world works from the lens of your own experiences. No matter how skewed or tainted that lens may be, there's still value in it. We have to learn how to cope in order to survive.

Like all human beings, I grew up with an ego, the idea that everything that *happens* to me is *done* to me. As I grew older, time, distance, and experience taught me life wasn't that simple. Nothing had happened *to* me, specifically. I just happened to be part of a family caught in a horrific circumstance. I had to let go of my ego and remove myself from the situation before I could see the cause and effects of an unfortunate chain of events. When I was able to cast off the emotion and become an intentional observer rather than an active participant, I could view the situation through a brand-new pair of compassionate lenses.

Don't get me wrong. I'm not saying that stepping out of the "active participant" role is easy. On the contrary, it's more like casually trying to step off a moving train.

Think about it like a line of dominoes: when one person reacts, the next person reacts to that reaction, causing the next person to turn around and chastise the first person, who just started getting back up but now has to take their anger out on the second.

On and on it goes, an endless carousel of pain, trauma, and bitterness. Hurt people hurt people, either purposefully or unwittingly, and the only way to break that cycle is to see it as part of a greater pattern.

Please know I'm not trying to excuse inflictors, justify grievances, or say the casualties of the hurt train aren't completely legitimate. If you get knocked down, you get *knocked down*. Having a wider perspective of that domino line doesn't magically cure the pain or put things back to the way they were. Perspective may make someone else's actions understandable, but that doesn't mean those actions are forgiven. The real value in perspective is that it gives you *power*—power to see a pattern, recognize it, and remove yourself from the reactionary cycles you would rather not take part in.

The cold, hard fact is I was left in Panama at a very young age, and I had every right to feel scared, vulnerable, and abandoned. The beauty of this story is I don't *have* to stay in that moment. I have the power to remove myself as a victim of circumstance and place myself in the observer's seat. Instead of feeding into the cycle, I can simply call it what it is.

This isn't a story about me being abandoned. This is a story about my family suffering a grueling misfortune that shaped my beliefs as a child. As a Leading Lady, I don't have to continue playing the role of five-year-old AliceAnne just because I was there so many years ago. When I listen to what's actually happening—take a moment to pause and learn about these cycles—I unlock the power of perspective.

I get to *choose* to get out of the way of the domino behind me and *refuse* to knock over the next one in my path. When I create space by stepping back from the situation, I can break the cycle once and for all.

Of course, five-year-old AliceAnne didn't know all of this. Some days, a much older AliceAnne doesn't quite grasp it either.

But let's not get ahead of ourselves. There's still a lot to learn.

•••

Needless to say, I didn't stay in Central America forever.

After being stationed at the Panama Canal, my dad moved the family to Andrews Air Force Base in Maryland. I don't remember much about the East Coast—just that the girl who babysat me had a Bon Jovi poster and there was a little old lady who lived across the street—but that's probably for the best. At that young age, the adjustment was difficult, but not earth-shattering. My older brother Charles, on the other hand, barely spoke English.

All in all, I had a typical eighties childhood. My mom wasted no time getting a job, and she pulled in extra money by hosting tenants in our top-floor bedrooms. Everything was new and different, and my mom did everything she could to make the most of her American life. She worked tirelessly at our local convenience store and quickly got herself promoted to manager, on top of raising three kids and running a boarding house.

In those early years, the world revolved around my baby brother. Michael miraculously recovered from his SIDS episode, but there were always machines hooked up to him—monitors, wires, and tubes too complicated and alien for my young mind to grasp. While the bells and whistles were incomprehensible, I quickly became an expert at reading my mom for signs of irritation, overwhelm, and fatigue. Everything seemed to be hanging by a thread. My mom was exhausted, and it was a cardinal sin to upset her.

Once, I fell asleep in the bathtub. She walked in and thought I'd drowned. After the upset, blowup, and shakedown that followed, I remember sitting there thinking: *Hey, stupid! Be more careful. How stupid are you? You upset your mom!*

Things like that weren't just *stupid*—they made me bad. *Good girls*

23

didn't send their mothers into a tailspin. *Good girls* didn't cause a scene.

Thankfully, the tension slackened as my fragile baby brother grew into a healthy young boy. Michael went from being an untouchable glass doll to my loyal sidekick, my very best friend. Wherever I was, he was. Whatever I was doing, he joined in. Dark-skinned and handsome with jet-black hair, that boy could do no wrong.

My adopted older brother, however, remained an enigma. I remember Charles being grumpy and authoritarian, a life raft adrift from our family that bobbed just beyond reach. That relationship dynamic is a tough nut to crack, but here again comes perspective to the rescue.

I want you to imagine being a teenager. Yes—sweaty palms, pimples, and all. Now, I want you to imagine being a teenager adopted by your older sister then shipped off to a new country where you don't speak the language. Oh, and did I mention that on top of braces, you also get to be the only brown kid in school?

Of course, it didn't help that Michael and I (always the dynamic duo) teamed up against him or that he constantly had to look after us. With my mom managing the convenience store and my dad also picking up shifts *on top* of his military job, we were what has affectionately become known as "latchkey kids."

Were we loved? Certainly. Did we have rip-roaring good times? Most definitely. Were we always completely supervised? Well...

Let's just say we made our own fun.

It wasn't long before we relocated again—this time, to my dad's hometown in Haysville, Kansas, smack-dab in America's heartland. My paternal grandfather had recently been diagnosed with cancer, and with my dad's next deployment looming on the horizon, it made sense to be somewhere where my mom could have the strong, familial support she'd had back in the Philippines. My dad was the son of a farmer, the third of four boys from a God-fearing, Southern Baptist family. It was as if we'd traded one tight-knit clan for another.

In the beginning, everything was wonderful. We bought a house catty-corner to my grandparents', and with all my aunts and uncles living nearby, Michael and I spent our days romping around with our rowdy American cousins. We were always surrounded by family, and there was nothing but gratitude for my lovely, hardworking mom. My grandpa absolutely adored her and respected her work ethic.

I was seven when my grandpa died. That's when everything changed.

Of course, I'd seen racism before. When three out of five family members are noticeably brown, you really can't avoid it. But only in Kansas did I see just how deep those roots could run, how the slithering tendrils of prejudice could dig, latch, and fester crevasses that could rip entire families apart.

After my grandpa died, the facade of acceptance came down. It was as if an entire half of my family had been wearing smiley masks of tolerance, only to rip them off as soon as their prejudice could go unchecked. All of a sudden, my mom went from being "the Filipino daughter" to "the immigrant maid." Even at the young age of seven, I was keen enough to spot the difference between the American daughters-in-law and the outsider. To them, my mom was a second-class citizen, which made my brothers and me some kind of second-class mutts.

My dad left for Desert Storm around the time I turned eight. The invitations to family gatherings dwindled then stopped coming at all. We were pariahs *living right next door*, and I'll never forget walking into one of the local churches, only to be sent away because we were mixed-race "abominations."

Yes, you read that right. Kicked out. Of a *church*.

All because of the color of our skin, which, in my case, wasn't very dark at all. Here I was, the light-skinned daughter of a beautiful, Filipino woman. My mother was (and still is) gorgeous. She's always carried herself with distinctive poise and elegance. I remember racking my brain, trying desperately to understand why anyone *wouldn't* want to look like her. How could anyone be so hateful of someone so beautiful? Charles constantly made fun of my light skin, teasing that *I* was the adopted one. Apparently, I wasn't white enough for the family who'd rejected me, nor was I "American" enough to meet God.

I have to hand it to my mom. When caught between a rock and a hard place, she absolutely shines. After her husband's community rejected her, she didn't lay down and wallow; she went right to work building her own community. She reached out to one of her sisters who lived in Oklahoma City only a few hours away. This Filipino aunt had married a Black Air Force serviceman, which meant I was constantly entrenched in a world of vibrant color, a world where *I* felt like an oddball for being so darned white.

And my aunt was just the beginning. My mom saved her money to sponsor other family members immigrating to America, starting with her parents. My Filipino grandma and grandpa (Apo and Ingkong) moved in when I was eight, and they lived with us until I was a college student. Here I was in the Bible Belt, being raised up in the devoted, hardworking Filipino culture I'd grown to love. My mom was proud of her heritage, and I never once saw my grandparents ashamed of where they'd come from. I envied them; I longed to look and be more like them.

But this was only half of my world.

At school, things were much different. I remember Ingkong walking me to the front steps every day, sensing my dread at being teased by my classmates about my "weird" foreign family. Ingkong was a keen man and a compassionate one, at that. With a twinkle in his eye, he crafted stories about how I was secretly a Filipino princess, which of course, I immediately told my classmates in hopes they'd stop picking on me.

Lo and behold, it worked. For the first time in my life, I realized I could seize the helm of my destiny by crafting stories of who I wanted to be. There was no way my peers could begin to understand what my life was like, so I fed them snippets they could understand—the kinds of stories they wanted to hear.

All of a sudden, I had a secret boyfriend in Canada. So-And-So had her first kiss, so I did too. There was constantly a new, miraculous reason why my dad couldn't pick me up at school or why my grandfather was a different color.

Was I a little pathological liar? Oh, most definitely. My stories kept me safe. They made me interesting. They protected me from being so alone.

The teachers soon picked up on my sloppily crafted, elementary-level lies. My dad was often deployed, and even when he wasn't, he was working multiple jobs. My mom constantly worked, and my grandparents didn't speak English. I didn't go to Brownies or dance class. Instead, I learned to cook massive meals and pan for fool's gold with my cousins. There was even a time when my wild stories about being home alone prompted one of my friend's parents to call social services—much to the chagrin of my notably *not-absent* parents.

I was different, and no matter how hard I tried, I couldn't shake the aching need to belong *somewhere*.

This caused problems for me on a different level. As a latchkey kid in Kansas, there weren't a lot of biracial, Asian American role models to show me how to navigate the strange new world of womanhood. When I was young, my mother always permed her hair. Lush, luxurious curls looked magnificent on her, and she wore them with the effortless sophistication of a starlet. Back in the seventies, she'd even moonlighted as a Diana Ross impersonator. She kept those gorgeous curls while I was growing up, and whenever she'd go to the salon, she'd take me along with her.

Remember, I don't look *anything* like my mom. While she was dark-skinned, glamorous, and put-together, I was pale, awkward, and dirty blond. My mom got me a perm along with her own (yes, even the bangs), but she wasn't around the next morning to show me how to take care of it.

For those of you who haven't experienced the magic of an authentic, eighties-style perm, the absolute *last* thing you want to do is wash your hair the very next day. But I was young. How was I supposed to know that? My mom had taken off early to work, and as I was getting ready for school, I wet my hair as usual.

The result was disastrous. You're probably thinking something along the lines of a poodle. Take that image, add an unfortunate jolt of electricity, and multiply the shock factor by five.

That's what I looked like.

My mother was gone. My brothers were useless. Of course, my poor grandparents had no idea what to do, so I ventured out into the neighborhood, knocking on doors in search of someone—*anyone*—who could help me.

It was six thirty in the morning. Finally, my next-door neighbor answered in her bathrobe, blinking blearily as she took in the sight of the desperate, poodle-headed neighbor girl.

"Please," I said, biting back tears as I looked into her eyes. "Can you *please* help me?"

The woman was agitated (and rightfully so), but she didn't have the heart to turn me away. She invited me in, ushered me into her bathroom, and painstakingly began to try to puzzle her way through the mess of my hair.

I remember sitting there—helpless, cowed, and ashamed.

This will never happen again, I told myself. *I will never put myself in another situation like this.*

Never again would I go knocking on doors. Never again would I be reduced to begging for help. Never again would I allow myself to be this vulnerable.

I try to think of my own children going door to door like that, but I just can't conjure up the image. I had to have been little—fifth grade, at the oldest. As the half-white daughter of the "foreign family," I already looked ridiculous, and if I came to school with my poodle hair, the teachers wouldn't just laugh; they would start to ask the types of questions I'd come to dread.

Is everything okay at home? How's your family? Are you sure everything's all right?

If I could *look* polished—create the *illusion* of being normal, capable, and well-adjusted—I wouldn't have to answer those questions. I could keep up the charade of being a perfectly normal, perfectly happy, perfectly *good* girl, and I could fool everyone.

Maybe even myself.

These days, I'm very particular about my hair. I'm adept at fixing it just the way I want, but it's not an issue of vanity. For me, it all goes back to the hair story—those breathless, mortifying moments of knocking on doors, *desperate* for anyone to rescue me from my electro-poodle nightmare.

There was no one to help me. There was no one to save me. If I was going to make it through this life in one piece, I had to figure it out myself.

My childhood taught me how to survive. I don't say for better or for worse; I'm just glad I came out the other side. Good or bad, the skills I learned were the skills that helped me be successful, to face what I had to face at the time I had to face it. Right or wrong, hypervigilance became my reality.

This is where the *L* in my acronym—the learning mindset—came from. If I could pay attention, figure out what was safe, and "perform" in such a way that kept me in control, I knew I would make it to the next day. Because of this, I've always been a pragmatic problem-solver. I think fast, and I make decisions without questioning myself. If anything, I can be *too* hasty, but the moment I start feeling like a situation is getting out of my control, I shift into an unwaveringly decisive mindset.

People often ask me about this trait because they interpret it as confidence.

"You have the courage to do what no one else does," my husband told me one day. That really stuck with me.

Yes, it's confidence, an unwavering trust in myself that gives me the ability to make a quick decision and never look back. But the other side of confidence is control. My childhood wasted no time teaching me that if I rolled over and accepted my fate, I would be ripped to pieces.

The first man who sexually assaulted me was young. He was my elderly neighbor's grandson, and he knew *exactly* what he was doing, even when I didn't. After he was finished, he threatened to do worse— to murder my family if I breathed a word of what he'd done. This was the moment I learned that not everyone who wanted to play with me was safe. I also learned what it felt like to be called a liar. When my older brother didn't believe me, I was truly on my own.

I was six years old.

Days after, I saw that boy again. I remember the stupid expression on his face—calm, placid, like he *hadn't* stolen someone else's innocence.

In that moment, I knew exactly what I had to do. I picked up a stick, waited for an opening, and flung that pointy sucker straight into the mother-lover's eye. The little creep hadn't been expecting that, and he ran home, sobbing. But I wasn't going to sit there and cry. I knew he couldn't *actually* hurt my family. I refused to be his victim ever again.

I remember being forced to apologize to that piece of human waste. I said the word *sorry*, and he did too. But I didn't really mean it, and there was no doubt in my mind that he was just as disingenuous as I was.

An eye for an eye, I thought.

Right or wrong, that's what was going on in my six-year-old brain. Crying wasn't going to save me. There was no point in getting mad or trying to convince anyone of something they didn't want to believe. Ignoring it wasn't going to make anything better. No one was going to save me, so I had to do it myself.

30

This instance taught me there's always something you can do for yourself. *Always*. When bad things would happen to me, I'd run through the same two questions, over and over: *How can I get out of this?* and *How do I keep this from happening again?*

These key questions shaped the crux of my learner mindset. As a child, I only had so much power to influence my situation, and no amount of anger or self-pity was going to change the past. The only thing I *did* have control of was prevention—observing the situation, reading the key players, and assessing what I could do to take back control.

I refused to lay down and take it. I refused to be an easy target for life. If I was the only one I could depend on, so be it.

As a child, this was the lens that tinted my world. I don't regret it. I wouldn't change it. This mentality was exactly what I needed at the time.

That isn't to say it made the world sunshine and rainbows. Ironically enough, strong people are the ones who set themselves up for the most hurt. When you're your own defender, you're also the one responsible for every ounce of pain. Just as I criticized myself for falling asleep in the bathtub, I was constantly beating myself up for failing to anticipate others' malevolent actions.

Stupid. How did you not see that one coming? Stupid. How have you not learned?

My unwavering trust in myself wasn't born out of pride. It was a defense mechanism.

It's hard not to cringe at those memories, but over the years, I've learned to have compassion, both for myself and for others. When you're a victim, you're in the moment. Things happen *to* you, and there's no space for compassion towards anyone, least of all yourself. But when you're able to take a learner's mentality, to step off the crazy train and look at the situation with a bit of empathy and emotional intelligence, you might be surprised what you find.

Believe it or not, I end up coaching successful women through victim mentality and into compassion on a regular basis. When a client comes to me reeling from what has been done *to* her, I encourage her to take a step back. Of course, her grievances are valid and completely justified, but as long as she stays on that other person's pain train, that woman will forever be at her offender's mercy.

The first thing I do is ask the victim to apologize to herself from the perspective of the offender. For example:

I'm so sorry I did that to you. I'm going through blankity-blank, and I'm not very good at handling it. That manifested as blankity-blank, and I took it out on you.

The situation probably isn't that simple, but writing a mock apology is a good place to start.

The next step is to craft a story about that situation from the offender's perspective. For instance, let's say you have an employee who breaks all the rules. Maybe she's sloppy, constantly showing up late, and just doesn't seem to care.

Your first reaction might be: *Who is this gremlin, and who does she think she is to hurt my business?*

And, in all fairness, no one could fault you for thinking that. But what if you made things less personal? Took your hurt out of the equation and reframed your initial reaction?

You might shift your initial response to something like this: *The way this employee is acting is completely unacceptable. If we can get to the bottom of this, we can find a solution.*

When you take a step back, you can try to see things from your employee's perspective—to ask yourself *why* she's behaving in this harmful, unprofessional way. Would your perspective on this employee change if you found out she was a single mom struggling to get her kid out the door? What if you discovered she's been wrestling with depression after recently losing a close family member? Maybe she really is just a lazy, lackadaisical person, and there's no need to dig any deeper.

No matter what the reason for this woman's tardiness may be—whether she's floundering, grieving, or just plain unprofessional—you remove *yourself* from the situation. You no longer have to be the victim; you're simply an innocent bystander who happened to be in the way. By plucking your domino from the cycle of frazzled lateness, anger, and frustration, you can find the best solution to the situation. You can finally see that this isn't happening *to you*. It's just *happening*.

Maybe you need to fire this employee. Maybe you need to sit down with her and have a heart-to-heart about what she truly needs to show up as her best. Maybe you need to support her. Maybe you need to give her space. But how can you actually get a pulse on the problem when you're standing in the middle of it?

Victim mentality tells you that you don't have a choice. That's simply not true. No matter what the situation may be, you *always* have a choice. You might not like the consequences, but there's always something you can do.

Studies show that children's learning styles are developed before the age of five. Think about who you were as a person during those formative years. Were you subservient? Did you learn to be a problem-solver? What was your learning style, and what sorts of skills manifested themselves through that learning style?

When I was young, I became a learner to protect myself. As a five-year-old living with a strange family in Panama, I could already pick up on the small, subtle cues—the way the wife would jerk when her husband put his hand on her shoulder or the strained lines of tension that meant someone was lying. I was constantly reading, constantly learning, and constantly assessing the room.

Now that I'm older, I'm a learner to lead myself. Being able to read someone's emotions isn't a bad thing. Subtle cues can be an important part of emotional intelligence. I can tell by my children's postures—a slouch, a glance, or the light furrow of a brow—what kind of day they've had, and I can use these same abilities to spot a struggling employee. It's not a superpower; it's an intentionally developed skill.

Years of experience have taught me that some of the skills I picked up throughout my childhood no longer serve me. The need to control my surroundings can be completely destructive, especially when working with a team. I frequently encounter leaders who lack the trust needed to delegate, and I hate seeing them crumple when uncontrollable circumstances come crashing down on their shoulders. It's highly likely that these people learned the same sorts of childhood lessons I did—to trust *no one* but themselves. But as with anything else, we have the choice to keep our mentalities, refine them, or let them go altogether. These lifelong learning skills are like tools. We collect them, sharpen them, and learn how to use them over time. The tools in and of themselves aren't good or bad; it's all about how we use them.

A hammer can build a house. It can also crack a skull.

Often, I get frustrated for responding to situations with the default tools I learned as a little girl. Whenever life took a swing at me, I picked up a sledgehammer and swung right back. But as a grown woman, I've come to acknowledge that there are certain situations where you *don't* want to pull out your sledgehammer. Hanging a picture, for instance. Or trying to clean your microwave.

That's the value of hearing other peoples' stories. They show us new tools so we can learn how to address situations in new ways.

Not long ago, I was arguing with my son about his refusal to eat dinner. The poor kid burns thousands of calories a day but only has a short list of foods he'll actually eat. My husband was frustrated because he didn't know what to feed our teenager, and in *my* frustration with his frustration, I reverted to my default—my good, old-fashioned sledgehammer.

I don't think I need to tell you how terribly that went. After lots of shouting, wanton sledgehammering, and a good dose of mom guilt, my husband shared a timely article about apologizing to your teenager. After a quick read, I went back to my son and told him I was sorry.

The old me would have taken the old brain path: *Stupid, stupid, stupid! How could you not pick up on the correct way to handle that? You're a horrible mother.*

But just because I once operated that way doesn't mean I have to continue that cycle. As a woman who understands the pillars of leadership, I can *choose* whether or not to see that instance as a failure or as an opportunity to make things right.

Yes, I'm guilty of yelling at my kids. Years down the road, I don't want them to remember that "mom was a yeller." My honest, sincere hope is that after years of reflection (and probably some therapy), they'll be able to say, "Sometimes, my mom was a yeller, but then she would come back and talk to us about it because she didn't want us to carry that."

You *can* break the cycle. You *can* make things right. If you blow up at work, you can bring the team back and honestly confess that you didn't handle things correctly.

I refuse to let pride and fear perpetuate any sort of pain train in my life. That's not how I want to show up. That's not authentic to who I want to be. I may have learned to respond a certain way because of my childhood experiences, but I also have the power to take my ego out of the equation and find a better way to react.

When you take a learner's mindset, you're able to take a pause and ask the questions that matter. What sorts of pain trains or domino lines are running your life? What kind of cycles are you perpetuating? By action or inaction, what kind of lessons are you teaching?

I hope my children grow up to run companies and have families of their own. Chances are, somewhere down the line, they're probably going to get angry and yell. And when that happens, I hope my cycles of behavior have taught them not to beat themselves up, but to take the time to go back and apologize.

•••

Back to my phobia of chickens.

As a whole, I really don't like birds, which might seem strange if you know anything about the Leading Lady brand. When I started this program, I chose the flamingo as my mascot. Yes, they're pretty. Yes, they're pink. But the real story goes much deeper.

If you don't know anything about flamingos, I highly recommend you reserve an hour of your day to watch *The Crimson Wing: Mystery of the Flamingos*. This documentary illustrates the beautiful, tragic life cycle of the lesser flamingo on the desolate shores of Lake Natron in northern Tanzania.

I'm going to make a sweeping generalization and assume you're not too familiar with Natron or Tanzania. I certainly wasn't. Basically, it's a giant lake of salt water brined by a neighboring volcano. Every year, this vast body of water dries up into a sulfurous wasteland. The intense heat and barren, isolated landscape make it the perfect destination for two-and-a-half million flamingos to gather. They'll flock to the lake (which, by this time, is little more than a sprawling network of puddles), gobble up enormous amounts of red algae, mate, and then stick around through the dry season to nest their eggs.

As the salty puddles evaporate, the flamingo eggs begin to hatch. At this point, temperatures hover somewhere around 130 degrees Fahrenheit. The chicks are born into noxious, sizzling heat, and eventually, they'll have to make the long journey across the apocalyptic desertscape to the fertile wetlands beyond the shores of Natron.

The journey is long, and their environment does them no favors. As the lake dries, the salty puddles turn into craters of acrid mud so thick and gummy that it builds up on the chicks' legs as they're just beginning to walk. These salt "shackles" weigh the chick down. They make the young birds slow, clumsy, and vulnerable—nearly defenseless to the innumerable predators that venture out to Natron in hopes of an easy meal.

I can't help but cry as I watch these hobbled chicks stumbling across the desert, growing weaker and weaker as their burden drags them down. It's not their fault they were born in this cruel, harsh environment. They didn't intentionally stumble into the salty puddles, and they never asked for the weight around their spindly little legs.

But when a baby flamingo ends up in salt shackles, one of two things happen:

1. They succumb to the weight, collapsing in the hot sun, only to be left behind by their flock as hungry, razor-beaked marabou storks close in.

2. They make it to the wetlands where the cool, fresh water washes the calcified salt away.

Of course, I cry for the ones who don't make it. But I also acknowledge that the flamingos that do cross that desert are stronger. They've suffered, but they've overcome. They've carried the burdens they didn't ask for as effectively as they could, and once they arrive at their destination, they waste no time shedding those shackles once and for all.

This is why I love flamingos. They may be pretty, but they're a mighty tough bird. I can't help but look at those wobbling, hobbled chicks and think of my own childhood. I think of the weight of those shackles. I think of those tiny chicks' fierce, unrelenting will to survive.

Looking back, I'm proud of who I was. Young AliceAnne was a survivor. She set the foundations I would later come to appreciate as a lifelong learner. She did the best she could with some extraordinary circumstances, and (if I do say so myself) she did a pretty good job. Instead of judging her, I have the unique power to step back and observe the cycles she perpetuated. There are certain lessons I've chosen to keep—my ability to read others' emotions, for instance—while others I've refined or even jettisoned.

They're not good. They're not bad. They just *are*.

On New Year's Eve, I hosted one final Facebook Live for 2020. After slogging through that quagmire of a year, my message was simple: Regardless of how your life is, it's still *your* life. No matter what that experience may be, you get to choose what you do with it.

That's the power of taking the lead.

CHAPTER 2: THE GIRL IN THE BOX

It was my husband who finally convinced me to throw out the masks.

When I throw the word "mask" out there, your mind probably snaps through images of bedazzled cotton and smudged blue paper. I'm perfectly aware that this book is debuting post 2020, so I know what sort of loaded imagery masks bring up these days.

Before anyone gets their knickers in a knot, let me assure you that I'm not talking about COVID face coverings—I'm talking about those drooping, melodramatic happy and sad faces you find over theaters.

You know. Happy and sad. Comedy and tragedy.

I'd collected them for years, and they'd festooned my walls as a teenager. My mom must have taken them down and boxed them up during one of their many moves after I went off to college. I guess houseguests really didn't appreciate sleeping under the eternal watch of those gaping, eyeless faces.

I don't quite remember how the collection started. Somewhere along the line, someone must have gifted me a pair of those happy/sad, comedy/tragedy masks, and the theme stuck. As creepy as these hollow shells may be, I found a lot of solace and connection with all those different faces. I painstakingly hung them up, each in their proper place, along with Charles C. Finn's poem, "Please Hear What I'm Not Saying." The beginning lines are still etched in my brain:

Don't be fooled by me.

Don't be fooled by the face I wear

for I wear a mask, a thousand masks,

masks that I'm afraid to take off,

and none of them is me.

Pretending is an art that's second nature with me,

but don't be fooled,

for God's sake don't be fooled.

The poem goes on, and I highly recommend you check out the rest of it on Charles C. Finn's website, poetrybycharlescfinn.com. These masks—the inherent, ultra-adaptive ability to become *whatever* for *whoever, whenever*—were nothing new. My mother was a performer, and I'd been on stage entertaining as long as I could remember.

Hanging up drama masks might seem a little strange, but when you really take the time to look at the wider world around you, you'll find that they're pretty commonplace. Masks are protection. Masks are shields. We marvel at the way animals camouflage themselves to stay safe in their surroundings without realizing we spend our entire lives doing the exact same thing. What you wear, what you say, what you do, how you react—most of this is learned, and I would argue quite a bit of it is molded by our society. We grow up learning what sort of faces to wear in certain instances, and for better or worse, we use these different faces to make sense of the world. Sure, you may feel differently on the inside, but how you should look—the way you're *expected* to appear—can be completely fabricated with enough skill and practice.

I can't remember the first time I donned a mask. To be completely honest, I can't remember a time I *wasn't* trying to hide. Throughout my life, I've collected thousands of different faces—dutiful wife, obedient daughter, doting mother, professional entrepreneur, boss lady…

None of those identities are necessarily *bad* in their own right. In fact, these faces can make the complexity of life simple to swallow.

But let's get real for a second. In a world of filters, Photoshop, and airbrushing, is anything real? When you spend your life cycling from mask to mask, at what point do you forget your real face?

If your entire identity is tied up in a performance, what happens when the curtain falls?

When I say I've been an entertainer my whole life, that's exactly what I mean. Part of being a "good girl" was caring for my mom—not only staving off any extra stress, inconvenience, or drama but also making her feel happy and comforted. My mom had moved to America without being fully literate in English, so as soon as I learned to read, I shared all sorts of stories with her. I read the entire Boxcar Children series aloud, and steadily, she began to pick them up and read them on her own.

This was the quality time I got with my mom, the time I felt truly special. If we weren't reading, I was singing, dancing, or making up little plays for her while she did her nails on the couch. I was always entertaining, whether it was for my mom, my mom's friends, or even my grandparents, Apo and Ingkong. I truly lit up at the idea that I could make the people I loved happy. It was more than the idea that I could bring joy—I knew, deep down in the midst of all the hardship, it was my responsibility to do so.

I thrived on the stage. When I was performing, I could be whoever I wanted to be. I didn't have to be the scared, insecure, or awkward little immigrant girl. I could have a reprieve from my own emotions to totally adopt someone else's. Both at school and at home, I was already playing roles anyway, putting on the parts people wanted to see so I could keep everyone around me happy.

At home, I was the "good girl." I kept my mother entertained, looked after Michael, and took my place in my bustling, Filipino family.

At school, I was something else entirely. A princess, a rebel with a secret—the heroine of my own mangled stories. I'd already devoted myself to the careful study of human emotion and razor-edged empathy. To say I could "work a crowd" was putting things lightly. When I performed well, people loved me. They paid attention to me. They approved of and accepted the AliceAnne I set before them.

For the briefest wisp of a moment, I was safe.

Considering how much I performed as a young child, it's not a surprise that pageantry came up.

There's something else you probably didn't know about me. I was Little Miss Kansas 1991 and Miss Asia America in 1998.

Before you go wandering off imagining an episode of *Toddlers & Tiaras*, give me a minute to explain. Many aspects of the pageant circuit are portrayed accurately in shows and movies, but Hollywood leaves a few key details out for dramatic flair.

For instance, when I say I was Little Miss Kansas, don't let your fantasies sweep you all the way to *Miss Congeniality*. There are actually many different Little Miss Kansas pageants, each sponsored by separate companies for their own promotional reasons. Some of these pageants aren't as popular as others, and oftentimes, completely separate competitions will have the same title. These contests run in stages from the local to the national level, and often, more than one representative from each state shows up to compete at the higher levels. Pageants at the toddler and elementary level are completely different from the adult level, and oftentimes, all contestants get crowned with the same title after putting their best, Keds-clad foot forward.

So, before you go thinking I'm some superstar or famous model, think again. This was purely for the publicity.

It was my dad who decided I would be the perfect little pageant doll. He'd finally left the military to become a real estate appraiser, and the whole affair worked out well for his business and community connections. He would shuttle me along to sponsor after sponsor, solidifying the social network and picking up old prom dresses from coworkers. Oddly enough, my mom is strangely absent from those memories. She was an immigrant mother of three who worked full time. She didn't have time for the glitz or the primping—just those solemn, tranquil respites painting her nails. Pageantry wasn't a part of her world. She hadn't even been in America for five years.

This disconnection didn't help my view on things. From the very beginning, I hated the whole affair. I was ten years old and awkward— lanky, stone-knuckled, and not at all excited about this new venture. For years, I'd longed to do something *normal* like Girl Scouts or team sports, but coming from a traditional Filipino family, my mom didn't put value on those kinds of activities. She and my dad worked hard on maintaining appearances, and the pageant was a foolproof way to solidify the social clout my family so desperately desired.

In the end, it didn't really matter what I thought or how I felt. I was the "good girl," and the pageant was just another stage to mask up for.

The reality of child beauty pageants is much closer to *Toddlers & Tiaras* than I would ever care to admit. Even at the elementary level, there are girls (and parents) who run the circuit as *professional* competitors—fake hair, spray tans, and all. Sure, Little Miss Kansas didn't have a swimsuit competition, but we were judged by a litany of other categories: evening wear, talent, in-person interviews, dance…

It's a full three-ringed circus.

What I saw on that first day rocked my whole world. Some of these girls had been in the circuit their entire lives, and my parents had signed me up on a whim. Sure, I'd seen what my parents called "white trash," but this was the first time I'd felt like *yellow* trash—bad teeth, bad hair, and cheap, hand-me-down prom dresses my mom had altered to fit me. It was the first time I'd felt like trash of any kind.

The crazy thing was, we weren't poor by any stretch of the imagination. We had a nice enough house, and my parents appreciated the finer things in life. I'd always sensed they had champagne tastes on a beer budget, but the Little Miss Kansas pageant was the first time I really *felt* that.

No matter how beautiful I was, I couldn't compete with these girls who lived and breathed the circuit. I didn't have dentures. I didn't have professional hair and makeup. I didn't even own a pair of tap shoes. All the other girls had bright, shiny-white Keds, and I showed up wearing knockoffs from Wal-Mart.

I may have been young, but I knew enough about class and social status to be completely mortified. At the end of the day, I was unpolished, and I knew it. I didn't belong in this world. I had no business being there. I would steal glances at the other girls—the perfectly poised, bubbly princesses who took dance classes and brought in real sponsorships—and quickly turn my eyes away. There just wasn't enough spit in the world to make me shine the way those girls did.

The first step in the process was reporting to the check-in desk. I received a pageant shirt and instructions to change into my dance shorts, socks, and white tennis shoes. Then I was herded into a tiny room to learn a little dance with the other contestants—girls who had years of formal tap and ballet training—with an instructor who expected me to pick up the routine as fast as she could demonstrate it.

Needless to say, I was abysmal. I had two left feet, and no matter how hard I tried, I just couldn't get the moves. I couldn't pick up the spins, twirls, and kicks as fast as the other girls, and the further I got behind, the more awkward and ashamed I felt. Tears stung my eyes as I struggled to match their effortless grace and poise, but the harder I pushed, the more glaring the truth became.

I was unworthy. No matter how hard I tried, I would never belong. Compared to these cute, bouncy girls with their muscular legs and smooth hair, I was an ugly duckling.

This was the first time in my life I saw myself in a group of females and felt completely hideous. Growing up in Kansas, I was already different. I wasn't blond-haired, blue-eyed, and backed by a supportive, all-American family. I was already weird enough at school, but everything about the pageant seemed determined to highlight every single flaw I'd strived so desperately to hide with carefully crafted lies and fantastical stories.

Child pageants are supposed to make little girls feel like princesses. The whole experience had the opposite effect on me. How could you be a princess if you were competing? Princesses were supposed to be happy, safe, and secure. Princesses were *born* beautiful; they didn't need to win anything to make themselves worthy. Princesses didn't have to dress up and strut across a stage to prove they were better than everyone else.

At the time, I didn't realize the crust of sweaty makeup was slowly but steadily hardening along with noxious clouds of hairspray and blinding camera flashes. This performance mask—the one that kept me smiling, no matter how ugly, unworthy, and vulnerable I felt—would stay in my bag of tricks for years to come.

As long as I kept smiling, no one could see the pain underneath.

The pageant came and went. I did my little dance. I sang my little song. In the end, no one won (that's kind of how things work at this level). Different girls received ribbons according to their standout strengths, and at the end of it all, we posed under the dazzling spotlights with our crowns and trophies. We were all Little Miss Kansas, but I knew, deep in my gut, the competition wasn't over. Forevermore, I would be measuring myself up against girls like these.

Who's the prettiest? Who's the most talented? Who gets the most applause, attention, and adoration? When all has been weighed and measured, who's the real *princess?*

If there was one thing I did take away from the Little Miss Kansas pageant, it was an intense desire to be beautiful. I'd never felt ugly before that weekend, but I became *obsessed* with the prefabricated version of who I was supposed to be. And with a little makeup, good hair sense, and the right social cues, I could craft any illusion I wanted. There was a mask for every occasion. All I had to do was fabricate it.

That was the theory, anyway.

Shortly after the pageant, we moved to Maize, Kansas. It's pretty insignificant to tell you all the places I've lived because we only stayed in one place for about a year or so, even after my dad got out of the military. My new school was a little more affluent and noticeably whiter. Ironically, this experience had the same effect as my last performance debacle. Now, I wasn't just an ugly duckling—I was the weird, half-Asian ugly duckling who wore knockoff brands.

Junior high is a traumatic experience for everyone (I'll argue any day that it's an especially brutal experience for young women), but I *lived* in that space of unworthiness for years. It was constantly staying vigilant: watching for social prompts, reacting to the smallest changes, and rehashing my strategy. In the ruthless world of junior high girls, elaborate, make-believe stories weren't good enough. *I* wasn't good enough, and no amount of spit shine could hide that.

It was only when we left Maize that I got a new take on that mentality. One of the benefits of constantly switching schools was I had a chance to tweak my identity—fix the mask here, add or subtract something there—with every new town. For some bizarre reason, my fourteen-year-old self gravitated toward trying out for the dance team. I'm sorry to say no hidden dancing talents magically appeared after the Little Miss Kansas competition, but it was a small town, and the talent pool was pretty limited. I was just good enough to get by, which ended up securing me a spot on the pom-pom team.

This changed everything. No longer was I an ugly duckling. Now, I was part of a team. Finally, I had something I could identify with that connected me with my peers. I met my best friend on that team, and she ended up loving my Filipino family. She gobbled up the food, embraced the culture, and never made me feel weird or different because of where I came from. We couldn't have been in that Podunk town for more than eighteen months, but for the short time we did live there, it was nice. Not spectacular. Not world-altering. Just *nice*. For me, it was a reprieve—a breath of fresh air. Sure, I was still wearing a mask, but this time, it felt a little looser.

And then there was my boyfriend.

Maybe it was the comfort. Maybe it was my naivete. More than likely, it was my insatiable, gnawing desire to be worthy that led me to that kind of hapless, hopeless love. Regardless of what it was, I somehow caught the eye of a senior football player. He was seventeen, but I didn't care. When he picked me, he flipped my world upside down. No longer was I ugly, yellow trash. Now, I was chosen—I was the most beautiful girl in the pageant of our high school drama. I fell so deeply in love with him I felt like my guts were being ripped out. I couldn't breathe without him. I was head over heels.

Looking back, I see all the red flags. If my fourteen-year-old daughter showed up in the back of some testosterone-charged senior's muscle truck, I would probably raise an eyebrow. But my boyfriend wasn't a bad person; he was just a hormonal teenage boy. I didn't look like any of the other girls at school, and I was starving for any semblance of love. He made me feel pretty. He made me feel *wanted*.

Unfortunately for fourteen-year-old AliceAnne, my parents didn't share my romantic view of the situation. In fact, they thought it best that we leave town—pronto. I didn't get to say goodbye to anyone at school. I didn't even get to return my pom-pom uniform. My parents gave our dog and cat away (they only let us adopt strays, and now I see why). Then we took off into the night, headed for a brand-new town, a brand-new school, and a brand-new life.

This is what taught me not to count on anything. If there was one thing to learn from this experience, it was not to get attached to something I could lose—which was, in fact, everything. Each new town was just another rug to yank out from beneath me, another nail-biting occasion to watch the other shoe drop.

To make things worse, my parents shifted the blame right back to me.

"You're starting down a path no fourteen-year-old should ever be on," they said.

In other words, this was my fault. *My* doing. Yet another example of what happened when you were a "bad girl."

Now that I'm a parent, I realize that I only knew half the story. My dad's work situation wasn't stable, and my teenage relationship was an easy scapegoat to disguise circumstances unbeknownst to me. But at the time, I was devastated. I carried this narrative for years, and it seared a hole straight into my heart. My little brother, Michael, who'd always tried to protect and shield me, had to leave his friends and become the new kid once again. Because of my actions, the whole family had to start over.

My brother's life was ruined. *My* life was ruined. What was the point of caring about anything if it was just going to get ripped away?

The next thing I knew, I was in a new school. In the snap of one car ride, I went from a class of sixty-three to *sixteen hundred*, and it didn't help that I had to make my first impressions with a broken heart. In my mind, I'd lost everything: my friends, my pets, and the love of my life. I showed up to the dance audition to try out for their pom-pom team, but it was a total replay of Little Miss Kansas. I ended up walking out during the middle of the tryout, fuming and mortified. Somehow, I'd managed to become the ugly duckling all over again.

I yearned for an escape—somewhere, *anywhere* I wouldn't have to feel like this. But deep down, I couldn't help but feel like such a place didn't exist.

I didn't make the mistake of embarrassing myself by trying out for the dance team again. Instead, I got into theater. If you've never been around theater kids, let me tell you, it's an absolute treat. Sure, they're quirky (obscure musical references, random harmonization, frequent lapses into dramatic overtures, etc.), but they're also accepting to a fault. For me, the stage was the perfect escape.

In theater, I could be *with* people without actually being present. I never had to take off my mask. I never had to bare my true self. Between all the singing, dancing, and acting, every interaction with my friends revolved around the latest musical or show. We didn't have to talk about my family; we were too busy rehearsing lines. We were so preoccupied pretending to be other characters, no one really cared about the truth back at home. My parents weren't terribly involved with my chosen extracurricular, but that was just fine with me. I was driving by that time, which afforded me some small shred of independence beyond their disapproval and judgment. I spent hours in the auditorium, and nothing made me happier.

Here, I could wear any mask I wanted.

There was only one flaw in my perfect, prefabricated world, and that happened to be my best friend. Being a theater kid herself, we did everything together. She was my closest friend and greatest confidant, but she also happened to be my archrival.

Even as a high schooler, this girl was good—I mean, *really* good. She was professionally trained as a singer and dancer, and she commanded the stage like no one I'd ever seen. Invariably, she would land the lead role, and I would end up as her second. I was always the sidekick, the Aunt Sue to her Nannette, the chorus girl to her shining star.

Oddly enough, I was never angry with her about it. She was deserving, and I think a wiser, more mature part of my teenage soul understood that at a deeper level. It was my parents' comments that really began to grate on me. I remember exactly how those conversations would go.

Parents: So, what part did you get?

Me: I'm a principal character. One of the leads.

Parents: But not *the* lead?

Me: Well, not really, but...

Parents: Why aren't you the lead?

No matter what role I landed—how many lines, songs, and scenes I appeared in—it just wasn't good enough. It would *never* be good enough.

Of course, I didn't blame my best friend for this, but that's not to say there wasn't tension between us. For our school's baccalaureate, all the seniors had the opportunity to audition to sing the senior song during the program. She and I both auditioned, but everyone knew she was going to receive the honors. Much to everyone's surprise, I was picked instead. This should have been a joyous, supportive moment, but in the beginning, it was hell.

Of course, I was excited about the performance, but that happiness was tainted with guilt. My friend was the better singer, and it wasn't fair she'd been passed over. She knew it. I knew it. *Everyone* knew it. By landing the song, I couldn't help but feel like I'd taken something from my best friend, something she rightfully deserved.

When the fateful day finally came, I walked up to the microphone to face the audience. The music swelled, I opened my mouth...

And promptly forgot the words. Oh, yes. *Every. Single. One.*

It just so happened my friend was sitting in the front row. She could have pointed and laughed. She could have just sat there with a smug, satisfied smirk, affirming the deepest, darkest fears I'd been wrestling with since stepping on stage for Little Miss Kansas.

You're not good enough. You'll never be good enough.

But my friend didn't do any of those things. Instead, she began mouthing the lyrics to me, every single word of "Wind Beneath My Wings." I started crying. She started crying. We sobbed as we sang that song together—her from the audience, me from the stage.

We were always best friends, but that was the moment we became sisters.

I'm blessed to say this woman has remained one of my closest and most treasured friends. She's the only classmate I really still keep in touch with, which makes her the friend who's known me the longest. To this day, she still graces the stage as a professional performer, and I couldn't be prouder of her. In that critical moment of our high school baccalaureate ceremony, she chose to support me rather than put me down. As much as we competed, she made the active, conscious choice to set aside her own disappointment in order to lift me up. She was the friend I didn't know I needed, and she taught me a pivotal lesson I'll never forget: *Life isn't a pie.*

As women, it's so easy to put down other women. Our society relishes this. Products, institutions, and even communities love nothing more than to pit us against each other. This was the root of the poison that infected me during my time in the pageant circuit. Only one could be the prettiest. Only one could be the most talented. Only one contestant could truly win, and that meant all the others had to lose.

This is a painfully accurate illustration of scarcity mentality. Or in terms of pie, *if another woman gets a particularly scrumptious slice, then there has to be less for me.*

This line of thinking is absolutely ridiculous. The universe is infinite and bountiful, but if you start seeing resources and opportunities as limited, you inevitably *put those same limitations on yourself.*

Think about it this way: When has there ever been a finite amount of creativity? Happy marriages? Healthy lifestyles? If another woman has something you want, is there *actually* less for you? Or are you purposefully boxing yourself in a victim mentality so you don't have to take responsibility for your own life?

More often than not, it's women—not men—who spend their time tearing other women down. It's trendy and fun to hashtag "empowered women empower women," but I can't even begin to tell you how many times I've sat down for an honest conversation with a Leading Lady, only to have her tell me I intimidated her sometime in the past.

This is why women are so quick to dismiss each other. This is why we love to box one another up and compartmentalize each other's successes. This is why we're so quick to point out one another's faults.

If she's winning, then I must be losing. If she's succeeding, there must be less for me.

We do it by default, and I'm just as guilty as the next woman. Growing up feeling less-than taught me to assess other girls by two distinct parameters: *Is she a threat? And is she going to get in my way?*

Maybe this is a natural law of the jungle, the "survival of the fittest" or some other competitive rigamarole. Maybe this mentality has tinted our worldview, telling us that any role but the "lead role" is shameful and unworthy. But no matter where this mindset comes from, we *do* have the ability to make conscious shifts out of it. Just because this way of thinking was our reality doesn't mean it has to stay that way. When we start tearing down walls—when we dare to *live* the hashtags we post—we begin to see opportunities we never thought possible.

My high school baccalaureate ceremony reminds me that I have a deliberate choice to live differently. We don't have to live in a world of scarcity, cattiness, and rivalry. And frankly, I don't want to. Every woman has value, and every woman has something to contribute. When we put our efforts into making room on the stage instead of trying to push others off, something amazing happens.

We rise by lifting others.

•••

But, again, these are things I only realized in hindsight, and my high school drama lessons were far from over. The pageant circuit wasn't done with me just yet.

This time, it was all my mom's doing. There was nothing maniacal or sinister about that. She had a beautiful daughter who could sing, dance, and command a stage. Why *not* capitalize on all that social credit, especially after working so hard to build up a proud, Filipino community? Every day, I wore the mask of the happy, well-adjusted, first-generation daughter. I had an American dad, and my skin was much fairer than my mom's or my brothers'. For all intents and purposes, I already *was* Miss Asia America. All that was missing was the crown.

I was seventeen years old and a senior in high school. I had other things on my mind: theater, college, boys—*normal* high school senior stuff. To me, pageants were stupid and silly, and I'd spent the last seven years filing my Little Miss Kansas experience away with all my other traumatic childhood memories.

But Miss Asia America was bigger than me, and it had nothing to do with what I wanted. For my mom, this was the ultimate symbol of the life she'd worked so hard to achieve. From her beautiful nails to her beautiful daughter beaming down from the stage, the pageant was a glorious pinnacle of achievement. My job, of course, was to be the good girl. I'd been performing my whole life, and it was time to get back up and do it again. This wasn't just for my mom and the rest of my family. This was for my *community*. I wasn't very happy about getting back into the stifling world of hairspray and rhinestones, but all I had to do was dress up, shut up, and smile.

The experience ended up being completely different. Where I had been the rough, unrefined lump of coal in Little Miss Kansas, I was the diamond in Miss Asia America. I tried to be nice to the other girls, but even then, the difference between our lives was astronomical. They were full immigrant. I was half American. For the first time in my life, my whiteness afforded me privileges I never knew existed.

I was under no illusions—winning was my job. *You go up, you do it, you do it right, and you don't complain.* All that mattered was getting out there and winning. I remember being so miserable the pageant directors handed out Vaseline for my teeth to ensure I kept smiling through it all. Even when my cheeks burned and my face started shaking, I just kept smiling.

Just keep smiling. Just keep smiling. Just keep…

I felt like a big, fat impostor. Here I was, primped, poised, and dressed to play the part, but I'm not even fluent in my native language. At the end of my performance, I was supposed to say, "Thank you, ladies and gentlemen," in Tagalog—*"Maraming salamat, po."*

Three little words. Easy, right?

Standing there, blinking in the stage lights with my million-dollar smile stretched wide across my face, I said, *"Maraming salamat, ha!"*

The audience thought it was adorable and laughed amiably at my blunder. I became something of a 1998 meme. Random strangers would approach me after the show and repeat my mistake like a bona fide greeting. I would just flash them my perfect, pretty smile and laugh, completely masking the burning humiliation coursing through my veins. No matter how beautiful I looked, this was just one more place I didn't belong, the kingdom my mom wanted me so desperately to reign over.

I won the pageant. My mom was *ecstatic.* The crown was a huge win for the Filipino community. Someone opened up their home for the afterparty, and the celebration raged for hours on end. There was food, drinks, vendors, and my mom's riotous community of supporters that had come out to see me take the crown. My mom partied all night, but I was exhausted. Dazed, bleary, and utterly spent, I searched the house for a quiet place to rest. There was a small room of bunkbeds covered in clothes, and I spread a little clearing so I could finally get some sleep.

To this day, my mom still tells people about that competition. Visit her house, and you'll still find a picture of me—primped, preened, and dolled up for the stage—centrally displayed for all to see. Of course, it looked great on college applications to say I was Miss Asia America. I received minority scholarships for being able to represent the Filipino community with such poise, beauty, and polish.

But the pageant world was a completely separate world, a fantasy world I could visit but never fully reside in. I couldn't talk to my friends at school about Miss Asia America. They made fun of me every time I brought it up. How could they ever understand what something like this meant? The pageant was just one more thing that made me odd, one more thing that separated me from my peers.

Have you ever seen Filipina Barbie? She's pretty hard to come by, but she's worth a quick internet search. I had my very own Filipina Barbie when I was a girl, but she never came out of her box. She was too precious for that. To me, she was pure magic.

I had many Barbies, and they all came in typical Barbie colors—blond and brunette with lily-white skin. They were pretty, but Filipina Barbie was by far my favorite. I valued her so much I kept her locked up so she would never get worn or frazzle-headed. Finally, I had a doll that looked like me, the Filipino princess Ingkong had always told me about.

I still have that Barbie. She reminds me that the world is both a mirror and a window. Sometimes, the world reflects your reality back to you. Other times, it gives you a glimpse of someone else's. That's why representation is *so important*, especially in the fundamental years of childhood. As a young girl, it meant everything to me to see myself in a world where I didn't seem to fit in anywhere.

All of a sudden, I'd stepped into the role of my most treasured possession. Up on the Miss Asia America stage, sparkling in my dress, my Vaseline smile scintillating for all to see, I was a living, breathing extension of Filipina Barbie and everything she stood for.

What I didn't realize was I was putting myself in my own box.

Nowadays, I try to steer clear of the bitterness I felt toward the whole pageant experience. I've been asked to come back to speak at the Miss Asia America pageant, and I've respectfully (but firmly) declined.

It took a long time to realize my parents weren't intentionally setting me up for failure. I truly believe pageant parents are doing the best they can. More often than not, it's *their* dreams that are irreparably tied to projections of fame, fortune, and beauty. Maybe my parents didn't feel beautiful. Maybe they didn't feel shiny. Maybe they thought, just for a moment, they could live those elusive dreams vicariously through me.

There's a lot of weight in that but also a lot of forgiveness.

Believe it or not, I still love the stage. I still love singing and dancing. I still take roles in our neighborhood performances. Recently, my mom was feeling especially down, so she asked me to record myself singing a song I used to sing for her back in high school. You would think that would be triggering, but the moment came and passed without any great emotional significance. There was no reconnection to the past. No stinging wounds, dark memories, or seething bitterness.

Here's what I know to be true: I love my mom. If she's lonely and craving connection, I can step into a role of comfort without putting on a mask. I can be authentic in my talent and my love.

I sent her the recorded song, and you would have thought I'd just bought her a brand-new house. She was *elated*. Her face lit up like a beacon. Sure, my song was a "performance," but it wasn't the same as getting up on stage when I was a girl. As a teenager, I was a puppet. As an adult, I have the ability to see that I did what I did out of love.

What have I learned from all this?

I get to decide how to view the wide world around me. *I* get to decide what to do with every life experience. To this day, I love the stage, and I love to perform. I can take a theater role or belt out a karaoke song with nothing but pure joy. My performance isn't me; it's just an *extension* of me. When I entertain, I do so to support my own values of connection, enjoyment, and creativity.

My gifts don't make me worthy. I'm *already* worthy.

There's no denying I've got glitter in my veins. I'm a girly girl with a proclivity for sparkles, but don't mistake manners and poise for weakness. I'm just as apt to giggle as I am to whack someone over the head with a Prada bag. A lot of people don't understand why I'm such a froufrou girl after all my pageant experience, and that's okay too—so long as they don't take my femininity for weakness.

A few years ago, the "don't call me a lady" campaign marched its way across the internet. Truthfully, I find it myopic and even offensive. I just so happen to like the values of a lady, and I just so happen to think kindness, appreciation of beauty, and manners are wonderful traits. Whether a woman wants to be decked out in frills or roar down the road in leather motorcycle chaps, *her* own authenticity is *her* own femininity—and no pageant in the world has the right or the power to redefine mine.

But again, these are musings years in the making. For seventeen-year-old AliceAnne, the lesson from Miss Asia America was curt, sharp, and salient: If you put your mind to something, you can do it. You *can* win anything you set your mind to, and if you show up and act like you know what you're doing, people tend to believe you.

Everyone wants to see a winner—the beautiful princess, the intrepid prince. We're all looking for someone we can look up to, and we're always hungry for a good ol' rags to riches story. As long as you play the part of the winner, people will see you as one. If you just keep smiling, you can fool them all.

I carried my burning, Vaseline smile for a long, long time.

Trouble with your marriage? *Just keep smiling.* Woes at work? *Just keep smiling.* Insecurities about your motherhood, your career, or even your own *soul?*

Just. Keep. That. Smile. LOCKED.

If you tell people you're winning, you're winning. And who doesn't love a winner? If I constantly had to pretend like I had everything together, so be it. I was all too good at wearing masks anyway.

No one likes a loser. No one wanted to see I was lost, vulnerable, or scared. From then on, I made it my job to win at absolutely everything I did. So long as I kept up the illusion of perfection, switching from mask to mask to hide any sign of weakness, I was safe.

This carried into my twenties and far beyond. No matter what I achieved in my business, my home life, or my hobbies, there was always that sly gremlin of insecurity—that nasty, sneaky little blackhead on prom night—waiting for the chance to spring. To make up for all these faults, I simply had to overperform at everything else. *Every single endeavor* was a rush to squelch the pain with a win.

This took all sorts of forms in my life.

Doubting your mommy skills? Become a breastfeeding champ. If you don't breastfeed your children, you're not giving them the best.

Body issues after baby? Get ripped, sign up for a bodybuilding contest, then walk across the stage in a piece of dental floss while a panel of strangers judge your physique. Fat moms aren't lovable. Loser *moms let themselves go.*

Worried people dismiss you as a gold digger after marrying a successful entrepreneur? Open your own childcare business while you're eight-and-a-half months pregnant. That will show them what a hard worker you are!

The critique never ends, so the perfectionism can never end either. It's a vicious, unforgiving cycle, but let's remember the self-preservation skills I learned in Chapter One. According to *those* little life lessons, this was what I had to do to keep myself safe.

It was only years later, far away from the glitz and the glam of pageantry, that I really went back to look at these lessons. Of course, there's nothing *wrong* with wanting to win. We all want to be the best versions of ourselves; we all work hard for those proud, shining moments. The question isn't whether or not we want good things for ourselves, our families, and our endeavors—it's what we use to fuel those efforts.

While working my way through my professional coaching qualifications, my instructor made us create a totem to represent our gremlins—a physical manifestation of our deepest, darkest fears and insecurities. To illustrate my gremlin of perfectionism, I made a cape. I covered one side of the beautiful material with stars of my achievements, including accolades I'd won and praise I'd received.

She's so charismatic, one star would say. *She's so smart. She wins this and that!*

The adornments were beautiful. Shiny. Sparkling. But looking at the cape from the outside, you couldn't see that those stars were safety-pinned to the fabric. On the inside of the cape, each star was pinned to its own corresponding insecurity.

She's a fraud. If she were so smart, why did she make a mistake like that?

She only won that because of this-and-that and so-and-so.

My cape is my shield, my mask, and my armor. Those safety pins might be uncomfortable from the inside, but as long as I was over-succeeding, over-accomplishing, and overachieving, no one would be able to see the ugliness underneath. If I just kept playing the role, I would never have to face my true self.

As you've probably guessed by now, this mentality had a breaking point. It turns out you can't live happily in a lie, and you can't live in truth until you've found your own authenticity.

That was a journey for me. It's a journey for everyone, and each woman's pilgrimage looks completely different. I'll be the first to confess the underside of my cape hasn't really changed. My gremlins of insecurity are always there; I'm just more aware of them. That's forty years of thoughts, pinned and pressed into the fabric of my mind, and it takes a constant, conscious effort not to hide behind all those shiny stars.

There was a lot of loneliness in my childhood. I didn't have any heroes or role models, so I had to become my own. Far too often, I would catch myself zoning out as I doodled the same drawing over and over again—a strong, confident woman clad in shining, impenetrable armor. Her chest plate protected her fragile, aching heart. Her sword slayed the naysayers and the monsters braying at the gates. From head to toe, she was covered in every lesson she'd accumulated to protect herself. But armor gets heavy. Carry it around for too long, and you'll end up exhausted.

When this book debuts, I'll be forty years old. It has taken me this long to go through the process of shedding my armor and putting on something else. I'm not quite sure what that "something else" looks like yet, but instead of protecting my heart, I've started to open it.

As for the happy/sad masks I collected as a teenager? I found them a little over ten years ago, boxed up in my mother's house with other childhood memorabilia.

"What are these?" my husband asked. A wry smirk tugged the

corner of his mouth as he inspected the dull, eyeless faces.

"Throw them out," I said. "I don't need them."

They went straight in the trash.

I'm done wearing masks. I'm done living a life of pretending. When I step out into the world, I want people to see my true face.

CHAPTER 3: TO LEARN, YOU MUST LISTEN

If you had the power to alter anything in your past, what would you change?

For years, I had it all mapped out. I would go straight to the hurt, all those instances of pain, confusion, and loss. With a clean, trauma-less slate of happiness and confidence, I'd venture forth into a carefree, happy-go-lucky life without making a single pain-fueled decision I would live to regret. There would be no abuse, no brokenness, and no capes. Just the shiny, glowing narrative of the fantasy I'd built for myself—a triumphant, heroic journey where getting what I wanted meant winning in the end.

I never wanted to spend my life trapped behind a mask. I never wanted to be the villain in someone else's story. For years, I was convinced that if I could just fix that one moment, I could fix everything. And in the fairytale world of "what-ifs" and "if onlys," the tangled threads go on and on.

If only…

If just…

If this hadn't…

If I had…

For thirty years, if you would have asked me what I would change about my childhood, I would have had a definite answer. I wanted to change my past. I wanted *desperately* to be someone different, and I could directly pinpoint each and every abuse in my life—be it my fault or someone else's—that made me into the person I am.

Nowadays, my answer is very different. I wouldn't change anything about who I've been, even when the howls of memory echo up from the deep, dark holes of my yesterdays. It's taken me a long time to learn that being a real leader is learning to embrace your story—discovering how to treasure the horrible, unsightly instances you've spent so long hiding. If only it were as simple as removing a mask, unclasping a cape, or shedding a suit of armor.

This is a mindset shift decades in the making.

It all boils down to forgiveness. If the word makes you flinch, don't worry. You're in good company. So often, we talk about forgiveness in terms of the other person: *you need to forgive so-and-so to move on with your life*, or *everyone deserves a second chance.*

For the record, everyone does *not* deserve a second chance, and just because someone apologizes doesn't mean that person is entitled to your best self. Forgiveness isn't about the other person. Quite the contrary—forgiveness is about *you*. It's not up to you whether the other person is shamefaced, sorry, or even bothers to change their behavior. All of that is completely out of your control, and you have every right to wallow in that unfairness for as long as you'd like. Life is arbitrary, cruel, and unfair more often than not. But the more time we sit and languish in this place of bitter helplessness, the less time we have for other truths—the fact that life is also beautiful, bountiful, and progressive.

Every experience has taught me a new skill. Every mistake has shown me who I don't want to be. I can cling to that pain as much as I need to, but the moment I choose to let it go, I find there's a whole wide world waiting for me to grow.

The fact is, we're all born in pain—every single one of us. Our parents had pain. Our grandparents had pain. *Their* grandparents had pain, and I'm pretty sure the further you get from indoor plumbing, the bleaker the picture becomes. We're all dealing with decade after decade of emotional dead weight, years of baggage our ancestors chose to deny, obscure, and struggle with far before they passed that burden down to us.

As a child, none of this made sense to me. It was raw. Painful. *Personal.* After my grandfather died, my father deployed, and my grandmother shunned us, I couldn't make sense of the hurt. My grandpa had been a Southern Baptist choir minister, and two of my uncles were preachers. I just didn't understand how my grandmother could be so cruel to my family, how two men of faith could stand at the pulpit, preaching the love of God while shutting their doors in my mom's face.

Even then, the hypocrisy was too much to stomach. These were broken people, and I took a lot of that on myself. When I was a "good girl," people loved me, so it only made sense that when people didn't love me, it was because I'd done something bad. When I finally realized my own pain wasn't a punishment but rather, an inheritance, something magical happened.

All of a sudden, *this* mess wasn't *my* mess.

Author and teacher Eckhart Tolle calls this "the pain body"—the concept that we're born with the pain of our ancestors, inheriting insecurities passed down from generation to generation. I used to be so angry at my parents for the choices they made and the unfair responsibilities they shoved onto my shoulders. But as I studied Tolle's work, my ironclad mindset began to shift. Instead of crafting a narrative of *my* childhood pain, I was able to trace the roots back— back to where my own parents had been made to feel less-than through racism, physical abuse, and outright rejection. My father hurt me because his father hurt him, and my grandpa was hurt by his father before him. This is just another cycle of behavior—a "sin of generations" that, if left unchecked, will follow our families for centuries to come.

Accepting that kind of pain is never easy. I'm not talking about justifying, forgiving, or healing—just *accepting*. Let's say you burn your hand on a hot stove. The wound will hurt terribly for a time, but eventually, the pain will fade while the scar still lingers. Whenever you look down to the scarred skin, you have a choice. You can either go back to the scorching, searing agony of the moment you touched the stove, or you can see the mark the same way you see a mole, a freckle, or a thumbnail—just another part of your hand. You can never peel off the physical reminder of what happened, but that doesn't mean you have to experience the same intense suffering each and every time you glance down.

To put things simply, you have to remove yourself from the pain in order to see the pattern.

The concept sounds easy enough, but the reality couldn't be any farther from the truth. There's a reason we've got memes, bumper stickers, and tea towels that cheekily proclaim, "I opened my mouth, and my mother came out." It's everyone's inevitable nightmare.

Of course, no one is *exactly* like their parents. We develop customized coping mechanisms through the perspectives of our own experiences. We have our own stories and our own ways of looking at things, but it's pretty easy to see how our default mannerisms get passed down through generations. In all fairness, how can we expect our kids to behave any differently? Most animals are born with rapid-fire instincts, the inane survival skills that enable puppies to leave their mothers at only twelve weeks and baby snakes to never even meet their parents before slithering off on their own.

Our children, on the other hand, stay with us for *eighteen years*. That's a lot of time for habits to rub off.

This is one of the reasons I'm so passionate about my preschools. The way an individual sees themselves—the origins of self-esteem, identity, and self-worth—develops well before those tiny humans turn eight years old. At that point in time, you've spent far more of your life with your parents and/or guardians than any other human being.

Think about that for a moment. What were your early years like?

What did people say to you? What did you say to yourself? What did these experiences teach you about the world and your place in it? Whether you felt shame, betrayal, guilt, or even love, these lessons have been hardwired into your worldviews.

Like I've said before, I'm pretty darn proud of young AliceAnne. She not only survived everything up to this point—she learned that she *could* survive everything up to this point. Even as a child, I knew that if I just put my mind to making it through, I would come out on the other end every single time. Maybe I was just born that way; maybe it's my experiences that made me so stubborn. Whether it was fashioning ad hoc weapons, dreaming up impossible tales to explain my strange family, or plotting my after-school schedule to keep me safe from the dangers in my own home, I knew that everything was "figureoutable." I had everything I needed. I wouldn't just survive—I would make it to the next level.

To this day, one of my strengths is a love of learning, and what started as a survival tactic has grown and matured into a passion. I absorb information feverishly; I'm constantly looking for ways to improve and figure things out. Ironically enough, the refuse-to-die fire that spurred me to spear a rapist in the eye is the same fire that's kept me navigating multiple businesses through COVID. That boy from so many years ago isn't excused, nor were his actions justified by any sort of success on my end. But that doesn't mean I can't look at that scar with a fierce sense of pride. I survived that. And I'm going to survive this too.

In the L.E.A.D.E.R. acronym, L is technically for "learner." But it's so much more than that. To be a learner, you also have to be a listener. It's about recognizing that there's more to life than just you— that if you step back, zoom out, and listen to what's happening around you, you can actually get deep insight into yourself.

I find it pretty ironic that you have to shrug off your own ego to keep from getting caught up in someone else's. Coming from a bicultural family, I had a lot of opportunities to be an observer. I didn't understand a lot of what was going on, but I recognized how my insatiable curiosity could serve me. I was always puzzling out why things were the way they were—why certain people acted a certain way and why so much of my life was different from what I saw outside. With every new school came a new mask, but the bright side of that was learning to be adaptable.

The truth boils down to this: The world is constantly growing and changing. If you're not growing and changing with it, you're falling behind. Birds stay attuned to the seasons. Dogs learn their owners' commands, and the deer on River Road constantly listen to traffic to determine when it's safe to cross. Nature is progressing with or without you.

If you can't be open to listening and learning, you will fail. If you can't give up on trying to fit the world into your own perspective, you will fail. You will stay small. You *will* stay behind. At the very least, you're going to be crushed and disappointed. At the worst, you'll just be lost.

The fundamental core of a survivor mindset is a learning mindset. Every experience has something to teach us if we're only willing to listen. The survivor mindset does have its perks, but you can't thrive *and* survive at the same time. Unfortunately, this is something I learned the hard way.

After coming up through life as a survivor, I tended to approach everything with that same mentality—friendships, job responsibilities, and even intimate relationships. If there was one thing my abandoned pets, boyfriend, and pom-pom career taught me, it was not to let people get too close. Yes, I was adaptable and congenial, but the good-girl facade was only an inch deep.

If I grabbed onto something, chances were, I was going to lose it. If I let anyone get too close, they might just catch a glimpse of my scars. If I never let anyone in, no one could ever hurt me. I'd been vulnerable before, and I swore to myself I would never get trapped in that place again.

There are a few problems with this logic, and I'm sure they don't surprise you. Here I was, listening, learning, and soaking up information from the wide world around me, only to find that all of it was useless when I wasn't engaging in life. My cape of accomplishments was so shiny—my armor so thick and protective—I couldn't feel anything at all.

I always joke that professional coaches end up coaching their younger selves. Ironically, a lot of high-achieving women I end up working with exist in this defensive, energy-guzzling survival mode. And who can blame them? After being looked down on, bullied, or even told how worthless they were their entire lives, they had to find some way to shield themselves from the beatdowns in order to move forward. If you've worked yourself up to a certain level—both in life and in business—you've probably had to develop some sort of high-response defense mechanism, ready at a moment's notice to protect you from harm. There's nothing wrong with that. I'd even argue that a good defense mechanism is essential for certain situations. The real problem is *when* and *how often* we use those defenses.

I have a colleague who was bullied and excluded as a child. She's a beautiful, incredibly successful businesswoman, but that doesn't validate or change the harsh lessons she learned as a girl. When she was only ten years old, she helped her friend plan a birthday party—only to be omitted from the guest list when the invitations finally went out.

This woman is now in her fifties. While the schoolyard bullying and birthday parties may be in the past, the lessons she learned lingered far after. Every time her clients undermine her work, the old defense mechanisms immediately fire up. These cruel experiences were so deeply ingrained in her mind, they've colored the way she thinks about conflict. What does this look like?

Situation: *Why did my client not tell me that key piece of information?*

Brain: *Because even after all the work you've done, your input isn't valued.*

Situation: *Why wasn't I included in this email?*

Brain: *Because everyone else is important, but you're insignificant.*

In the lens of this woman's past experiences, this logic makes perfect sense. No one can pull the rug out from under you if you pull it out first. No one can beat you as long as you refuse to play.

But this isn't thriving—this is surviving situations that aren't even a threat. A healthy, trust-based working relationship isn't possible when you're constantly trying to outflank the other person in order to protect yourself. If you spend all your time building walls around your heart, the love you experience is never going to expand. No one can touch your life, and you can never touch anyone else's.

Stories like these remind me that while we may have no control over the way others treat us, victim mentality is a choice.

Before you go clutching your pearls and seething about victim blaming, please hear me out. I'm not saying this flippantly. I don't believe anyone deserves pain, harm, or cruelty, and I'm not saying bad things never happen to good people. What I'm trying to communicate is that, while you can never hold yourself responsible for others' actions, you have a choice to stay in the "burn stage" of victim mentality. *You* are responsible for your own happiness, and that's both liberating and intimidating. Having lived a significant chunk of my life in "survival mode," I know victim mentality is pretty darned comfortable. I see my clients choose this mental model time and time again, and it makes perfect sense why it's their default.

Nothing ever goes right, but that's not your fault.

Of course, your life is awful. Look at what that person did to you!

How can you ever be expected to get over any roadblocks if you never had that sort of confidence in the first place?

In victim mentality, it's over before you even begin—the zero-sum solution to a zero-sum game.

When you grow up surviving, living on the assumption that tomorrow will look like today for the rest of eternity, you grow up waiting for the next bad thing to happen. You find what works, and you stick to it no matter how much it hurts you. You're not learning to grow; you're learning to follow patterns, reacting to your life instead of leading it.

This is what I like to call "the default." When I talk to women in leadership, it usually sounds something like, "Well, she set the precedent of doing it this way, and he did that over there…"

Blame-shifting runs in infinite loops. It may feel like absolution, but every twist and turn tangles you up tighter. At its core, victim mentality is a shrug of responsibility. Complete and utter surrender to the actions of others. While protocols, systems, and cycles can be extremely useful, default mode makes the assumption that they're immutable, built-in cogs of fate. In other words: *this is just the way things are, for better or for worse, and it's never going to change.*

Default mode is inherently a refusal to listen, to truly put an ear to the engine to hear what's running smoothly and what may be creaky, squeaky, or even just plain harmful. You have to pay attention to the rhythms of life in order to identify patterns, and only then can you determine which cycles you need to break. There's a reason default mode feeds right into victim mentality, and more often than not, I see the two come hand in hand. If you're living in victim mentality, you can't put in the effort required to create real, lasting change because admitting you have the power to take the lead also means you have the responsibility to do so. Being the victim (theoretically) absolves you from that responsibility. If you're constantly at the mercy of your circumstances, how can you celebrate the power to triumph in the wake of ugliness?

This mental armor seems like it's a safe, defensive mentality, but it's ultimately a stagnant one. At the end of the day, learned helplessness is still helplessness. There is such a thing as being powerless, but there's also the default of victimhood—the illusion that you can never have any control of your life because that control was taken from you sometime in the past.

There are days I find myself back in this place, wandering the aimless corridors I swore I'd left far behind. I have to be gentle to myself in these moments. Everyone has bad days. No one (not even a

Leading Lady) makes a choice to be different then magically wakes up to find these tangled mental pathways have disappeared forever. But before I start beating myself up again, I have to remember that reverting to my old cycles of victim mentality doesn't mean I'm weak. It means I'm *hurt*, and that makes me human.

There are instances in my past that have resulted in post-traumatic stress and depression. That's a combination of my brain chemicals and my experiences—a salient cocktail of both nature *and* nurture that, while not my fault, is a reality I have to deal with each and every day. There are days I'm sad, broken, and tired. There are days I regress to responding in my trauma default. There are days when I crumble under the weight of it all. When I finally reach the end of this harrowing mental labyrinth, there's nothing left to do but admit that I'm helpless to change what happened to me.

That may come off as pretty fatalist, but it's actually extremely empowering. Yes, I was a victim. Those things were out of my control. That is, after all, the definition of a victim—someone who doesn't have control. But I can find a way to honor that hurt without letting it own me. I don't want to live in the default of who I've been. I don't want the lessons I've learned to dictate who I become. I want to pick and choose from the vast array of experiences I've collected in my crazy, colorful life. I want to be discerning about the skills I've developed, and I want to trust in my own abilities.

I don't just want to survive. I want to thrive.

•••

There's a beautiful Japanese art called kintsugi, literally, the "golden journey." The artist takes broken pieces of a certain medium—usually glass, ceramic, or pottery—and fills the breaks with golden lacquer, repairing the vessel while honoring the crack from the shattering.

In essence, it's the art of precious scars.

I remember when my scars made me feel unworthy and broken. I hid them any way I could. My masks shielded my face, my cape covered my insecurities, and my armor protected me from the chaotic forces of the world—ridicule, jealousy, and even love. These false faces were my coping mechanism. I could never let anyone see anything less than the perfect, put-together image I wanted them to see. Cracked things were ugly, useless, and broken. Who could ever love something like that?

Kintsugi flips all of these beliefs on their heads. The broken pieces of these vessels aren't pitied, hidden, or left helplessly in the rubble. They're *celebrated*. Every single crack makes these pieces beautiful, and the story—the golden journey—comes from every place that vessel was decimated.

I've been asked how I manage to forgive others for the wrongs they've done to me. I've also been asked how I'm able to forgive myself for the wrongs I've done to others. When I recall these instances, the stories bear a lot of weight. Each one has heroes and villains; each experience comes with its own heaping mound of baggage. My own golden journey was realizing that baggage wasn't mine to carry. Every last crack is a testament of the lessons I've learned as I've put myself back together, time and time again.

There's so much worth in these crooked, golden lines. When I truly began to recognize that, I realized that the wholesome, "put-together" parts aren't the only ones worth celebrating.

In fact, the chips and cracks just might be the most beautiful feature of all.

Even after wrestling through all of this, I revert to my own default mode more than I like to admit. Oddly enough, acknowledging my scars does help. There's something strangely breathtaking about making a mistake, looking back at the gold, and seeing the growth in your life. I've come to terms with my past, but that doesn't mean the memories don't come back to haunt me. It's not distressing; it's just another thing that makes me human. We all revisit those deep, dark corners of who we've been. Whether we acknowledge them or not, our own cycles of behavior have made seismic impacts on the world around us.

I wasn't a very good mother in my twenties. When my daughter Marissa was growing up, I was still determined to make every meal a delicious, perfectly balanced, home-cooked miracle. I was still living under the pretense of perfection—still juggling the "boss mom" persona while desperately trying to keep my flaws hidden.

I was a young mom. I was wading through a lot of my own trauma. I know beyond a shadow of a doubt that if I'd had my kids now instead of way back then, their childhoods would have been completely different.

In those days, I was still hiding behind my cape of accomplishments. I put a lot of emphasis on perfection, and my expectation was that my daughter needed to be perfect as well. I never set out meaning to shrug my own insecurities onto her, but no one exists in a bubble. When you're living in default—following the rut of patterns and behaviors you've been living in for so long—you can't help but impact your children with those same habits.

These patterns stick out to me as painful barbs of memory. When Marissa was around four years old, I spotted a photo kiosk during one of our trips to the mall. You know the ones I'm talking about, those big, boxy booths that take a series of successive snaps then frame your pictures in order with cute designs or funny text. Marissa saw the kiosk and wanted her own photo strip, so I obliged her. I, too, wanted a nice, adorable memento of our lovely, mother-daughter outing.

But the moment we stepped into the booth, something in Marissa snapped. Maybe it was the excitement. Maybe it was the claustrophobia of that cramped, plastic box.

Whatever that spirit of craziness was, it descended on my daughter in a rush of tiny, toddler fury. She started kicking and squirming, bicycling her little feet like a madwoman. At this point, I'd been working with little kids for years. I was used to toddlers being—well, let's just say *unpredictable*—but after paying for the pictures she so desperately wanted, this was the last straw. I grabbed her by the arm and slammed her down, hissing and red-faced as I pinned her wriggling body to the seat.

"Settle down," I snapped. "You're the one who wanted these pictures. We already paid for them."

What I didn't know was that this kiosk also took videos. The very same camera that snapped the pictures was recording us the whole time, and the thirty-second clip of visitors scrambling to rearrange their cute, funny poses would be left up for passersby to see until the next customers recorded their own video.

Only when I exited that photobooth did I see what I'd done. I watched in open-mouthed horror as the video played on repeat. There I was, berating my child, shoving her into that seat over and over again. I looked like a monster.

The image is still burned in my brain.

We left the mall quickly after that. Honestly, I'm surprised no one alerted child services. I called my best friend, sobbing, horrified by what I'd seen on that screen. This wasn't who I wanted to be. This wasn't the *mother* I wanted to be. After all I'd been through as a little girl, was this really how I wanted to show up?

Sometimes, it takes a bit of distance to see our own patterns for what they really are. Watching myself from the outside changed everything. If we had that sort of space in our everyday lives—if we could watch our own behavior, over and over on repeat—we would live very differently. This instance showed me exactly why I didn't want to be a victim, helpless and hungry for any means to keep up the illusion of perfection.

I never want to pass that down to my kids.

I often wonder about the seeds I planted during those early years. Did I affect the way my daughter sees herself? Did my criticisms, anger, and need for control pass on baggage she has no business carrying?

It took a full view of the damage for me to listen and learn about the destructive cycles in my life. Now, I know perfectly well I was in default, and from there, I had to make the decision to change. Perfectionism is *not* a pattern I want to continue. It hasn't served me in my own life, it has never served Marissa, and it's definitely not serving our mother-daughter relationship.

I remember driving her to school one morning. We were cruising down the winding stretch of River Road when it hit me all at once.

"Will you need therapy because of me?" I asked.

She caught my eye in the rearview mirror and snickered. "The very fact you're asking me that is going to put me in therapy."

That wasn't the response I'd expected, but I couldn't help but smile. At least we'd settled that I would be paying for both college *and* therapy.

Perfection has never been a prerequisite for thriving. You can't grow if you can't acknowledge your starting point. If you're still living in survival mode, the absolute first step is to accept yourself for exactly who you are, wherever you are. When you start filling in those cracks, you're going to uncover more hairline fissures than you could ever imagine.

Trust me on that one.

If you think of your life as a vessel, that makes you a cup for all the goodness, love, and beauty this world has to offer. But if that cup cracks—and, unless you happen to live in a fantastical fairy dreamworld full of ponies and guileless pillow-people, you *will* crack—your vessel will never be full. You'll forever be leaking, constantly grasping at fistfuls of water as events beyond your control seep away the joy and happiness that should have always been yours.

It's not your fault that you're broken. It's not your fault that someone damaged you. This world is full of reckless, heavy things.

If you're struggling to fill a cracked cup, the oversimplified solution is to replace your broken vessel with a new one. A perfect cup won't leak water. An undamaged, intact vessel can hold anything life brings. You might yearn to go back to before your cup was cracked, to

74

stop anything in your life from ever breaking. Another strategy is just to keep the water running, flooding your life with success, business, and entertainment in hopes that the overflow will mask the brokenness.

Yes, you can stand at the sink, wishing for that new, perfect cup. Yes, you can run that faucet to the max until your water bill skyrockets. But if you ignore the leaks in the vessel you're holding, you're never going to see how it can be whole again.

That's why the first step in filling your cup is accepting and acknowledging those cracks. It doesn't matter where they came from. It doesn't matter who's responsible for them. *You* hold the power of *kintsugi*, and you and only you have the ability to fill the brokenness with beautiful, golden lacquer.

As I raise my own cup to the light, I can't help but admire it for exactly what it is. I don't celebrate the ones who hurt me. I don't pass my gilded vessel into the hands of anyone who asks. But if I had the power to pick and choose any life to live, I would take this one, exactly as it is, from start to finish. The scars of my past are some of the most beautiful parts of me. They remind me I don't have to be a victim— while my trauma may leave a mark, it doesn't define me and the future of my children. These little gold veins are a testament to who I was and everything I've overcome to get here.

I can't think of anything more beautiful than that.

E is for engagement.

CHAPTER 4: THE AGREEMENTS

People make a lot of assumptions about a young woman marrying an older man. And when I say "a lot," I mean, *a lot*. Maybe it's the stereotype, or maybe it's just easier to assume a woman has ulterior motives than it is to accept she's truly confident with making her own decisions. We look at couples with what we perceive to be "suspicious" age gaps, and our minds light up with the labels that make us most comfortable: gold digger, cradle robber… Take your pick. There's no lack of options.

But labels are funny little boogers, aren't they? For the life of me, I can't explain why they show up in the midst of my own raging insecurities, but they're just as quick to attach themselves to my judgments as I am to make those judgments in the first place. I admit that I'm just as familiar with labeling other women as I am with being labeled. For years, nothing terrified me more than the judgments I couldn't control. I became obsessed with the idea that my teachers, my family, my classmates, and everyone else in my world was constantly weighing, appraising, and evaluating me. There was nothing I could do to escape their judgment. It only made sense to try and eke out the best label I could.

And, if I do say so myself, I got pretty good at the whole song and dance. The only issue was, by devoting myself to controlling labels and meeting other peoples' expectations, I never took the time to think about how I wanted to show up in my own life. Sure, impressing people and dazzling them with a cape of perfection made me feel in control, but driving your own car doesn't afford you any freedom when you spend all your gas driving everyone else where they want to go.

Labels are inevitable. Judgments are unavoidable. No matter what we do or don't do, there's always going to be someone, somewhere who slaps down an unfair assessment for the sake of their own comfort. I've been flippantly told far too often that I should simply shrug off the snide comments—that I shouldn't care what other people think because others' opinions don't matter—but we all know the issue just isn't that simple.

Others' opinions do matter. They impact the world around us.

They have just as much potential to heal as they do to wound.

But at the end of the day, the only thing truly in our grasp is reality. No matter what forces are beyond our control, we get to choose how we engage. We can live to please others, or we can strive to show up as our authentic selves.

By the time I met the love of my life, I'd been living for others so long, I had no idea what my true self looked like.

Most people don't realize that I started my business without completing my degree. After high school, I spent a lot of time bopping around from college to college. I had no idea where I belonged, so I struck out at it blindly. The University of Missouri, Northwest Missouri State, Central Missouri State… I was so indecisive and anxiety-stricken, I couldn't keep myself in one place.

Anytime there was a hurdle, I withdrew, packed my life up, and tried somewhere else. My childhood had taught me nothing was permanent anyway, so why did it really matter? My parents and I had always been nomadic, skipping from town to town, making tenuous connections we could easily slip away from the moment things went wrong. Throughout my childhood and teenage years, I'd attended thirteen different schools. I couldn't control the tumultuous flow of my parents' wanderlust, but it was my responsibility to keep myself safe, no matter what the cost.

When I heard about a girl being raped in a local parking garage, I stopped going to class altogether and opted to take my courses online. When I was nineteen years old, I had my first full-blown panic attack on a Missouri interstate. I remember pulling over to the side of the road, struggling to keep a grip on my cell phone as my hands trembled. I called 911 screaming and sobbing. Nothing was life-threatening, but I didn't know that. As I sat there, wracked with trembles as my lungs constricted, I could only assume that I was dying prematurely of a heart attack. My thoughts raced in frenzied circles, blurring behind my eyes as they twisted themselves into hideous forms:

I don't know what to do. I don't know where I'm going. I don't know what to do with my life...

At that point, I finally had to acknowledge that I was *not* okay. I had no idea what it was I actually wanted, and not having direction or goals for my future was fueling my anxiety like kerosene on a campfire. I was truly living in default—surviving without any plan, intention, or directive. I had no idea what I was doing or what I wanted to accomplish. As far as I could see, life was about reacting to everyone else.

This total lack of self-confidence didn't bode well in the relationship department. My longtime high school boyfriend was a complete loser—the kind of guy perfectly equipped for a relationship based in victim mentality. He was a liar and a cheater. He opened up bogus financial accounts in my name and completely ruined my credit. Despite all of this, I stuck with him for years. Sure, he was a complete idiot, but at least I knew what I was getting.

In the midst of all this gaslighting, I handled things the best way I knew how—overachieving. After-school enrichment programs are commonplace in Missouri, and at the ripe age of nineteen, I was the supervisor for seven different locations. Here I was, excelling in these programs as a leader of my peers, wielding significant authority at a shockingly young age. I should have been happy. I should have been thriving.

I'd never felt so lost. No matter what I accomplished or how much praise showered down from above, nothing was ever good enough.

Nowadays, I can look back and recognize that this time in my life was riddled with impostor syndrome. I didn't value myself, so I overperformed to compensate. I don't know if I was running on praise or the sheer fire of adrenaline, but I knew that as long as people liked me, I would be okay. If I could just make it through the workday looking clean, put-together, and completely competent, I could go home and hate myself behind closed doors.

The house of cards came crashing down when I found out about my boyfriend's cheating. It wasn't just anyone—it was a family friend. This ended up triggering my mental breakdown on the side of the road. Sure, I was "winning at life" as a young professional, working hard day after day in a job where I excelled. But what did any of it matter if I *felt* this way—mortified, miserable, and completely exhausted?

The episode ended up putting me in outpatient therapy where I promptly received a diagnosis of post-traumatic stress disorder—PTSD. At the time, it didn't make any sense. I wasn't a combat veteran. I'd never been in a grisly accident or witnessed a horrific murder. For the life of me, I couldn't identify the trauma I was supposed to be *post*.

Unfortunately, my lack of understanding didn't qualify me as being "above" or "unfit for" the diagnosis. While PTSD has come to be associated with a specific type of trauma, it's not necessarily the trauma itself that constitutes the illness. Two people can witness the exact same thing, and while one person walks away mentally unscathed, the other can end up scarred for life. It wasn't as much about what had happened to me as it was how I'd learned to cope. Rape and abuse throughout my childhood had taught me to be careful and hypervigilant, to ceaselessly strive for perfection in hopes for a modicum of control over situations far beyond my grasp.

I'd been operating as a victim for so long, I didn't realize I wasn't living my own life. I was living in response to someone else's.

At this point, there was nothing I could do about my cheating, pathological liar boyfriend—nothing but take my licks and nurse my wounded heart. Once again, I'd been incredibly, irreparably *stupid*. How had I not seen this coming? No wonder the relationship had failed. If I was really this gullible when it came to relationships, nothing was ever going to change.

To add insult to injury, I was supposed to go with this guy on his family vacation, but he *conveniently* forgot to tell his parents he'd invited me at all. Instead, he told them I was going to house-sit for them. Feeling broken, shamefaced, and completely devoid of any self-worth, I did what I always did and gave in to please them. I told him I would watch the house but only with the complete understanding that he and I were finished.

As it turns out, being stuck in my ex-boyfriend's house didn't make me feel any better. (surprise, surprise) While I was wallowing in my misery, a friend of mine suggested I distract myself by checking out MSN's newest feature—*chat rooms.*

If you're younger than thirty, you're probably laughing at me right now. But you have to understand, this was a big deal. For the first time in my life, I could instantly connect with people around the world and exchange messages in a matter of seconds. I immediately gravitated toward the music and theater groups, and it was in a random, jazz-themed chat room that I noticed someone using a registered trademark symbol in their name.

Yes, that was it. The big, romantic draw: an R with the circle around it.

I messaged the user, asking him how he'd managed to finagle the symbol into his profile. I didn't hear anything for hours, but that night, my computer chimed. Mr. R had written me back with detailed instructions. I wrote him back and thanked him. He replied. So, I wrote to him again, he wrote back, and pretty soon, we were chatting about everything and nothing.

This went on for hours. Finally, he asked if he could call me on the phone, and we stayed up all night until my phone battery spluttered out and died. So, he called the next day. And the next. And the next.

His name was Marty. He asked what he should call me. Ever since I was a little girl, my family had called me Annie, and I went by Alice at school. For some reason, people seemed to have trouble with the double name. But Marty wasn't interested in what other people called me. He was fascinated by the fact that I had two names because he'd never met anyone like that before.

"What do *you* want to be called?" he asked. Honestly. *Genuinely.*

I was dumbstruck. No one had ever asked me a question like that.

Marty was the first person in my life to call me by my real name, and I loved him for it. I'd always gone by the name other people had been comfortable with, but all of a sudden, here was a complete stranger who didn't want to put me in a box. So, we talked the next day. And the next.

Those three or four days were an absolute whirlwind.

"I know this sounds crazy," he said one night. "But there's a plane ticket waiting for you on US Airways. I'll be waiting on the other end of it in Baltimore."

I tried to talk myself out of it. Really, it *was* crazy. Here I was, sitting in my high school sweetheart's house, talking to a strange man I'd never met who was literally twenty years older than me. This wasn't safe. This wasn't *expected.* To run off to Maryland and meet up with a random MSN mystery man was the farthest thing from "smart" any young woman could do.

But I suppose that's what makes this story so incredible. Despite all of this, I drove to the airport and got on the plane. I didn't tell my family where I was going, but I did ring up one of my friends.

"If you haven't heard from me in five days," I said to her, "tell my mother what I've done."

I immediately knew Marty was different from anyone I'd ever met. He called me by my name; he genuinely desired to know who I was.

For the next three weeks, we were on and off planes back and forth from Kansas City to Baltimore. After the first visit, we couldn't be apart for more than four days.

Like me, Marty was insatiably curious. He wanted to know anything and everything there was about me—my likes and dislikes, hopes and fears—and he was constantly peppering me with questions. The problem was, I hardly knew the real me. He would ask what I liked to eat, and I wouldn't have an answer. He would prod and push, trying to learn about my ambitions and interests. He took me to new places and introduced me to beautiful new things. When I was with him, I felt like I could finally *exhale*. I could breathe—settle into my own skin—and it was absolutely terrifying.

It was as if someone had lifted a veil off my life. I now saw everything through a completely different lens. Marty seemed to take all the *shoulds* and *musts* in my life as a direct personal challenge. Sandwiches, for instance. For my traditional Filipino mom, sandwiches just weren't a thing. Coming from a culture of big, loud, and elaborate dishes, serving a sandwich for a major meal was nothing short of sacrilege.

"You can't have a sandwich for dinner," I told Marty, taken aback by the very suggestion.

But he didn't rile. He didn't laugh. He just looked at me calmly and asked, "Why not? Who says you can't?"

Who says you can't?

That question rattled me to my core. *Who says these are the rules? Who says it has to be this way? Who says this is how you have to show up?*

The floodgates of possibility crashed wide open, and what lay beyond was endless space—space to grow and be myself. There were no expectations, nor were there any chains binding me to my past. By asking these simple questions, Marty invited me into a relationship where I could write my own narrative. *I got to decide what I liked. I got to decide who I wanted to be and where I wanted to go.*

This was my narrative—my choice. And this man truly cared about how I felt, what I wanted, and how much space I needed to dream.

At first, I didn't know what to do with all that space. One of my family values was valuing the family above all else. I'd always done what other people had expected of me, and over the years, the expectation had become my reality. I remember coming back to Kansas City after my first Baltimore visit, breathless and dazed by the sheer notion that my life could be different. I happened to be sitting next to an adorable older woman, and we struck up a chat.

"I think I just met my husband," I told her.

Three weeks after we'd first met, Marty asked me to move in with him. I promptly told my ex-boyfriend we were finished for good this time. Then I told my family (and pretty much everyone I knew) that my life was really *changing* for good.

I was moving to Maryland.

.•.

If they find your mask suitable, most people don't bother to peek under it. As long as other individuals can be assessed, classified, and labeled—as long as they operate in the realm of our expectations—we can take them at face value and think no more of it.

But Marty never accepted face value. He's never been interested in the superficial. When he was a young man, he chose to forego college and work in masonry. His father was appalled and told him he would never amount to anything in his life, but Marty has never been the type to let others' expectations define him. He knew himself, and he knew what made him happy. His masonry business has thrived in Annapolis for the last forty years.

Don't get me wrong—monetary success is great. But no amount of money could ever measure up to the pride I feel when I think about the kind of man Marty proves to be time and time again. It takes an unbelievable amount of courage to stand up for the person you want to be. From the very beginning, he's been unshakably confident in what he wants, and he's never let anyone sway him to be anything other than the person he is.

Meeting Marty was the first time I realized I had the very same ability. Back then, I hadn't fully stepped into my power, but being with him threw me a glimpse—maybe even a foreshadowing—of the endless possibilities waiting at my fingertips. After living under masks for so long, I'd forgotten my own face. Marty showed me things didn't have to stay that way. With patience, space, and understanding, I found myself in this incredible place devoid of expectation, but rife with potential.

There's not necessarily a negative correlation between expectations and potential. You don't automatically surrender every ounce of potential just to set an expectation of yourself. However, it *is* important to recognize that expectations have the ability to sap your potential, depending on the role they play in your life. When you let expectations from others (and even from yourself) become concrete parameters rather than growing, shifting guideposts, you're forever limited by a single idea. There's no growth in that—no room to change, shift your beliefs, or mature.

If you want a more grounded example, think about asking a small child what they want to be when they grow up. There are going to be a lot of firefighters, ballerinas, royalty, and (in one specific case) maybe even a duck. Even young children have expectations for what they want their lives to be and what they want their futures to look like. But what if we didn't allow those expectations to grow—to change and mature alongside the rest of the world? There are those among us who discover their calling at a young age and stay dedicated to the idea, but most of us find that our childhood expectations evolve with the rest of our lives. Can you imagine what our world would look like if we had to base our entire life's expectations on our childhood perspectives? If we became so married to one idea of success that we wouldn't let ourselves feel happy or complete otherwise?

What would our world look like if we all ended up as firefighters or ballerinas?

When I was little, I wanted to be a teacher. I had a collection of old school desks, and I would gather all the used textbooks the schools threw out so I could "teach" my playmates over the summer. From a very young age, I possessed a passion that would stick with me for the rest of my life. No matter how much I grew, the thrill of learning and teaching others grew along with me.

When you think of a teacher, you probably have a very specific image in your mind. It may have something to do with a classroom, a young, smiling woman with an apple on her desk, and a group of gap-toothed youngsters gathered around on carpet squares. If you take the idea a little further, you probably assume this woman has some sort of degree in childhood development and/or education and gravitated her studies toward a specific age group. In our minds, her success involves putting in thirty to fifty years of loving, patient instruction until she can finally retire, beloved by generations of students.

You know—a *teacher* teacher. The typical, straitlaced woman who stands at the front of our classrooms.

The funny thing is, I've never been that woman. It took me ten years to finish my bachelor's degree, and I only wrapped it up *after* I was the owner and director of two separate childcare facilities. While I love working with kids, most of my days don't involve standing at the front of a classroom. I don't work at a school every day, and I sure as heck don't keep an apple on my desk. While my friends were on traditional paths, sailing through amazing colleges, joining sororities, and graduating with honors, I was floundering.

This used to be a major point of insecurity for me. Even after I opened my first successful business, I held so much embarrassment and shame because I hadn't done things *the right way*. In my mind, being a "professional teacher" meant you followed the "professional teacher path," and that included a professional teaching degree. Never mind my years of experience. Never mind that I was running my own thriving childcare business. I had a very specific expectation of what it meant to be a teacher, and since my path wasn't conventional, I couldn't allow myself the satisfaction of success.

It's ironic to look back and realize how much time I pined away, wishing for the life I already had. With or without a degree, I've always been a teacher, and I always will be. I don't just instruct the students at my preschools. I'm constantly teaching employees, other instructors, Leading Lady coaching clients... My entire *masterclass* revolves around a curriculum that I wrote myself.

My own expectations had blinded me. Everything I was wishing for was already in my grasp—it just looked different than the "traditional" image in my head. I was chained by my own beliefs, and no matter how much I accomplished, it was never good enough. I missed out on so much joy and satisfaction because I couldn't see what was right in front of me. I didn't need a degree to be a teacher. I'd been a teacher all along. Here I was, chasing the end of a rainbow when all I really needed to do was sit back and enjoy the view.

When I finally did complete my degree, I was already a mother of two and had been running two preschools for almost four years. I'll never forget calling up my mom to tell her.

"Great!" she said. "Now you can finally be a real teacher."

A real teacher.

I have to admit, those words stung. They pressed deep down into every aching insecurity I'd been wrestling with since starting out on my teaching journey.

Right then and there, I had a choice to make. I could continue to buy into the narrative that "real" teachers followed the same strict career path, or I could open my mind to the possibility that different teachers' journeys looked... Well, *different.*

The truth is most of us dream small. We have no idea what life holds for us; we can't fathom an inkling of our own limitless potential. We desperately cling to stale, predetermined expectations—not because we *have* to but because of our own fear.

It's always been done this way, our doubt whispers to us. *There* is *no other way.*

Our dreams may be small, but our fear and impostor syndrome makes them seem much bigger—insurmountably bigger, so huge and overwhelming that we can't imagine our lives any other way. Don't believe me? Take a moment to pull out your "Happiness List." Whether we're aware of it or not, we all have one, and they usually start with, "I'll finally be happy when…"

I'll finally be happy when I reach six figures.

I'll finally be happy when I'm married to Mr. Wonderful.

The bullets on this list don't necessarily follow a specific format. They can get pretty creative.

When my kids get into good colleges, I'll know I'm actually a good parent.

Traveling is for retirement. I'll save that dream vacation for later.

Or even…

If I just accomplish (insert fantastic feat here), *my life will finally look like* (insert insta-perfect, airbrushed image here)*!*

Whether we see them or not, implicit and explicit expectations are always there, hissing in the back of our minds about all the things we think we *should* be doing. In my opinion, "should" is a dirty word. Who says your life has to follow a specific, traditional path? Who says you can't have a sandwich for dinner?

The truth is, I could have written a book about all the ways I failed my own expectations. I never planned on falling in love with an older man and having a family. I never thought my career would look anything like this. Even after all the success, joy, and happiness, there are days I feel like a failure because my life isn't exactly what I'd planned—as if I somehow failed by not sticking to an arbitrary, made-up narrative I foisted on myself. No matter how much money I make, how many women Leading Ladies touches, or how amazing my family may be, when I live in the prison of my own expectations, nothing is *ever* enough. We choose whether or not to hold on to our own skewed *shoulds*. More often than not, *we're* the only things that are keeping ourselves from being happy.

The good news is, if we can choose to chain ourselves to our own expectations, we can also choose to unchain ourselves. We're all fully capable of stepping away from our own distorted images of what our lives should look like. We all have the power to cast off the *shoulds* and replace them with *already haves*. Instead of chasing the fictitious gold at the end of the rainbow, can we take a moment to sit back and admire the breathtaking sky?

By letting go of expectations, we unlock our true potential. That doesn't mean giving up your dreams, goals, and aspirations. It simply means relinquishing the contrived image in your mind for the sake of endless possibility. When you live your life in accordance with your values—when you finally let go of your expectations to live, love, and lead on your own terms—you make space for opportunities beyond your wildest dreams. Sure, you may have wanted to be a firefighter (yes, maybe even a duck) when you were a child, but when you step back and see that every path of possibility is beautiful, bountiful, and full of success, you'll find fulfillment, no matter where you end up.

Once I stopped pining over the life I thought I wanted, I realized I was already living the life of my dreams.

•••

There's a difference between expectations and agreements.

Marty is (and always has been) a man of unwavering honesty. When he said he would do something, he followed through. If he made you a promise, you knew he would go to the ends of the earth to fulfill it. He could never stand to be anything other than his authentic self, and early on in our relationship, that brought about another unexpected lesson.

When we pulled up to a restaurant together for the first time, I expected Marty to come over and open my car door for me. I sat there and waited until it got awkward then climbed out myself, miffed. I was used to a certain degree of chivalry and showmanship on a first date. This was, after all, the time for the man to be on his best behavior.

Marty must have noticed my annoyance, and we struck up a discussion about it.

"Do you *need* me to open the car door for you?" he asked.

It was a moment of painful honesty. *Did* I expect him to come to my beck and call whenever a handle or a hinge blocked my path? Did I *want* him to put on a show for me, or did I want to learn about what he truly valued? Was it fair of me to expect him to fulfill an arbitrary request I'd never actually vocalized? It wasn't that Marty wasn't thoughtful; he'd proved that time and time again in other ways. He just didn't see the point in helping me with something I really didn't need help with in the first place.

This is an idea we brushed up against early in our relationship, but it's taken years to understand just how poisonous expectations without agreements can become. So often, we base our expectations of another person on who we think they *should* be—there's that dirty s- word again—rather than agreeing on actual values. Everyone has needs in any sort of relationship, but until we articulate to others and ourselves what actually *matters,* the pain and disappointment will never end.

It's another classic case of being chained down by our own preconceptions. I *expected* Marty to come open my door on our date. Why? Because I'd been told this was the "proper" thing for a man to do. I'd never asked him to open the door. I didn't expect him to open the door every single time I got in and out of the car. My indignation was based on my own myopic image of who Marty was supposed to be, and had I let that color our first date, I would have missed the amazing person he actually is. My expectation was completely based on my own experiences.

Of course, I was disappointed when he failed to fit into the perfect, gentlemanly image I'd been cultivating since girlhood. Disappointment is an emotion; it's not something we actively choose. But when I was honest with myself about *why* I felt that way, I was finally able to see my anger stemmed in my own prejudice—not anything Marty had done to me. When we got down to the core of the issue, I was able to let that disappointment go.

If you've ever interacted with another human being, you've probably been disappointed by another human being. It's completely valid to have wants and needs in any kind of relationship, whether that be at work, with your spouse, or even with your kids.

Let's say you get a new personal assistant, and you open your email the next day to find your inbox in a state of utter chaos. Before you get angry and yell the poor girl's ear off, could you take a moment to think: *Did I ask her to organize my inbox? Did I clearly communicate I wanted this type of email starred and this other type color coordinated? Did we actually agree on what she needed to do for me, or was this an expectation based on my last assistant?*

If you and your new assistant sat down and agreed that organizing your inbox was one of her morning tasks, we have an entirely different situation on our hands. In that case, she has failed to uphold her agreement. However, if the agreement was never made, then we're operating on the basis of assumption—that this young, starry-eyed girl *should* have shown up with magical mind-reading powers.

And now we're knee-deep in the realm of sheer ridiculousness.

The night of our very first date, Marty challenged my preconceived expectations. He was authentic about who he was and what mattered to him, and he invited me to share in that same level of authenticity. Whenever I'm frustrated, disappointed, or angry with someone, I try to remember to take a pause before reacting—to truly assess whether my reaction is based on a broken agreement or my own unspoken expectation.

There's nothing wrong with wanting the best from others. For the most part, it's pretty safe to assume that individuals in our society operate by rules and mores we've agreed upon as citizens. You know—don't steal things, murder is bad, that kind of thing. But when we start letting who we think others should be blind us from the potential of who they are, we're shackling ourselves to our own expectations.

How can anyone expect to grow in a relationship like that?

Marty and I were married in 2003. Today, my mom will admit the whole thing made her nervous. I'd told my family Marty was ten years older than me—not twenty. My traditional, close-knit family just couldn't understand why I would pack everything up and move to Maryland.

But that never bothered my husband. It's a rare occasion indeed when he makes a decision based on what someone else thinks.

Of course, there are challenges in our marriage, just like there are challenges in any other relationship. My business is in its prime; Marty is beginning to think about retirement. Back then, our age gap meant we were coming into our relationship at different milestones in our own journeys. He'd had years of experience running his business when I'd just started mine. I would be a young mom, and he would be an older dad.

What kept us together in spite of (maybe even *because of*) these differences was the fact that we stayed intentional about keeping our core values in alignment. We've always been at different waypoints in our personal journeys, but that brings us back to our agreements— being honest with one another about what we need. I never had to change for Marty, and he has never changed for me. We grow and change for *ourselves*, and we're always coming back to revisit those agreements to make sure we're still supporting one another as our best selves.

Of course, I've changed in the last twenty years, but Marty never asked me to change the core of my being. I still have nomadic tendencies. I still love to travel and get antsy if I'm cooped up for too long in one place. I have to have a separate office because I need to be on the move, and Marty accepts that wholeheartedly. He, on the other hand, loves the house he built for us. It's a pure representation of his art and his craft, and I respect that he's a creature of habit. I'm a rolling stone and he's a homebody, but that's not a point of contention. We validate and acknowledge what the other needs; we're constantly circling back to our agreements and knocking down expectations to reimagine compromise.

When you're able to understand another person's needs, you can start asking the questions that matter: *What are you willing to do? What are you willing to learn? How can I support you in that?*

These answers aren't eternal or immutable. They're constantly shifting as we grow and mature as a couple. I'm a person who loves moving and changing, but even my "change has changed." Gone are the days when I would run away, transfer schools, and completely restart my life whenever I became uncomfortable. Sure, I'll retreat to a different building—maybe even a different city, if I have time for a quick vacation—but I'm no longer running. I'm giving myself the space I need to regroup and return as my best self.

Change isn't a bad thing. I would even argue it's a healthy thing when embraced for the right reasons. I'm so grateful I have a partner who gives me the space I need to rediscover myself over and over again. If I were to boil our relationship down to a single thread of truth, it's that a healthy relationship is where each partner accepts the other for exactly who they are while allowing them the space they need to be their best.

And that *does* take space. That takes time. It takes patience, love, and letting go of expectations. If you're not showing up in a relationship as your true self, you're going to be miserable, no matter what you think that relationship should look like.

My marriage is teaching me to let go of the *shoulds*—that I *should* guard my heart, *should* keep my defenses up, and *should* bolt at the first sign of trouble. While learning from life's experiences is important, we can't let those lessons become diehard expectations. Yes, I might have learned difficult lessons in the past. Yes, I may have learned to constantly keep my guard up, not to trust anyone, and to perceive others' expectations before taking my own authenticity into account.

But just because I learned these lessons doesn't mean I have to live by them. No matter what I've experienced in the past, *I* choose how I want to show up in my own life.

Now that I'm a bit older and a lot wiser, I'd love to say that the whole "label thing" just isn't a thing. But then I'd be lying—and that's the farthest thing from the heart of this book.

Marty and I don't have a perfect marriage. We never have, and we're not going to start now. What we do have is a *healthy* relationship—an honest, loving agreement that refuses to put our own needs above the other's. We love each other fiercely for exactly who we are, and we refuse to begrudge anyone in our family the space they need to grow, change, and engage as their best selves. Our engagement with one another is based on agreements rather than expectations. We strive to lead by values instead of internalized assumptions.

As for the age difference? People still talk. I've just stopped listening. Marty and I know exactly who we are, and no label in the world could ever change that.

CHAPTER 5: CHANGE YOUR SHIRT

All I needed to know I learned in a supermarket.

Okay, maybe that's a bit of an exaggeration. "Everything I needed to know about customer service, collaboration, and khaki pants" is much closer to the truth. I worked at the same chain of grocery stores for eight years throughout high school and college, and while it wasn't the high-paying, purpose-fulfilling career of my dreams, the experience planted seeds in my young mind that didn't fully bloom until years later.

If you're not from the Midwest, you've probably never seen a Hy-Vee. Think of it as an upscale, mid-sized grocery experience—a clean, synthetically lit establishment less niche than Trader Joe's but notably more upscale than Walmart. When I started working at our local Hy-Vee, I was so young my parents had to sign a permission form. I desperately wanted Z. Cavaricci jeans (if you don't know what those are, look them up; it's totally worth an image search), and getting a job was the only way I could ever hope to afford them. My hardworking parents were all about the idea.

As far as grocery stores go, Hy-Vee is a pretty classy joint. I was required to come to work in khaki pants, an ironed white shirt, a belt, and a tie. The standards were high, and I absolutely loved that. *Standards* were something I understood. *Clear company expectations* were music to my ears. The rules were fair, the work was straightforward, and the pay was pretty good for a teenager. What's not to love about any of that?

I valued the standards and excellence of that chain. No matter where we moved, I would find a Hy-Vee and submit an application as soon as I could. Being one of the few teenagers on earth who reveled in punctilious restock and expertly ironed uniform creases, I was quick to rise through the company. By the time I was seventeen, I was in charge of the multifaceted customer service desk. Refunds, dry cleaning, movie rentals, post office services—I did it all. Sure, I had my share of cranky, vindictive, and downright nasty customers, but that was just another part of the leading role I'd chosen to play. I wasn't AliceAnne—I was the Hy-Vee customer service representative. This position gave me an identity. It came with a full set of rules and protocols.

Hy-Vee was also near and dear to my heart because the company constantly gave me opportunities to showcase my strengths. I wasn't very happy at home, but at work, I felt valued and appreciated for the things I did well. When the manager of the store found out I could sing, he asked me if I wanted to star in our brand-new store jingle. The approval-hungry teen in me was *thrilled* to oblige, and so I recorded the song. For months after, I'd be checking people out, and my little tune would come on.

"Oh, what a sweet voice," an elderly woman commented one day.

My grin must have been a mile wide when I told her that was *my* voice.

My experience in the grocery store taught me that people were so much more than their jobs. If someone did a particularly good job at selling Valentine's Day teddy bears at the register, they were recognized and rewarded. If you had an employee who was also in the school choir, you could give her a unique opportunity to shine. There was the job description, and then there was the *standard*. I felt like that company always demanded excellence from me, not just as an employee but as a human being. They took the time to notice what I loved; they capitalized on what made me unique.

As a bright-eyed young professional, I felt seen.

Jaunty ties and tucked-in shirts might not mean much to some, but they meant the world to me. Here was a place that saw me as the sum of a whole rather than one mundane part. They opened up this brand-new, positive space for me to show up as someone special. They created an intentional place where I could step into my best self.

As I mentioned before, this lesson didn't hit me in its entirety until much later. I knew that it *felt* good to be acknowledged, appreciated, and seen as an individual, but I wasn't yet in a place of trust and security where I was comfortable relinquishing the control I so desperately craved. That takes time, maturity, and perspective. No one wakes up one magical morning knowing how to lead with their values.

Between directing the Missouri after-school programs and my Hy-Vee adventures, I'd been fortunate enough to take on leadership roles relatively young. But that didn't mean I saw myself as a leader. The potential was there, lurking below the surface, but I had yet to look beyond my own insecurities to see what I was actually capable of.

After moving to Maryland and marrying Marty, I became pregnant much earlier than either of us had anticipated. Of course, we were excited, but the new baby left me in a bit of a professional quandary. Since my professional credentials didn't transfer from state to state, I couldn't work in after-school programs at public schools. I took up a part-time job in a private preschool instead—a small, local business called Safe Harbor. The owner was looking for me to step up as a managing director, which required further certifications, so here I was, working as a teacher, taking classes to get my credentials as a director, *and* frantically trying to keep up with the "perfect wife" facade.

All the while, there was a nagging, prickly feeling in the bottom of my gut. I loved what I did, but *something* was wrong. When I became pregnant with Marissa, I started looking for childcare options, but nothing felt good to me. As a teacher, I wanted a structured, growth-oriented program. As a new mother, I wanted a loving, nurturing environment. I scoured local childcare facilities, but I couldn't find one that met my expectations for both.

Then, it hit me: Safe Harbor didn't *feel* right because I didn't agree with the way it was being run. There had to be a better balance of instruction and nurturing—a subtle but critical line between curriculum and care. The children's meals weren't nutritious. Naptime was all too often shirked in favor of other activities. As a teacher, focusing on education only seemed right. But as a mom, I couldn't make peace with compromising healthy meals and sleep training. Having worked with school-aged children in the public sector, I was constantly trying to assess how well our curriculum prepared students for kindergarten. If our program wasn't preparing the kids for their next big step, what was the point of a curriculum at all?

When I found myself at a crossroads of conflicting values, I sought advice from my childcare management instructor. She calmly informed me that I had two options:

1. I could approach the owner and speak from the heart, hoping she would see things from my perspective and compromise for change.

2. I could quit my job and seek out another establishment more aligned with my values.

Neither option had my incredibly pregnant self jumping for joy. Of course, I'd had experience with after-school programs, but when it came to an independently owned childcare center—a private institution with professionally qualified teachers—I was up to my ears in strange waters. I had confidence in myself and my own abilities, but the lingering claws of impostor syndrome kept cinching tighter. What right did I have to tell the Safe Harbor owner how to run her business? Sure, it *looked* like I knew what I was doing. But did that actually make me *qualified?*

I ended up going for Option 2. Here I was, twenty-two years old and eight-and-a-half months pregnant, waddling to my boss's office to tell her I had to step down as the Safe Harbor director. Ironically enough, the owner was having an even worse day than I was. I don't know if she saw my resignation as the beginning of the end or had been planning it before I decided to leave, but she confided in me that she was closing her doors and shutting down Safe Harbor for good. The same Friday I resigned, she sent out a message to the parents, informing them they needed to find alternate childcare. And for those who worked nine-to-five jobs five days a week, that meant they needed to find a solution by *Monday*.

Parents started scrambling. One of them reached out and asked me if I would be interested in taking over the business myself. The owner of the building called and offered to sell me Safe Harbor if I would continue to run it as a childcare center. Our community needed a preschool, and all of a sudden, Option 3 magically appeared. It was a dangerous option—a risky, daring opportunity. If the previous owner couldn't compromise and I had trouble finding a school that aligned with my values...

Why couldn't I start my own school?

I lay awake that night, tossing and turning as a flurry of expectations and possibilities swirled through my mind.

This is crazy, I kept thinking over and over as I stared at the ceiling. *This is genuinely insane.*

I rolled over and nudged Marty awake. He stirred groggily then started up in a panic.

"What?" he asked. "Is the baby coming?"

"No," I said. "I think I want to do this."

And as the words left my mouth, I actually believed them.

Ten days before Marissa was born, I bought the Safe Harbor building and incorporated my own business, Bright Beginning. The paperwork was the easy part. If you've never had the pleasure of working with small children, let me assure you that the job involves *a lot* of sanitation. The old preschool had been carpeted, which meant that nearly a decade of olfactory offense was trapped within those raggedy fibers—particularly the ripe smell of pee. Marty and his team worked around the clock to give the place a facelift, and after long hours of tearing out carpet, power washing grime, and scrubbing away years of neglected buildup, he would have to shower twice to get himself clean.

I remember him muttering under his breath as he shambled through the door after a particularly grueling day of renovations. "The day our program smells like this is the day you go out of business."

But I never allowed myself to even think of getting to that point. As a new mom, I had a precise vision of the childcare center I wanted for *my* baby. I wasn't just going to slap down some new carpets and call the place clean. Even though I couldn't clearly articulate my personal values back then, I knew from all those years pushing a broom along the Hy-Vee grocery aisles that I valued excellence. Any business with my name on it was going to have standards—bow-tie and khaki-pants kind of standards.

Which brought me, full circle, back to the original problem—the same tedious conundrum that became even more glaring when Marissa was born.

I just bought a new business. What in the heck do I do with this new baby?

By this time, I'd come way too far to settle. If I didn't like any of my choices, why couldn't I step out and create my own? Marty taught me I could eat sandwiches for dinner. Safe Harbor taught me there could be more than two options. At the time, my business was only licensed to care for children between two and five years old. But that qualification said nothing about *my* center caring for *my* children.

I took my new baby, dressed her in her swankiest clothes, fastened her into her tiny bucket seat, then drove all the way to the Maryland Department of Education. When I asked for permission to bring Marissa to work with me, the board immediately pointed out that my qualifications didn't cover infants. I replied with a gentle reminder that the infant in question was, in fact, *my* infant.

The board ended up granting me a variance—a leeway in the rule under special circumstances. From that day forward, I refused to choose between being an entrepreneur and a mom. With enough tenacity and imagination, you can defy expectations in favor of limitless possibilities.

This was another lesson that stayed with me for the rest of my life. Why not compromise? Why not *ask* if you can do something a little differently? Why not stretch? Why not explore creative solutions?

Instead of agonizing over the options you've been given, why not blaze your own path?

Getting rid of that pee-sodden carpet and gaining permission to bring Marissa to school were both resounding victories, but there's more to running a preschool than carpet squares and carrot sticks. I immediately dove into teacher interviews, many of which were conducted while I was breastfeeding. Thankfully, quite a few of the Safe Harbor teachers stayed on board for the transition. I knew and trusted these teachers, but after working beside each other for so long, the leadership change came with its own baggage. These people had seen me at my best; they'd also seen me on days when I hadn't been my best. I came to the program, guns blazing, advocating for change, and that built up some resentment. Who was I to waltz in and change everything they'd been doing for years on end? My grand vision clashed with other personalities, but my eyes were so full of stars, I wasn't able to see how these sweeping changes negatively affected my team.

Believe it or not, I've gotten younger as I've aged. Back in the beginning, I carried quite a bit of my grocery store mentality into my preschool. And when I say, "a bit," I actually mean, *a lot*. Yes, my staff were required to wear khakis. Yes, it was mandatory for them to keep their shirts tucked in. The dress code was stuffy and uncomfortable for many of my teachers, but I was convinced that uniformity equaled professionalism.

I'd never grown up with fashionable or fancy clothes. In fact, I often downplayed what I wore in order not to stand out so much. That's why I loved having drab, everyday work attire, and that's why I never hesitated to belt up my trusty khaki pants. To me, that starched, uniform look was a symbol of the pride and professionalism I'd learned during my time at Hy-Vee. And since I valued quality and professionalism, I decided that was what my whole staff needed to look like.

It's easy to dismiss the whole "uniform thing" as me just being a dork, but there's a darker side to this mentality. When I opened my first business, I was twenty-two. I was so young, and it didn't help that I was married to a forty-year-old man. Part of the reason I dressed the way I did was because I was terrified of what people would think of me if I dressed like other women my age. Even then, I could hear the "gold digger" whispers over my shoulder. While my peers were finishing their degrees, I was opening my own business. I didn't come from money. I didn't have the clout or life experience to justify how this all worked out.

No matter how hard I tried to shield myself with success or professionalism, my worst fears inevitably came true. There were those who assumed my husband had gifted me the building as a vanity project—that I was using his money for my own personal gain. The deep, dark dread of women whispering to each other became one of my most haunting insecurities.

"You know," they'd say in my daydreams, lowering their voices into snide chuckles, "it really isn't her business. Her husband did all of this for her, and she just lives off the cream."

In my mind, they saw me as an opportunist—a fraud, a parasite. Even when I was winning, I would forever be losing under the perception that none of these accomplishments were actually mine.

The thought left me terrified. For the first three years, I didn't take a single paycheck. I was determined to pay back every penny I owed on both the business and my student loans, and I wouldn't rest until I'd ripped down every single reason that anyone else could ever fault me.

But that was the irony of it. Even when I did pay back my bills, the whispers didn't stop. Once again, I was caught in a vicious cycle of trying to outmaneuver other people's judgments. I was living my life in response to their perceptions instead of leading with my own values—trying to change the narrative they'd already fully fleshed out in their minds. This was a painfully difficult notion for me to accept. Some people are devoted to disliking you, and there's nothing you can do about that.

While writing this book, the dark horse buzzword that kept rearing its ugly head was *misunderstood*. When I hear that word, there's still a little part of me—a piece of deep, heavy sadness—that reacts with visceral pain. I feel like "misunderstood" has encompassed my whole life.

People have always crafted their own narratives of who I am. In their minds, I check all the boxes of a gold digger—maybe even a spoiled princess. Some of that I contributed to. I didn't want people gawking at my flaws, so I put on masks of power and perfection to hide the parts of me I didn't want anyone else to see. That was my fear, my defensiveness.

But misunderstanding is a choice. It's *always* a choice. It's a choice for someone not to look deeper, and honestly, it's a shame. It's a shame for the judger. It's a shame for the judged. All the friendships, learning lessons, and benefits of knowing a person and the good things they have to offer are squandered for the sake of a little personal comfort. Because that's what it is, isn't it? Personal comfort. If someone makes us feel less-than or uncomfortable, it's much easier to pass judgment than question our own insecurities.

I told myself my staff wore khakis because I valued professionalism. But really, do pleated pants *actually* translate to that kind of quality? *Must* one wear a suspiciously grocery store-esque uniform to provide a loving, growth-centric education for kids?

My current executive director has worked at Bright Beginning for seventeen years. She has been with me since the very beginning; she's a Leading Lady and one of my best friends. Nowadays, we look back at those early years and laugh. She hated the uniforms, and she can attest to the personal growth she saw in me when I realized beige pants weren't topping the list of my personal values. The khakis were more about me and my own insecurities. They were, in a way, my own whacky attempt to shield myself from judgment.

But the people who are going to judge you are going to judge you.

They'll judge you if you show up in a tucked-in polo; they'll judge you if you show up with a Louis Vuitton handbag. Knowing that there's really nothing you can do about that, the only thing you *can* do is refuse to live your life according to someone else's hang-ups. If someone chooses to take a judging mindset rather than a learning mindset, that's their loss. If you choose to shove someone into a preconceived box instead of opening your mind to their true value, that's *your* loss.

Every relationship has value. From your spouse to the garbage truck driver, the way you interact with others *matters*. You may not be able to control what other people choose to think about you, and if that thought is worrisome, "control over others" isn't the sort of power you're missing.

What you need is to realize the power you have to control your own narrative.

•••

Most people wouldn't assume that I have a lot in common with Abraham Lincoln. I mean, him being six-foot-four, me being five-foot-five; him with a proclivity for giant top hats versus my extreme hatred of chickens.

It's not necessarily an easy comparison to make.

We do have one very important thing in common though; we stacked our teams with people who possess very different worldviews. Lincoln famously packed his cabinet with his political enemies because he wanted differing—maybe even antagonistic—views of his decisions. I wouldn't go so far as to say I filled my Bright Beginning administrative team with enemies, but I have been very deliberate about making sure I don't fill my roster with professionals who are exactly like me. To be perfectly honest, I don't *want* an entire team of AliceAnnes.

When staffing my admin team, I quickly learned there's infinite value in differing perspectives. Good leadership isn't hiring people who are exactly like you. Good leadership is bringing together team members with multiple strengths then giving them the space they need to engage as their best selves.

To this day, I host weekly meetings with my team to discuss what's going on in the business. Whenever I pose a question, I get three different answers from three different people, and that's how I like it. No one is wrong, and no one is necessarily right. We're just looking at the problem from different viewpoints, which ends up affording everyone a more comprehensive picture of the situation. We certainly don't always agree with one another on the best solution, but we still have an inherent trust that each team member can move forward in her own authentic way.

I kind of think about us like the Care Bears (yes—even the magical tummy part). Each of us shows up with our own special skills, whether that be kindness, ingenuity, or even a strategic mindset. Another less retro way to look at it is to see our individual strengths as an assembly of construction tools. I may show up to the meeting ready to tackle the problem with a hammer, but after looking at the situation a little closer, I might discover that my teammate's wrench is better suited for a comprehensive solution. Maybe we *do* need a hammer, but that work will go better if we do a little sawing first. Maybe we don't even need the hardware at all. A hot glue gun would be the simplest, most elegant solution, but we had no idea our teammate carries one in her back pocket until we expressed a need.

That's the dirty little secret of successful collaboration: in order to truly acknowledge where you need support, you need to be honest with yourself about your own strengths and weaknesses. A good leader isn't good at everything—a good leader is able to pull in other players who support her best while also balancing out her worst. If you're not authentic with yourself, you may know what you *want*, but you'll have no idea what you *need* to achieve what you want.

My current executive director, the lovely woman I mentioned before who's been working with me back when Bright Beginning was Safe Harbor, has been by my side for nearly twenty years. She knows all too well that the hotheaded, Filipino Scorpio in me has days where she wants to tear down the curtains and fire everyone in the establishment. But my executive director also recognizes this isn't me showing up as my best self. In these moments, she knows my anger needs to be acknowledged and validated. She'll take a deep breath, and I can practically see her nodding over the phone as she says, coolly and calmly, "Okay, I hear you. But let me give you another perspective..."

Let me give you another perspective. Those six little words are a game-changer.

Strengths in excess—*anything* in excess, for that matter—are going to lead to heartbreak. Balance is the name of the game, and we can never forget that balance is an active verb. It's not something you achieve. Balance is something you're constantly working for, striving towards, and attending to. When you're stuck in your own head, wrestling with what seems to be an insurmountable circumstance, your first instinct is to dig in to your strengths.

I'm good at that, you tell yourself. *I should just do more of that.*

But when your strengths start doubling down on themselves, creating an endless feedback loop of trial, stress, and panic, you're going to work yourself into overdrive.

Think about it this way. If you've ever heard feedback from electrical speakers—you know what I'm talking about, when a microphone screeches like a dying banshee dragging her tungsten-tipped fingernails across a blackboard—the solution isn't to turn up the volume. Speaker feedback happens when the microphone picks up on sounds from the speakers, which then replays the speakers' own sounds *back* through the speakers, which amplifies the wavelengths, heightens the noise, and...

Well, let's just say it's not pleasant for anyone.

To break that feedback loop, you have to bring the microphone *away* from the speakers. Resurfacing from our analogy, that means we have to step *back* from the situation. To continue feeding that loop is to perpetuate the problem, and that's just getting in your own way. Not every strength fits every circumstance, and no leader has a surefire solution to every issue.

Taking a moment to pause, reassess, and recenter your perspective is often the solution you never knew you had. Your team members should be the ones who yank you out of your destructive loops, the ones who ensure you never become your own worst enemy.

My admin team is an excellent example of a well-balanced team. We may have totally different personalities, but their strengths constantly temper my weaknesses and vice versa. As long as the core value of our mission—to provide a safe, loving, and nurturing environment where children can grow and develop—remains on track, we keep Bright Beginning in balance. We may not go about our missions the same way, but we're all working together and striving toward the same goal.

There's a reason Care Bears, Power Rangers, My Little Ponies, and even Charlie's Angels aren't clones of one another. You need a variety of skills to triumph through a variety of circumstances.

I'm often asked if I only work with Type A women. This is the wrong question to ask. Leadership doesn't have to look a certain way. You don't have to be outspoken, gregarious, or extroverted to effectively lead a team. I recently worked with a client who definitely wasn't Type A. She was creative, competent, and passionate but also scattered and lacking any semblance of procedural accountability.

Was she a bad leader because she wasn't a typical, Type A "boss lady?" Absolutely not. Her team was struggling because she kept hiring people who were similar to her. Her hands-off personality is by no means a negative thing; it just means she needed a team that was willing to take initiative and flourish in the space she provided them. She needed people who could manage themselves, employees who could take her vision and start acting to make it reality.

The lesson? When you take the time to truly reflect on your own attributes—how *you* engage best, according to your authentic self— you can honestly assess whether or not your team is effective. Do you give people the space they need to grow into their own power? Or are they stifled by expectations? If you're opening up an expansive space but getting nothing in return, can you glance back and realize your team needs a little more direction?

Some people work better with rules and regulations. Some people thrive in a *laissez-faire* environment. Rather than shoving someone into a box of preconceived expectations, an effective leader takes the time to discover *who* their team members are in order to determine how they work effectively—what they *need* to show up as their best selves.

It's not that my business thrived. The people *in* my business thrived, which bolstered a strong, supportive community. I've never seen Bright Beginning as an enterprise; it's always been part of a larger social ecosystem. If children are in a safe, happy, and growth-oriented environment, parents have the peace of mind to go out into the world with their best foot forward. And when the community is strong, my business—which comes straight from the parents we support with childcare—is also strong.

When I started this business, my aim was to create the childcare center I wanted for my own children. What I didn't realize was that I wasn't the only person in the community who shared this vision, and ironically enough, it was this shared vision that ended up building our community.

It's kind of mindboggling when I think about how organically it happened. As a working parent, I knew what it was like to want the best for my kids—educational opportunities, emotional development, and diverse cultural experiences—but not have the daylight hours to make everything happen. If my toddler wanted to take ballet, chances were, there were other preschool parents facing the same conundrum: *How do I get my little one to daytime classes when I work all day? Do I quit my job? Tell my kid it's just not possible?*

How about Option 3: hire a third-party contractor to come to Bright Beginning and offer lessons during the school day?

Heck, it was my school. I had the freedom and the resources to make these things possible. Dance classes, sign language, music lessons, toddler PE… It not only opened a whole new world of learning and experiences for the kids; it also created an amazing space for other community members to shine.

I'll never forget the day the woman knocked on my door. I had no idea who she was. She'd just moved into the neighborhood, and she barely spoke English. She needed a job, but she couldn't drive, which meant her options were limited to whatever was in the neighborhood—working at the preschool or trying to get a job at the local mini mart. I knew this woman wasn't certified as a teacher, but that didn't mean she didn't have a place at our school. She spoke fluent Spanish, and I just so happened to need a foreign language teacher.

Bright Beginning got a brand-new Spanish teacher that day. The woman at the door created a whole program for the kids, speaking to them in her native language, singing songs, and exposing them to rich cultural experiences. She ended up loving the job so much, she earned her teaching certifications and started her own business, marketing her Spanish programs to other preschools around the area. To this day, her company touches hundreds of young lives, and my preschools still have an incredible Spanish program.

When it comes to my employees, I don't care whether Bright Beginning is a career or a stepping-stone. Many of my teachers end up leaving to take jobs at public schools, and that's completely fine with me. I refuse to see any investment in my educators as a loss. If I can play a small part in supporting another person's passion, *everyone ends up winning.*

Altruism has never been pity. It's not glory-hounding or even seeking a return. When you have the opportunity to give, *just give.* In fact, give more than you think you can give. The results will blow you away.

There was a boy in my preschool whose mother had just lost her job in the corporate world. The woman came to my office and explained that she had to withdraw her son because she couldn't continue to pay tuition while she was applying for a new position. I didn't have to think. I didn't have to question my decision.

"Don't worry," I told her. "We've got you. Keep your son here until you're back on your feet."

Do we advertise free childcare? Absolutely not. Do we give free tuition to every single person who runs into trouble? No, that would be impossible. But in this situation, I went with my gut. Any sane person would know the last thing this woman should have been worrying about was what to feed her toddler for lunch. To pull him out of an environment that was constant, stable, stress free, and fun wasn't doing anyone any favors—especially his frazzled mom.

In this instance, my company had the opportunity to give this woman a little space to re-enter the world as her best self. She didn't end up returning to her corporate job; she opened one of Annapolis's most popular, locally sourced restaurants that supports farmers and vendors in our community. She also went on to found #FeedAnneArundel, a partnership of local restaurants and donors that have come together to provide food, basic supplies, and toiletries during the COVID pandemic.

This woman has served tens of thousands of people in the community. She's won multiple awards and now owns her own successful business. That's not about money, nor is it about any sort of material return. I'll continue investing in my teachers' educations, my preschool programs, and my community because, when the people around me are winning, I'm winning too.

But it's not just about space. If you're going to succeed, you need those around you to succeed, and that means providing them with the resources they need to make that success a reality. I had an amazing woman from Pakistan apply for a job right after 9/11. Crownsville, Maryland, wasn't the easiest place to walk out in a hijab, and she'd applied to many other centers without success. Apparently, no one wanted to hire her, for "indeterminate reasons."

I offered her a job on the spot. I'll never forget her jaw dropping.

"Wait," she said. "Don't you see my wrap? I'm a *Muslim*."

"Are you a good teacher?" I asked.

She nodded.

"Great," I said. "Then you start tomorrow."

She instantly became a member of the Bright Beginning family. We applied for every grant we could to help her get her college education, and what was left, we paid for. This woman taught for years at my preschools. My son loved her so much, he would pretend *to be* her. I know for a fact that I wasn't the only parent to walk in on my child with his blanket wrapped around his head, proudly proclaiming that he looked just like his favorite teacher.

"People don't do this," she said one day as we were applying for her grants. "And they don't do it for women."

But people *can* do this, and the right people *do*.

She was terrified of what parents would think of her being Muslim, and a few couples did come to me with "concerns." When that day came, I invited them into my office, closed the door, and stared them straight in the eye.

"What's the real problem here?" I asked. "Is this woman loving your children too much?"

But anyone who's prideful enough to be a bigot is usually far too prideful to admit that they're a bigot. While I had no control over someone else's hateful mindset, I *did* have control over Bright Beginning's stance on prejudice.

I didn't care if this teacher prayed at work. I didn't care if she fasted. It wasn't her job to make me comfortable with her culture; her job was to provide a loving education for her students. To this day, I still get letters from parents talking about how this extraordinary woman changed their whole family's perspectives. Their kids would come home talking about Eid, Ramadan, and fasting. For many of these families, it was their first real exposure to Islam beyond the fearmongering in the news.

All of a sudden, our sheltered community opened up. The world became a little less dark because this woman had the courage to shine her light. While she's no longer working for Bright Beginning, she left with her degree fully completed, armed with glowing recommendations. Now, *she's* a director at a childcare center in Silver Spring, and I couldn't be any prouder of her. When you give your people intentional space and resources, you give them the power to take the lead in their own lives.

That's why I never begrudge paying for my teachers' educations, even if they choose not to stay at my program for the rest of their career. Any investment in my staff is an investment in my students. When Bright Beginning children are rooted—when they're happy, safe, and supported in a place where they feel loved—I've done my job right. That's the value I choose to lead with, and though my staff and my teachers may have different personalities and perspectives, when we all lead with that common goal in mind, our community preschool becomes something much more than a childcare center.

I've seen my teachers bathe dirty children in our kitchen sink. I've seen them deliver meals, bring in fresh pairs of socks, comb through tangly hair, and even advocate in court for victims of child abuse. Quality childcare providers are quiet heroes, and whether they stay in my company or not, I'm dedicated to doing everything I can to help them show up as their best.

I've learned so much from my Bright Beginning family. I've learned how I want to show up as a leader, a wife, and a mom. I've learned that money is just another tool to provide space and resources for the things we truly value. And, yes, I've learned that it doesn't take pleated pants, a tie, and a tucked-in shirt to maintain a standard of professionalism.

While Hy-Vee did spark a vision of what I wanted my business to look like, I also came to realize that khakis weren't the secret ingredient to success.

I take a lot of comfort in the idea that I can change my shirt (or, in this case, my pants). That's why 2021 has been "The Year of the Pause."

Yes, pause. Stopping. Hitting the breaks. Waiting. Reconsidering. Taking a moment to double-check the systems before I slam the lever into overdrive. Before I react to anything, I have the power to take a second—maybe even a *microsecond*—to think about whether or not that's the way I want to show up. And, if it's not, I have the power to change.

Just because you try on one shirt from your closet doesn't mean you have to walk out of your bedroom wearing the first thing you grabbed. (For the ladies who change their outfits at least five times before stepping out, can I *please* get a witness?) Just because a top looked good on a Monday doesn't mean you have to wear it every Monday. Fabric stretches. Colors fade. Circumstances change as you grow and mature.

If your shirt doesn't fit right—if your attitude isn't what you want it to be or you feel like you're not acting in line with your values—change your shirt. You have power over how you show up. You have power over the precedents you set in your community. If you glance in the mirror and don't like what you see, don't be afraid to hit that pause button.

The attitude you wear matters. The way you show up matters. If you think the shirt you're wearing isn't important, you've made a gross underestimation of your own potential. In any given moment, you're either teaching or learning—and more often than not, you're doing both.

When I was a teenager working at Hy-Vee, I walked the giant push broom up and down the aisles near closing time. One night as I was making my broom rounds, my eyes glued to the floor as I looked out for pesky dust bunnies, a super-cool pair of shoes stopped me dead in my tracks.

"Hey," I said to the cool shoes guy. "I like your shoes."

I looked up into the face of a blushing boy. He seemed to be about my age, and it seemed like he was there with his mom. What I didn't know was that this boy was new at my school, accompanying his mom on her shopping quest to stave away the gnawing dread of becoming the new kid the very next day.

I wasn't in a classroom. I didn't have an apple. But in that moment, I became a teacher in a way I hadn't expected. When I got to school the next day, this same boy recognized me and said hello. The grin on his face must have been a mile long.

"Hey," he said. "You're the girl who complimented my shoes."

Years later, this guy found me on Facebook. He was now grown up, married, and had kids of his own. We connected, but it was the reason *why* he sought me out that surprised me the most.

"When we moved to Kansas City," he explained, "you were the first person I interacted with. It was a new school, but I knew there was a nice girl who went there. That made things easier."

Never underestimate the potential of a kind word. That night, I never would have guessed the cool-sneaker guy would take that compliment as a comfort. Unwittingly, I'd taught him there were kind, friendly people waiting for him at his new school. I'd been the new kid so many times in my own life. I knew exactly what it meant to face that kind of uncertainty.

I taught, and I learned. I showed up, and I grew. To this day, I carry those Hy-Vee lessons into my businesses. If you like someone's shoes, tell them about it. Say hello to every person you interact with. A smile, a wave, or just an acknowledgement can reshape someone's entire perspective. You have no idea what sort of impact even the smallest action can make on a broader community.

The shirt you choose to wear—the way you choose to show up—matters. Whether you know it or not, your engagements are teaching lessons and establishing precedents. Maybe I didn't learn *everything* I needed to know while working at a supermarket, but those khaki-clad days made me realize how significant my day-to-day interactions really are.

If I don't like my shirt, I can always go back and change it.

CHAPTER 6: THE CULT OF HUSTLE

Everyone serves something.

Regardless of what philosophy you embrace, how religious you may be, or what sort of spiritual background you relate to—if you're a human being with time, treasures, and talents, you're wired to believe in something. What that "something" ends up being is different for every person, and the worship of the "something" varies depending on personal circumstances. But the "something" is there whether you know it or not. And if you truly believe you're an atheist, your god might be hiding in the strangest of places.

We all have values. We all have beliefs. We all have fantasies about what would make our lives better, richer, or more fulfilled. We tend to put our time and effort (intentionally or otherwise) into the things we think will make us happy or deserve our laudation.

Think about it this way. When we spend quality time with our families, we're serving them with precious moments of our own lives, moments we could spend doing *literally* anything else. When an entrepreneur puts money into her business, she's doing so with the faith that bringing her dream to life will bring her fulfillment, her ingenious idea will bring a great return on her investment, or that her efforts will bless her community—maybe all three outcomes if she really pulls things together. When an alcoholic spends night after night guzzling down drinks, that person is truly entrenched in a ritual of pain, despair, and placation. And when a friend drudges on, day after weary day, in a job that depresses and drains her, she's paying homage to the idea (be it accurate or not) that this job is what she should do—*must* do, even—to keep her life together.

Service, no matter how loathsome or begrudging, is still service.

If you're reading this book, I highly doubt you fritter away your days doing nothing. You probably spend your time in different places with different people doing all sorts of different things. You probably use money or manipulate resources to buy, barter, and trade for other commodities. I would even go so far as to presume that you possess some sort of specialty or talent, a trait, skill, or insight that not only makes you an individual but empowers you to make an impact on the world. If you didn't serve anything—if there was nowhere, nothing, and no one worth your time, treasures, and talents—you would probably be lying in the middle of your kitchen floor, staring at the ceiling as you waited for the inevitable end of the world.

And if you're anything like that, you're probably not reading this book.

It's much more likely that you're a dynamic person with hopes, dreams, aspirations, and people you just so happen to love. Serving these things—investing your time, treasures, and talents into things that *matter*—isn't a bad thing. Service doesn't have to be particularly religious, and by no means does having an afternoon picnic or spending a lazy day in the sunshine make you some sort of heretic. In other words, caring about "something" doesn't make that something a cult.

Inevitably, you're going to put your time and efforts into some sort of service, but it's not the service itself that needs a good dose of scrutiny. After all, we're human, evolved over millions of years to build, create, and make progress. It's the *why* behind our actions—the mirror we raise to the face of our own ambitions, patterns, and motivations—that shows us the truth.

The things we invest in speak volumes about what we truly care about, and the things we serve on a day-to-day basis give us insight into what sort of values we're engaging in. Notice I didn't say, "what sort of values we wish we had" or "what sort of values we think we should have." We're talking about engagement, and how we *want or wish* to show up can often be very different than how we *actually* show up.

But that's the tricky part. In order to know how you want to show up, you need to know what you value.

It's the classic motif from any Hallmark movie: The way-too-busy female professional is called away from her fancy-pants, big-city job, and when she finally returns to her homemade-apple-pie-Midwest hometown, she realizes everything she has been looking for has been right back home all along—usually in the form of the muscular mechanic/firefighter/underwater basket weaver. What she wanted wasn't what she needed, and now that she knows that, she can live happily ever after in the arms of her furniture-whittling beefcake. Add a dramatic kiss, give Dolly Parton a cameo, then roll the credits.

If only "discovering yourself" were that simple.

Even when I make an active effort to engage according to my values, there will always be something in my life I don't want to be there. Balance, after all, is a verb. Anyone who has ridden a skateboard, walked across a fallen log, or braved a mechanical bull knows you have to make constant, corrective movements in order to stay on top. If you're putting too much weight on any one side, no matter how lovely, noble, or wholesome that side may be, you're not going to like what happens at the end of the fall. Sure, I may *say* I value connection, excellence, and safety, but if my time and resources aren't reflecting that, my life is out of balance. And a life out of balance—a life in service to something you don't truly believe in—is bound to be deeply unhappy.

"Hold up," you say to me. "Don't even pull that crap. You were just talking about opening your business ten days before giving birth to your first child. Don't you dare tell me *that's* balanced."

And to that, I say, "Touché."

Yes, there's a time for hustle. Yes, there's a time for sixty-plus-hour workweeks as you do what needs to be done while getting your feet off the ground.

Yes, there's a time for sacrifice. There's a season when your time, treasures, and talents will be spent on things you're not passionate about.

But that's where balance becomes critical.

•••

I'm not going to lie and say starting my business was Zen and kale smoothies. It was more like eating a bowl of rusty tacks. When I started Bright Beginning, I *was* looking at seventy-hour weeks as a new mom. There was a lot of groundwork that came with renovating the old building, hiring a new staff, and molding the business to my vision. This was the heavy-lifting stage—the *oomph* to get the whole enterprise off the ground and into some sort of system. I wouldn't say that onboarding, conducting interviews, and developing corporate policies are intrinsic passions that light my soul with inspirational fire, but I understood that these were the things that needed to be done. It would be a season of hard work and personal sacrifice before I got to the "yummy goodness" of making my dreams a reality.

There are myriad reasons why entrepreneurs, ideas, and endeavors don't last beyond their first season, but this is one of the biggest. There are so many bright-eyed dreamers who have a burning desire to hang curtains—to immediately dive into the fun, personally rewarding aspects of the business that play to their strengths. And if you're trying to build a business (or build a house, according to this analogy), there's nothing wrong with hanging the curtains, so long as you have a sound structure to hang them *in*.

When I started my preschool, I was hiring and onboarding, getting enrollment up, and working on a brand-new set of protocols with my brand-new team. Creating systems and processes was just as time-consuming as it was mentally exhausting. Of course, I wanted to get to the fun work, to wave my teachers off with a wink, promising we would get to the boring stuff some distant snack time in the future, but

I also knew my business relied on cash flow. Without a functioning preschool, there would be no students. Without students, there would be no money. And as much as we loved lesson-planning, crafts, and extracurriculars, none of those things could happen if we weren't making money.

Before we got to painting and interior design, we had to build a solid base for our house. This kind of construction work isn't glamorous. Unless policies and protocols are the stuff of your wildest dreams, this kind of work isn't fun or particularly enjoyable. Most entrepreneurs I know didn't start their business because business is their passion. They became an entrepreneur to make a business *out of* their passion. And while this is a completely legitimate aspiration, it leaves us with a critical question: if business isn't your passion, who runs your business?

This is what we need to ask ourselves about our enterprises; this is what we need to ask ourselves about our lives. If our investments aren't centered in the things we value, what "something" is actually in charge here? If you're not doing the work to build up your house, who the heck is?

There are several colossal mistakes I see from entrepreneurs—pitfalls I have to watch out for even after running my own businesses for decades. The first has everything to do with the curtains. Far too often, I see people so busy working in their business that they don't work *on* their business.

I get it. It's not easy to zoom out and take a broader view of what you're constructing if construction isn't your cup of tea. But this is where we start to see what I (lovingly) call entrepreneur firefighters: high-achieving, well-meaning business owners who spend their days rushing from fire to fire when their slipshod systems start splintering. Even if you initially do have the money to outsource things like payroll, the procedural systems—the strong, sturdy lumber beams that make up the frame of your house—have to be yours. You're the one who has to set the tone of your operations. You have to be the one to decide what the house looks like and how the interior layout functions.

Shingling a metaphorical roof might not be what you *want* to do, but you're never going to be able to lay beautiful carpet or bring in fabulous furniture pieces if you've got a leaky ceiling.

You don't shingle the roof because you like shingling. You shingle the roof so it *protects* that gorgeous carpet and handcrafted coffee table.

And this isn't just true in business. This is a truth of life. Too often, we want the glory without the guts. We want the fairytale ending without the backstory. We want fully actualized, well-mannered, and independent children, but we don't want to tell our kids no. We want a joyous, fulfilled marriage, but we're much more apt to point out our partner's faults than dare to look at our own. We want the beautiful house, but we certainly don't want to expend our sweat and tears building it. We want the "something" we serve to make us happy, but we never dare to question if we're the ones who are making ourselves *un*happy.

You see this frantic, almost desperate busyness everywhere. Now more than ever, women's lives are on fantastic display via social media and hyperconnectivity. We see what other people have, and we're able to manipulate the image of what we *think* we have like never before. If one woman builds a business or posts photos of her adorable family, there's an automatic judgment—an assessment on where *we* stand within the perceived dominance hierarchy. And when we see our neighbor's beautiful house, the first temptation is to keep up with the Joneses.

It's scarcity, not production, that lies at the root of our hustle culture.

The disease is everywhere, and we've got the hashtags to prove it. #momboss, #hustlelife, #hustleandglow… It's all tied back to some sort of perceived effort. It's not the aim of the hustle, the reason behind it, or even the end goal. It's merely the idea that someone, somewhere, is hustling. And if you're not on the hustle train, obviously, you don't work nearly as hard as you should.

It's a frenzy—a mad dump of spastic energy toward an illusion and not a concrete goal. Building a business (building anything, for that matter) does take an agonizing amount of groundwork, but you lay that groundwork for a reason and not for the sake of the work itself. Posting pictures of your office is so much easier than making concrete progress, and the temptation makes perfect sense. The hustle culture makes us feel good. We feel seen, acknowledged, and appreciated. If we look like we're busy, others assume we're productive and give us positive affirmation. And once we're hooked on the hype, it's only natural to hustle harder to *keep* receiving that kind of intoxicating affirmation.

It's all about the illusion of "effortless struggle"—working hard, taking names, and keeping a perfect face of makeup while you do it. We glorify this hustle, focusing more on the act of building than what we're actually trying to accomplish. And when we lose sight of why we're even building something in the first place, we begin to worship the hustle.

In real life, it goes something like this: A well-intentioned woman announces she wants to build something. Everyone claps, and the clapping feels good. The woman reflects on how nice it is to have others applaud her efforts. So, she starts building in earnest, and the people clap louder because she's building so fast.

Look at that success!

Look at how hard she works!

Look at how productive she is!

Look at how she does all of this while also doing that!

This is where we see the bait and switch—the subtle but insidious encroachment of the superficial over actual value. When you glorify the hustle, you glorify how fast that house is being built over how sturdy the house actually is. In a world where you need to move fast and build even faster, there's no time to do the heavy lifting, not when your audience is watching, waiting with bated breath to see how quickly you can build something beautiful. Never mind if the floorboards creak, the door hinges rattle, or the roof leaks. Those are "maintenance" projects, the nitpicky things you can see to later.

But that's the irony of it all. When you're constantly attending to maintenance, flitting around from project to project while putting out fires, there *is* no later. If your systems are faulty, there will always be something out of place, and as those tiny faults compound, you'll forever be one step behind. You're always going to be fixing, mediating, and adjusting. Your time will be spent patching floorboards instead of enjoying the beautiful house you built.

But the cult of hustle doesn't want you to live a balanced, fulfilling life. It wants you to keep hustling.

Don't get me wrong—I'm not against hard work, and I don't want to disparage the women who are busting their asses twenty-four-seven to make things happen. There is a season of life where hustling isn't only good, it's necessary. When I opened Bright Beginning, I was working around the clock. However, I was also in a unique position where my children were able to come to work with me. My situation wasn't like anyone else's. *No one's* situation is like anyone else's. There were a lot of other women who disparaged me for spending so much time at work without even bothering to learn that my new baby was right there with me.

I put in those excruciating hours at the beginning of my business knowing that those systems and procedures—the bedrock of my house—would enable me to outsource, scale, and build Bright Beginning without having to maintain that grueling pace. Once I got a few sturdy walls up, I could slow down and take a breath. I could be strategic. I could be intentional about what I wanted my childcare center to look like. Working my tail off was never the aim; it was merely a season, the conduit base I needed to start building the life I wanted. I didn't serve the hustle. My hustle served me.

Business doesn't equal productivity. Production doesn't equal profit. And if your efforts aren't building the house you want—the *life* you want—what's the point of it all anyway?

That's why resting is an art. There's a season for hustle, but it must be followed by a season of recovery. Any woman who doesn't understand this is a woman who's going to burn out. Nothing has illustrated this concept to me more vividly and painfully than training for and running a marathon, an endeavor I embarked on back in 2014.

Anyone who knows me knows that I'm not a particular fan of running. I tend to enjoy the people I run with more than the running itself because (let's be honest) who actually *likes* the running part? It's hard. It hurts. It takes discipline, time, and the reluctant sacrifice of your lazy Saturday mornings. Every morning during those marathon days, my alarm would honk me awake, and I'd roll out of bed still half-asleep to join my running group in the merciless cold or scalding heat, depending on how the Maryland weather happened to feel that day. Then we would be off, step after painful step, up hills, across roads, mile after mile as we built up our strength.

While I don't consider running to be particularly fun, I learned something different about myself with every new mile, something I never would have discovered had I not pushed myself so far. I learned, for instance, when I needed a bite of a delicious power waffle to re-energize my legs and boost my morale (if you haven't tasted a power waffle, I highly recommend you go pick one up; they're delicious *and* give you a boost of yummy-waffle power). I also learned I needed to sprint myself out of the tight-knit pack at the beginning of the race then reel my pace back before I overexerted myself and burned out.

In addition to delicious waffles and frenzied sprinting, my training showcased my athletic strengths and weaknesses in visceral clarity. I'm a natural powerhouse on hills. When our group of eight women approached a particularly nasty incline, they'd put me at the front of the group so I could coach the others through it. I would remind them to be light on their toes or to dig through their heels—to keep pushing, even when they thought they had nothing left to give. After we conquered the hill, another woman would take the lead and encourage me through something I wasn't good at. We all had different body types and different levels of experience, so we combined our strengths to balance out our weaknesses.

That's not hustle. That's collaboration.

When the New York City Marathon rolled around in November 2014, I had confidence in my abilities because I *knew* myself. I came out of the gate two minutes faster than my target pace, but I knew from experience with smaller races that I had to pull away from the crowd before I could start cruising. I knew I had to check my watch and slow myself down. I knew I had to stop for water breaks, nibbles of food, and the morale boost of seeing my husband at different mile markers.

Of course, it was painful. Of course, I wasn't the fastest runner there. But when I scaled back, took the time to listen to my body, and focused on *my* race, something incredible happened. I truly began to marvel at the boroughs as I ran through the city. As exhausting as it was, I could glimpse something beautiful in each and every neighborhood. I was comfortable with my pace. I was comfortable with myself. I hadn't particularly enjoyed the grueling training regimen, and I wasn't terribly pleased about my rubbery legs and throbbing blisters. But despite all the hard things, I ended up enjoying myself.

That's when I realized mile eighteen could be just as beautiful as mile eight.

Everyone out there is running their own race. Every woman on earth is keeping her own pace. I remember running through downtown Annapolis, constantly getting lapped by various Naval Academy sports teams.

"We're not slow," my group would call after the midshipmen, laughing. "We're just running farther than you!"

Maybe we were. Maybe we weren't. In the end, it doesn't matter. Our race was *our* race. We had to find our own cadence and strategies to make it through the training run by run. We didn't keep up with the midshipmen—and why should we have even tried to keep up with them? Their pace didn't affect our race. Their speed didn't change the fact that *we* had to get through twenty-six miles.

This is why hustle just doesn't work. Keeping up with the

#bossladies may feel like an obligation, but keeping up with anyone isn't a goal. Comparing yourself to the woman next to you does you no good; you're not running the same race she is. You don't have the same body type, strengths, and needs. If you look down and compare your feet to hers, you'll realize you're probably not even wearing the same brand of shoes.

"Hustling" for the sake of hustle doesn't get you anywhere. "Busy" isn't a badge of honor. If you're in an endeavor for the long run (no pun intended), you'll end up spending much more time training than you will in the actual race.

The hustle culture also doesn't account for the indifference of reality—the cold, hard fact that life is full of surprises. A dislocated pelvis, for instance. *That* was something I couldn't control. The injury happened during a training run leading up to the marathon. I stubbornly pushed through it and ended up suffering painful consequences for years afterward. No matter how hard I hustled, there was no way around it. I couldn't keep running with that kind of injury.

After coming so far after so long, I was upset that my injury had thrown a wrench in my running career. I missed my running group. I mourned the runner I used to be. But at that junction, I had two choices. I could give up, lamenting that the universe and all my karmic balance was somehow against my athletic endeavors, or I could find another sport that made me happy. I took up TRX, tennis, paddleboarding—anything that got me out and about. I still missed the camaraderie of my running group and the boost in my day from seeing them every morning, but just because we didn't run together didn't mean we couldn't be friends.

Just because I couldn't run like I used to didn't mean I had to lay down and die.

The cult of hustle doesn't hold space for setbacks—only ultimate defeat. When your only goal is to keep up with everyone else, you're doomed to fail when life throws an obstacle in your path. Bringing ourselves out of this mindset gives us space to pause, grab a breath, and then truly take inventory of what we can and can't control. More often than not, blocking off adequate time to rest and regroup is the most productive thing you can do when your plans go off the rails. You can still be mourning a loss while making a plan to move forward.

The last year of my life has been a powerful reminder of what I can and can't control. When COVID pummeled the globe in 2020, I had just as much power over the pandemic as I did over a spontaneous injury. And believe me when I tell you that 2020 was just about as fun as a dislocated pelvis.

There was one night I woke up in the throes of a full-blown panic attack, wondering how my business was ever going to survive. But in that moment, I took time to pause—to calm down, check in with my five senses, and clear productive space in my head—before racking my brain for the things within my control. Yes, the terrain was uncharted. Yes, the odds were dismal. With stringent restrictions on groups and parents working from home, I honestly had no idea how I was even going to pay my teachers.

But that didn't mean Bright Beginning was over. There were things we could do to survive. We could pivot our structures, apply for loans, and redefine the way we did childcare. At this point, these changes were possible because our centers had fostered relationships beyond systems and procedures. After years of nurturing our shared values, we weren't going down that easily.

The night my fears shook me awake, I got up and went to work.

This was one of those "cookies for breakfast" kind of mornings, the ones where you eat too much sugar and drink obscene amounts of caffeine. I started mapping out pragmatic, doable action items my team could accomplish immediately. Instead of using the downtime to fret over the things we couldn't control, we got busy utilizing that time to map our next steps. We started prepping and training, rehashing our systems and procedures to be sustainable in the world of the "new normal." There were essential workers who needed somewhere safe to send their children, and we weren't about to close our doors on them.

During the early days of the pandemic, my business was barely surviving. I own that. I don't think any preschool owner is about to climb up and shout from the rooftops how amazing, expansive, and profitable childcare has been in the age of COVID. But in the midst of all the unknowns, I knew there were two things in my life I had ultimate control over—my attitude and my effort. My attitude was going to be indomitable. I wasn't giving up. And the effort I needed to expend was everything it took to keep showing up as a leader, day after day, for my teachers and students.

In a way, the pandemic has been my mile eighteen, the point in a marathon where runners claim to hit "the wall" of exhaustion. If you've ever run this far (or run any distance at all, for that matter), you'll know this is the point where the race totally sucks. If there's any gradient, you know it will be uphill. If you've got a blister, *now's* when it starts stinging. Most likely, it's also the point where there's no one cheering you on from the sidelines, distracting you from the soft, oily voice in the back of your head.

You still have over eight miles left, it whispers. *Do you honestly think you can make it?*

For many of us, 2020 was our mile eighteen. This is the point where we keep putting one foot in front of the other—when the pretty hustle hashtags fall away and all you're left with is half a soggy power waffle.

It's times like these when I remind myself I'm a survivor. I've survived every single day of my life. Every horror, disappointment, and pain has passed—and this will pass too. Nothing lasts forever, whether it be the good days or the bad, so when the going is good, *celebrate it.* Those good times will come and go, and by the time you reach the other side of the bad times, they'll feel like a drop in the ocean.

That's why successful businesses are built on values, not hustle. Hustle is finite and fizzles out quickly; shared values aren't so easily bested.

As grueling as COVID has been, nothing can dampen the pride I have for my Bright Beginning team. We applied and were approved to serve as an essential employee childcare site, and we revamped our entire program to accommodate the needs of essential workers and their families.

Was it a scary time to be in business? *Of course.* All businesses were suffering similarly. The numbers on the books were downright terrifying; we were only operating with the revenue of one-fourth of our normal student enrollment. But this was one of those times when success wasn't measured by revenue, and that kind of outreach isn't something the hustle culture accounts for.

In the end, it was the outpouring of love from our community—parents, alumni, and even families who no longer had children at Bright Beginning—that kept our heads above water. People donated money, school supplies, and even cleaning products so we could keep our doors open. As if operating during a pandemic wasn't hard enough, we were also hit by a flood. But when we came in the next day to find our library completely waterlogged, the community sent so many donations, we ended up with more books than we'd lost in the storm.

When I think about my team, my family, and my community, I can't help but look back in open-mouthed awe. Values are what matter. Values have kept us together through what could be the most trying period of our generation, and values are bringing us back even stronger than before.

When you truly and authentically build your foundation on what matters to you, you're willing to put in the work. You'll know how to build from the bottom up. You'll learn how to run your own race, and you'll do the hard training to get there. To strive and achieve is only one small stretch of the long, calamitous road ahead. You can't be so focused on the road that you don't take the time to look around you—to find beauty, express gratitude, and even change your direction, if you need to.

When I get stressed and overwhelmed by the things I can't control, my first inclination is to lean into my strengths. I'm wired to work hard, hit harder, and never take no for an answer. But when I get caught up in the hustle cult, sprinting and straining without knowing where I'm actually going, I always end up more lost, expended, and confused than when I started. Hustle has its place, but so do *resting* and *pausing* to take inventory of the "why" behind the "what."

Hustle is the means to an end. It should never be the end in itself.

•••

Most people assume I'm a business coach, which is only partially correct. Technically, I'm a business-leadership coach, which gets much more personal once you realize you have to take the lead in your own life in order to effectively lead others. In true life coach fashion, I find myself helping women work through the same lessons I had to learn before I could rip myself out of the cycle of endless busyness. Having been in thrall to the hustle myself, I know how hard it is to regain control when the weight of that hustle comes crashing down. It's no easy task to slow down that kind of frantic momentum. Once you get the hamster wheel going, you really can't help but feel swept along for the ride.

While sticky notes, colored highlighters, and meticulously notated calendars may seem a bit obsessive, these tiny illustrations reveal simple truths about our crazy, complex lives. Consider what would happen if you began to track how you spent the hours of your day. What if you highlighted your hours of sleep in green, your workday in yellow, and your time with your family in blue? Maybe you want to exercise for an hour a day, so you go ahead and mark that with pink. Do this for a mere seven days, and you might be surprised by what you find.

If you say you value connection with your family but your week is awash in yellow, it would be only natural for you to feel exhausted, frustrated, and tense at your job. If yellow and blue are dominating your days, you need to think carefully about how much you really want to prioritize your health. Of course, there are seasons where we skimp on a little green, chop off a bit of yellow in order to jam in more blue, or even skip the pink altogether. But as you start to track these colors, week by week and month by month, you'll begin to see patterns and habits. Sure, you say you want to exercise. And yes, you may be in your busy season. But if you're not getting to the gym months after that busy season ends, are you really valuing your health?

On my calendar, I outline health and wellness in orange. I know if I'm not taking care of myself, I'm going to burn out and crash hard. If I don't see any orange through my week, I've got to make room. My kids' color is blue, and as they've grown older and more independent, the amount of blue in my week has waxed and waned. Your values stay constant, but your priorities may change month by month and week by week. *And that's perfectly okay.*

Seasons are different. Life is unpredictable. But when you take the time to outline what you're doing then ask yourself why you're doing it, you can honestly assess whether you're showing up in life in accordance with your values.

I have my clients look at their lives like a wagon wheel. The Institute for Professional Excellence in Coaching (iPEC) illustrates this as a circle divided into slices where each slice represents a specific area of life. iPEC defines the eight categories as fun and recreation, physical environment, career, finances, health, family and friends, romance, and personal growth. When I sit my clients down, I have them rate the satisfaction in each of these areas on a scale of one to ten with ten being the highest and one being the lowest. Higher numbers are located on the outside of the circle whereas lower numbers gravitate closer to the center. The higher the satisfaction rating, the longer the wagon wheel "spoke" becomes.

After doing this exercise, many of my clients discover they have clunky, lopsided, or even oblong wheels with significant divots. When I did this exercise for the first time, I finally saw that there were elements of my life where I was deeply unsatisfied. At the time, I was throwing myself headlong into volunteer work, and no wonder. That was the place I felt most successful and appreciated. But my "shorter spoke" areas—my family, my husband, and my business—were the areas that needed my attention. If I continued to bury myself in the places where I felt good, I was never going to move forward.

This was how I started mastering my priorities. Once I acknowledged it was in my human nature to avoid the uncomfortable, I started putting conscious effort into investing my time where it was needed. If I was dealing with a "stumpy spoke," what did I need to do in order to fix it? How could I bring more satisfaction into that area of my life in order to achieve more overall balance? Instead of blowing off steam with my girlfriends over a few too many glasses of wine, I started sitting down with my husband and discussing what was and wasn't working. Just like we budgeted our money, we began to budget our time.

Being a business owner, a wife, and a mother came with a boatload of expectations. I couldn't ignore them. I had to manage them. If I wasn't intentionally prioritizing my time, talents, and treasures, they were at the mercy of every twist and turn life threw at me. But my kids needed my engagement. I needed to be showing up as my best self in my marriage and my business. I had to honestly look in the mirror and ask myself the question I dreaded most: *if you're not dictating your own priorities, who is?*

If you don't know where your values lie, you can't have priorities. And if you don't have priorities, your goals will always be shallow and arbitrary.

Here's one odious phrase I hear far too often: "all this 'self-discovery' sounds great, but I just don't have time for that."

No—you have all the time in the rest of your life for that. You just don't prioritize it. It drives me crazy when people ask me how I have time for this or say they wish they had time for that. Oprah and Beyoncé have twenty-four hours in their day, just like every other person on the face of the planet. Successful people don't magically create time. They don't get more hours in their day than you do. "Not having time" isn't a legitimate excuse for anything.

Time is finite, but you have to spend it somewhere. If you have twenty dollars in your pocket, you get to choose if and how to use that money. Maybe you want to buy a new top. Maybe you want to treat yourself to a decadent ice cream. Maybe you don't want to spend the money at all and end up tucking it into the bottom of your wallet for a rainy day. No matter what you do, you only ever had the potential of twenty dollars, and what you do with that potential will show what truly matters to you.

On Sundays, I sit down and map out my routine for the week, strategizing how I can puzzle in projects, calls, and Bright Beginning work with the other events in my schedule. When I wake up, I spend five measly minutes of my morning reviewing that day's schedule and assessing last-minute changes. This doesn't mean my day goes perfectly. It doesn't mean little things aren't constantly popping up and screwing with my color-coded plan. But because I have a plan, it's much easier to adjust my schedule when life gets in the way. No day ever goes exactly as I'd envisioned, but it's the vision itself that gives me direction when I have to make spur-of-the-moment decisions.

If your life feels out of control, the solution isn't trying to frantically control everything. Instead, focus on the things you *can* control. I would never say planning makes you immune from overwhelm (I have two teenagers in the house—enough said), but I never feel out of control. Stressed, exasperated, and close to scorched-earth tactics, maybe. But never helpless.

I can't control if my kids suddenly need me or something blows up at work. There are just too many variables out of my hands. But because I *know* at my core that I'm prepared, I know I can make things work. I know my bandwidth. I know how things can be moved, and I know the resources at my disposal. The events on my calendar will get bumped, swapped, and maybe even cannibalized, but there's always a way forward. Having been through these situations before, I can trust myself to take care of them now and in the future. Nothing is truly "un-figure-out-able," and that does a lot to ease the stress when life gets overwhelming.

I've learned to trust myself over the years, and it's a trust that's been hard earned every step of the way. You have to earn that kind of trust with yourself as much as you do with others. When I plan events in my day, I assign them to myself as a boss would pass on responsibility to an employee. There's no "I don't feel like it." There's no "maybe I'll get to it tomorrow." If I've worked that event into my schedule, I've made it a priority, and if it's a priority, it's somehow connected to my personal values.

Can you imagine waiting in a conference room for a meeting with your boss, only to find out she's cancelled at the last minute for no good reason? It's unthinkable—utterly unprofessional. Bosses don't cancel like that, and if I'm my own boss, *I* don't cancel on myself. When I find myself avoiding or procrastinating things I've committed to, I can't just beat myself up or dismiss myself as a lazy, sloppy person. I have to look for the deeper factors. If I can shrug this commitment off so easily, is it *actually* my priority? And if I genuinely think this project or endeavor is worth my time, am I actually being honest about my capacity to get it done?

If you're committed to your goals and honest with yourself, you'll take responsibility for creating a schedule that takes your bandwidth and abilities into account. You'll make sure the events highlighted on your calendar align with your goals and values. You're the one who decides to show up as your best self. You're the one with the power to engage as a leader.

But when you decide to take the lead of your life, make sure you're a good leader. That means being a "good boss" to yourself. A good boss doesn't overwork her employees. A good boss knows their emotional, energetic, and mental capacities for the day. Hypothetically, my employee (*i.e.*, me) could take six clients, an hour lunch break, and then an hour for office work Monday through Friday. But if I stepped into my office and told the *real-life* AliceAnne about that workload, she'd think I'd lost my mind. I've been a life coach for over five years and an entrepreneur for nearly twenty. I know for a fact that I can only manage two coaching calls a day then need an hour to decompress after each call. If I stretch myself beyond that pace, I'm going to burn out.

These parameters come from time, experience, and reflection. The personal boundaries I set on my workload aren't limitations or obstacles to overcome. This is the space I need to show up and engage as my best self. I know that AliceAnne is both a hardworking employee *and* a good boss, so I know I can trust her.

How can I expect to effectively lead others if I can't even be good to myself?

•••

These days, I have to be very careful about what I glorify. In a world that blindly lauds busyness over substance, it's all too easy to get sucked into the cult of hustle. But hustle is a cruel god. No matter how much you give, you're never going to get where you want to be. How can you reach the finish line if the whole point of the race is to keep running? How can you ever be satisfied if you can only feel good about yourself when others applaud you?

No one can run forever. No one can clap forever either.

We're all given a finite amount of time, talents, and treasures. Every second you breathe, you're expending those precious resources. Even the man lying in the middle of his kitchen, shaking his fist at the ceiling as he professes to serve no one and nothing, is sacrificing his potential on an indifferent altar of nihilism and despair.

Everyone serves something. Your time, talents, and treasures have to go somewhere. If you don't know what you value, you have no idea what to prioritize. And if you don't know how to prioritize, how can you ever engage as your true self?

I constantly have to remind myself that balance is a verb. Life is a symphony of seasons, and we're always evolving—always growing through dreams, goals, and aspirations. If you do have to hustle, go into it with the mindset that it's a phase, not a lifestyle. A wise woman once told me, "This, too, shall pass," both for better and for worse.

The only constant is change, so take time to honor where you are. Seasons of hustle build us up. Seasons of rest rejuvenate us and provide space for learning and reflection, the time we need to check in with our values and priorities.

Wherever you find yourself, you won't be there forever. Something, somehow, is going to change, and that's not necessarily a bad thing. Life is bustling, busy, and chaotic, but that's also what makes it beautiful, vibrant, and exciting. If you can stand firmly in your values knowing you have the power to lead yourself with both surety and kindness, you can venture forward boldly. You may not be able to see every obstacle in your future, but as long as you're guided by your values, you can move forward with the confidence of knowing you're headed in the right direction.

A is for authenticity.

CHAPTER 7: THE SHATTERING

Values are much easier than authenticity.

This probably seems hypocritical, seeing as the last chapter revolved around knowing your values so you can show up as your authentic self. And, yes, there's valuable truth in that. If you don't know what you value, how can you ever know how to take the lead in your own life? And if you never dare to peel back the layers—the armor, the masks, the capes—how can you ever find your authentic self?

For me, it's much easier to write these philosophies out as "lessons" than it is to unwrap those layers. I haven't always lived my life as a leading lady. I didn't wake up one beautiful, sunny day with a sudden revelation that I needed to start living my life authentically. More often than not, lessons are learned the hard way. They come from the dark times in life, from the places we would rather not talk about. I'm used to boiling down the L.E.A.D.E.R. acronym into points and principles when I coach or give seminars, but this book has been harder. *Much* harder.

Teaching a lesson is one thing. Showing the scars behind that lesson is something else entirely.

But values aren't just learned in life. They're lived through the best and worst of it. More often than not, people get uncomfortable when I bring up this subject because it involves a little depth. When another woman chooses to show her authentic self and step out of the prefabricated box we've shoved her into, she makes herself vulnerable. And that might even make *you* vulnerable.

Highlight reels and social media stories are easy to digest. They're happy. They show the winning moments we've come to expect. But a human life is far more complicated than that, and leaders are even more multifaceted. If you see a woman who's growing, I would bet money she has the scars to prove it. If you see a woman who's strong, she probably has an incredible story about how she got that way.

I imagine most of you know nothing about my sordid past as a serial killer. Yes, I must confess I've killed more houseplants in my lifetime than any one woman has a right to admit to. I could tell you it wasn't my fault, but that's not quite the truth. The fact is, I just love plants. They bring life to the rooms of my house, and I appreciate the splash of color and beauty they add to my office. It certainly doesn't help that my friends and family have taken it as their personal responsibility to keep buying me plants, sending their unwitting sacrifices along with pithy little instructions about getting plenty of sunshine or singing droopy leaves back to life.

Full confession: After many, many tragic losses, I've gotten better with my poor houseplants. Not *good* but certainly better than I used to be.

What I didn't know was that what these poor plants needed was a hearty shake. When I learned this, I went to each plant, picked the pitiful thing up, and gave it a gentle rattle. While this may seem strange and maybe even cruel, an old-fashioned shaking is actually one of the best things you can do for indoor plants. The stress of the vibration signals to their DNA that their environment has become threatening, and so the plant responds by growing thicker stems, longer roots, and even tougher leaves.

This phenomenon is called *thigmomorphogenesis*, and it doesn't just apply to house plants. While you won't see trees sporadically shoot upward during vicious thunderstorms, their roots have been shown to grow deeper and stronger beneath the soil. Adversity tells the tree it needs to burrow farther, slurp up more nutrients, and prepare itself for

142

the gales of the storm. Anyone who has tried to get a stump out of their yard knows just how much of a pain it is to untangle the gnarled roots of an old, burly tree. Anything that survives that much wear, tear, and weather has survived for a reason.

The lessons of my life run deep, but the stories behind those lessons run even deeper. When I'm speaking, coaching, or giving a seminar, we usually stick to the meat and potatoes of the subject—the *what* I learned without the *how* and *why* I learned it.

That's why this book has been so hard for me. It's different than anything I've ever done before. All of a sudden, I have stretches of long, blank pages to illustrate those *whats* with *hows*. What am I supposed to say? Where do I even begin? How can I even skim the surface of what it took to get here?

It's easy to be misunderstood. When we step back to admire a tree, we're probably not taking much time to give the roots a second thought. But learning to take the lead in my life wasn't some kind of revelation, jolt of inspiration, or even a burst of genius. I've worked through my acronym the hard way, and I have the golden *kintsugi* scars to prove it.

I didn't learn to be a leader because my life is perfect. I learned to lead myself during the shaking—during the times when my life was falling apart.

Just because a woman looks put-together doesn't mean she *has it together*. When I opened Bright Beginning, it must have seemed like I was living a fairytale. I had a handsome prince, a beautiful baby girl, and a thriving kingdom of entrepreneurial prospects. I was a business owner in my early twenties, happily married with the world at my fingertips. The highlight reels looked great. I was checking all the boxes of success and fulfillment.

But the cracks—those ugly, lurking gremlins I hid behind my cape of accomplishments and the mask of an easy smile—were starting to show.

It was a lot at once, and at the beginning, it was very lonely. Early on, I didn't want to talk about the struggles of being married to an older man. At the risk of being labeled as a gold digger, I didn't even want to mention I was married to an older man. But Marty was in his forties, and he'd been running his own profitable masonry business for years. As I set out to navigate my way through the ins and outs of being an entrepreneur, he tried to steer me away from failures or mistakes based on his own experience.

His heart was in the right place. Truly, he only wanted to protect me. But between being newly married, starting a new business, and being new parents, the pressure and resentment began to build. I was young and headstrong; I needed space to learn and grow. Masonry was a completely different ball game from what I was trying to do with Bright Beginning, and I'd already had years of experience in childcare and early education. When Marty would comment on my struggles or try to give me unsolicited advice, I would tersely remind him that, back when he was starting his business as a twenty-something, he didn't have anyone hovering over him, breathing down his neck.

"I'm just trying to protect you," he would say.

And we left it at that.

I felt stifled. Even then, I knew there was a difference between making minor mistakes and driving my business into the ground. I wanted my husband to trust I could do this—or at least, that I would come to him before things went completely off the rails.

But letting people make their own mistakes is hard, and letting the people you love make their own mistakes is even harder. The things that knock you down are also the things that teach you to get back up. When Marty shielded me from failure, I knew deep in my heart I was also missing out on valuable lessons.

It certainly didn't help that I was trying to learn these lessons at such a young age. Whenever someone in my business was upset at me or quit, I would be completely heartbroken. Marty, however, had already worked through setbacks like these, so he responded by giving me his perspective on the issue. To me, that felt callous and dismissive.

His forty-year-old wisdom didn't help me in the moment, and in the moment, I was hurting. All of a sudden, this person who had given me all this space free of opinions and judgments had a lot to say about what I was doing in my day-to-day life.

But things just weren't the same. We were married. We had businesses. We had a child to provide for. My husband is a strong, steady person, and when a person used to smooth sailing starts to list, they tend to grab on tightly to anything they can.

I, on the other hand, was all too familiar with the realities of a rocky boat. My past experiences had taught me just how easy it was to jump ship if things got hard. Nothing was permanent anyway, and I was still young. If I wanted to, I could move on and start over, just as my parents had done so many times before.

It was a rough patch in our relationship. It was a rough patch in both of our lives.

These growing pains made me feel unsuccessful in my marriage, and I hesitated to go to Marty with my struggles. He wasn't validating me; he wasn't hearing me out. He was just telling me how to fix things. Eventually, I stopped going to him with anything about Bright Beginning, which made it even worse as the little problems began to fester.

Then came the 2008 crash. Parents lost their jobs and started pulling their kids out of childcare. Our profits plummeted. I started to worry if I could even stay in business. To add to the stress, my second baby, Christian, announced himself in 2007. As joyful as we were, it was *not* a good time for a baby.

It didn't seem to be a good time for anything.

I couldn't get a break anywhere. My body was strange and uncomfortable. I didn't feel confident, appreciated, or seen at home. Work was just another endless circus of problems to be solved. I was floundering and vulnerable, so I leaned into what made the most sense at the time—the one place where I could feel good about myself.

The Junior League of Annapolis has been one of the most defining leadership experiences of my life, and I initially joined with the best intentions. I've always loved volunteering, and I appreciate opportunities to give back to my community. I'm a natural at organizing and executing events, and the women of the organization lauded me for my poise and success at such a young age. I saw my volunteer projects as places I could dump in work, turn the crank, and spit out the praise and validation I so desperately craved. Because of this, I threw myself headfirst into any project I could.

Through the organization, I made a group of friends, and outside of the League, we bonded over a salacious monthly ritual of wine, appetizers, and venting at Bertucci's. Every Friday, we would get together for drinks and complain about our husbands. Before I knew it, we had a little tribe of victims, each more downtrodden and unfortunate than the last. We would complain about our marriages, our jobs, and our kids. At the time, it felt like a safe place, a place where other women truly saw me, understood my plight, and legitimized my self-pity.

I remember going home after those get-togethers and feeling nothing but anger, resentment, and disappointment. There was never a night where I felt good about venting. I would return furious with Marty, convinced I was miserable because he was making me miserable. My friends had told me just as much. We had convinced ourselves that others were responsible for our own unhappiness. Misery, after all, seldom dines alone.

I've spent years trying to get to the bottom of why I spent so many nights at Bertucci's. The truth is, it was much easier to label myself as a victim than to make the hard, self-reflective effort to actually make changes in my life. Deep down, I think I knew that. I wouldn't be surprised if the other women did too. The atmosphere was toxic, but no one ever engages in destructive behaviors because they feel particularly good about themselves. Nights like these numbed the pain. They gave me someone to blame, and they shirked the realities of responsibility off one more day.

We weren't encouraging ourselves to be our best. We were just allowing ourselves to be our worst.

This is why I caution women about getting into "venting" relationships. I'm not talking about when a good friend needs to sit with a difficult emotion. I'm not talking about someone who just needs a shoulder to cry on or a listening ear to help her process a complicated situation. A venting relationship is fueled by blowing smoke over problems you never intend to solve. There's no forward motion; there's no attempt to find a solution, be better, or even look at the situation from a growth angle. These kinds of relationships reward misery and voluntary victimhood with positive affirmations (e.g., wine and doughy appetizers) that end up entrenching you even deeper into your own problems.

These friends didn't call me out for my negativity. How could they? Pointing out the problems with my attitude would have meant calling themselves out for the exact same thing. If there was one faux pas in the Bertucci's Venting Club, it was self-reflection.

This mentality poisoned my perspective. It poisoned my attitude and my relationships. I was constantly over-volunteering, shoveling my time and effort into the things that made me feel good. I lived for the validation of the Junior League. If everyone there was singing my praises and lauding me with accolades, I could ignore the places where I felt like a total failure.

If life is supposed to be a balanced wheel, I was basically riding a pogo stick.

But you can't live a lie forever. Eventually, these things catch up to you. Sometimes, it takes months. Sometimes, it takes years. Some people spend their entire lives living behind masks, capes, and armor, only to reach the end and realize happiness could have been theirs all along.

More often than not, it takes a big fall for us to finally see just how much our lives were tottering. Unfortunately for me, that fall was very public.

My marriage wasn't doing well. My business wasn't doing well. *I* wasn't doing well. But no one knew that. I was still living behind my masks. First and foremost, I was a performer and an entertainer. As long as I could make people think I was winning, I could fake my way through anything.

When the Junior League asked me to speak to a full conference room of women, naturally, I said yes. To say no would have implied that something was wrong, something deeper and darker squirming beneath my cape of shiny accomplishments. When the day finally came for me to give my talk, I walked into that room of women completely unprepared. I was frazzled. Disheveled. I stepped up to the podium, smoothed out my top, put on my shiniest pageant smile…

And froze. Completely, utterly froze. As I stood before those women, gaping out at the hundreds of eyes staring right back at me, I lost my words. I lost my breath. For a moment, I even lost my heartbeat.

"I…"

I choked. Faltered. Tried to start again. Finally, I found a breath, and something inside of me snapped.

"I'm sorry," I said. "I can't do this."

I fled that room through a chorus of hissing whispers, head down, gaze forward, tears stinging the sides of my eyes. I couldn't make out words, but what was said in that room inevitably made it back to me through the churning channels of gossip.

"Did you hear? AliceAnne cracked."

"She fell apart."

"Have you heard about her marriage?"

"I guess she's not as successful as she thinks she is."

Those women who had once praised and applauded me ripped me apart piece by piece. They saw my weakness, and they pounced on it. The relationships I'd invested so much time and effort in turned on me in an instant. I was battered, broken, and bleeding, so I did the only thing that made sense. I ran away and hid.

There's a strange sort of voyeurism that follows successful women. Celebrities, business leaders, and even the female royals constantly grace the front of our tabloids. We love to watch them succeed, but we love to watch them fail even more. When I fell from grace, I fell hard, and it seemed like the women around me relished that destruction. I can't assume what sorts of feelings of power, validation, or moral superiority my hardships gave them, but the reality of my superficial friendships came into visceral clarity when my room full of fans suddenly cleared out.

All the bad things, the secret, shameful things I'd hidden so carefully behind my facade of perfection, just kept getting worse. The humiliation within the Junior League was only the beginning. When I finally began to crack, it didn't take long for my whole world to shatter.

The details aren't pretty, so I'll suffice to say that everything collapsed in on me at once. My marriage, my business, and even my identity had all been built on the image of who I thought AliceAnne Loftus *should* be. When that mask was ripped away, I had to face the real woman in the mirror, and she wasn't the strong, put-together woman I wanted to see. She was weak, wounded, and wanting. She'd failed, and she'd failed *big*.

No performance in the world could save me from myself.

There were very few people who stood by me during my darkest hour, and the ones who did weren't the ones I'd expected. When I was too much of a wreck to even take care of my children, Marissa's preschool teacher came to my house at 5:30 a.m. to help me bathe the kids and get them ready for school. This same teacher was the one who pulled me into her office throughout the day to make sure I'd eaten and taken a shower. In one instance, she shielded me from serious consequences I truly deserved. This woman didn't pity me; she had compassion for my situation. She truly saw me at my worst, and she chose to help me.

It was women like her, women who didn't even know me any deeper than the perfectionist image I'd so carefully curated, who came alongside me. My Bright Beginning families saw what I was going through. My staff saw what I was going through. I have to imagine my executive director was disappointed in me, but she stepped up as my silent protector. She never took out her frustration on me. She never disparaged me for my failures. She saw I was fragile and had flaws, but she also chose to see the good in me. She chose to forgive me. She gave me the space and compassion I needed for a painful transformation.

Nothing was easy about this time, but tending to my marriage was the hardest of all. When you've neglected such an important aspect of your life for so long, the time and effort it takes to nurse the relationship back to health goes far beyond even the most heartfelt apology. Marty and I had work to do—deep, painful work. It involved going straight back to our original agreements. If we were going to keep our commitment to one another, we had to clearly communicate what we needed from each other. Which gremlins were mine, and which were his? What aspects of our relationship were non-negotiable, and where could we meet in the middle to make things work?

It was a lot to untangle. Progress didn't happen fast, and digging this far hurt more than either of us could have ever imagined. At this juncture, separating would have been easier for both of us. I even met with a lawyer, but after an hour of discussing how to even begin, my heart was aching. I could only think about how much I loved my husband and how I was willing to do anything to repair our marriage. But even with all the love and regret, it's no simple matter to renew commitments, rehash agreements, and heal betrayal. Add two kids and two businesses on top of all this, and you're looking at one heck of an overhaul.

There was no going into rebuilding this relationship lightly. Marty and I both knew that. That acknowledgement didn't make things easier, but agreeing on our commitment to one another was a solid start.

At the time, my best friend was actually my mother-in-law, Karen. While not Marty's biological mother, Karen was the one in the delivery room when I gave birth to Marissa. The fact that she loved me so purely and fiercely without a blood relation made her even closer than any traditional definition of family, and even if we hadn't been close, there was no denying that this woman was a total force of nature. After graduating from the University of Idaho, she'd been recruited by the CIA to create their computer systems. And we're not talking about the "fempowered" early 2000s—this woman was shattering glass ceilings while most of us were learning how to tie our shoes. She was the smartest woman I've ever met in my life, but on top of all this, she was so unbelievably kind. She must have been disappointed in the way Marty and I had hurt one another, but I'll never forget her gentle encouragement—the night she called to give me one of the most important messages of my life.

"I believe that you guys can get through this," she told me. "Marty loves you."

And Karen was right. She pointed to the high road—the hard road—and told me the truth. I think about her whenever I'm building things for the Leading Lady program. I think about the way she gave me space and loved me when I couldn't even love myself.

Karen died in 2010, and there's not a day I don't think about the fact that I lost her before she saw me put my life back together. That woman was truly a Leading Lady in every sense of the word. She was the first person in my life who showed me how to give and receive unconditional love.

My dad died shortly after. He passed in 2011 on my thirtieth birthday. I try not to judge myself too much for what happened during that time. It almost feels like an out-of-body experience, like I was watching a shadow version of myself living out a nightmare. Everything felt awkward and stiff. Even though part of me saw it coming, I don't think the premonition made it any better. I dragged myself through the funeral process, but it was the performance of a lifetime I'd never wanted to rehearse for.

As the ceremonies came and passed, my thoughts were a murky blur. Was I responding correctly? How, exactly, was I supposed to respond?

The reality finally set in that I hadn't just lost my dad. I'd also inherited the responsibility of caring for my mom. My older brother was absent, and my younger brother, Michael, dealt with things in his own detached way. We didn't come together to support one another. Truth be told, we were scrambling to keep *anything* together.

There was so much happening—so much chaos, pain, and despair—I ended up reaching out to one of my Bertucci's friends. I hadn't heard much from any of them since the Junior League meltdown. They knew I was trying to make adjustments in my life and in my marriage. They'd seen me fall flat on my face as my world went into a tailspin. Oddly enough, I hadn't been in touch with any of them. For the first time in years, they'd all been strangely silent.

I called this woman—this friend—to tell her about my dad, only to be surprised by the fact that she already knew. I asked her why she hadn't reached out to me earlier.

"I thought you weren't really close to him," came the reply. "You two had all sorts of issues, right?"

I was one second away from either hyperventilating or snapping the phone in half. I wanted to cry. I wanted to scream. Of course, I had issues with my dad, but this wasn't about him. This was about my family. This was about *me*. The surprise of her answer could only be bested by the pain of realization.

These women didn't actually care about me. At one time, I thought they did, but what we had wasn't true friendship—it was sharing in one another's miseries. These women only wanted to be there for my highlights, to share in the experiences they were comfortable with. As soon as I hit a patch in my life they couldn't understand or relate to, they couldn't accommodate my brokenness. When I came forward in an honest place of pain, they either judged me or popped a bag of popcorn so they could sit back and watch the show.

These friends couldn't embrace me through this. They couldn't give me the love and space I needed to grow as an authentic person.

That's the bitter truth about these types of friendships. When a relationship is built up from victimhood, there's no room for any real substance. You don't discuss problems to better yourselves or find solutions. You validate one another's victimhood with pity, platitudes, and blame. Any emotions outside the victim wheelhouse are far beyond the realm of comfort and experience.

Shortly after, I saw this same group of friends having one of their routine girlfriend gatherings. For a moment, I was confused. Had I missed something? Did they forget my invitation? Maybe I just hadn't seen the email or the text.

We locked eyes, and after a beat of excruciating silence, the group quietly informed me I was no longer invited to their monthly gatherings.

I would be lying if I said I wasn't hurt. It's one thing to get that message before walking into the party you haven't been invited to. It's something else entirely to be rejected in real time. But as painful as it was, I get it. At the time, I was hyper-focused on my own life and rebuilding myself. These women probably felt neglected and betrayed. As I worked through my own trauma, I'd inadvertently failed to show up for them in the way they were used to.

I needed space, but they had no space to give.

There was a bigger lesson to pull out of that situation. No matter what sort of pain I was going through, these women had their own burdens to bear. This was a group where everyone paraded their grievances. We didn't truly listen and hold space for one another. We just waited for the others to stop talking until it was our turn. But if everyone in the group is constantly going through hardship and wallowing in helplessness, no one will be there when the wheels fall off the wagon. When I look back on these relationships, I realized that none of us were there for each other. We couldn't have been there for each other. Living as a victim doesn't allow you the space or energy to truly show up for anyone else.

Thinking back to that group of women reminds me of my mother-in-law, Karen. That woman never lived her life in a victim mentality. She lost her mother when she was young, and her brother came out as gay when being a homosexual endangered his life. Karen shattered glass ceilings, fought through impossible prejudice, and died far too young at only sixty-two. But she never lived her life in a victim mentality. Despite all the pain and setbacks in her life, she was there for me wholeheartedly. I know that woman was able to give herself wholly and accept me where I was because she knew *her* authentic self.

If you're half a person—a person who doesn't know what she wants, where she's going, or what truly matters in her life—you can never give anyone your whole self. While I wasn't privy to Karen's personal reflections or what sorts of gremlins she'd battled in her past, the fact that she could love me unconditionally spoke volumes about her character. No one learns to love like that without a measure of pain. No one can stand that strong without learning how to get up after a fall.

Karen is, in her own special way, one of the original Leading Ladies. She never lived to see this program, but I doubt she could have imagined how many lives she would touch by touching mine. When my world fell apart, she was the one who encouraged me to put it back together. She was the one who taught me I have the power to fix the things I break.

She was the first woman in my life who challenged me to take the lead.

For all the heartache and hardship, this was a critical juncture in my story. My cape had crumpled, my masks had fallen away, and my armor had shattered. For the first time in my life, I had nothing left to hide behind, and that left me with a painfully clear choice. I could frantically try to scramble back to my defenses, throwing up walls, repainting masks, and pretending like none of this craziness had ever happened, or I could do the work to change. I could take the time and space I needed to show up as the person I wanted to be.

At this point, I knew living inauthentically wasn't a sustainable strategy. Hiding behind perfectionism worked for a time, but I was only delaying the inevitable. By ignoring the pains and shortcomings in my life, I was ignoring the things that needed the most attention— my family, my marriage, and my business. I needed to change, but it was going to take a bit of self-exploration to figure out what that change was going to look like.

For me, this involved going back to my own wagon wheel. I took a real, honest look at the things I'd been avoiding. It wasn't enough to say that I wanted to "stop doing this" or "start doing that." I had to tease out the *whys* behind my actions and motivations. What past traumas was I clinging to? What sorts of habits needed weeding out? What kind of person did I actually *want* to be, and what did I need to do to make those differences in my life?

Not a lot of my female friends stuck with me through this process, and that's completely understandable. This experience taught me I don't need a lot of people. I just need *my* people, the ones who love me enough to give me time and space because they truly want to see me thriving as my best self. These are the friends who encourage me to find balance in my life and put in the hard effort to engage authentically. In my experience, friends like that are few and far between, but the impact they make is nothing short of astronomical.

The worst part about losing Karen is that she never got to see the impact she made on my story. She'll never get to see me and Marty send our beautiful daughter off to college. She'll never see how much my husband loves to watch his son play baseball. She'll never see that her seed of unwavering faith in my marriage has matured into something stronger and more beautiful than ever before. My love for my husband is deeper. Our bond is forged by fire.

Karen never got to see the Leading Ladies either. I never got to sit down and show her the tens of thousands of women who have been impacted and encouraged to take the lead in their own lives because she encouraged me to take the lead in mine.

You never know the role you play in someone else's story. By the time the book comes out, you may not be around to pick up a copy. When I look back on my own life, I can't help but wonder what Karen would think of all this, if she could have grasped an inkling of her legacy while still here on earth.

I sit, I reflect, and I wonder. *Am I that person in someone else's life? Could I be?*

The questions come like a tidal wave. Do I hold space for other women to grow? Or am I a judger—a spectator, a bloodthirsty voyeur? Do I relish other women's misfortunes, or do I come alongside them with unconditional love? If I can't give wholly of myself, what might I be missing? If I'm judging, what could I be learning instead? If I can't forgive, what do I need to let go of? If my life is unbalanced, what can I do to fix it? If I feel lost, scared, or unsure, what values do I need to light the way?

In a world full of victims, how can I be a leader?

•••

There's a certain beauty to being broken. No matter how many times I try to backseat quarterback the worst years of my life, I can't come up with any regrets. There's pain, certainly, and most of the scars are still visible.

But if my life hadn't fallen apart, I wouldn't have been forced to change. If I hadn't broken, I never would have learned how to thrive.

After my public disgrace, I spent about a year hiding out in my "cave," licking my wounds and rebuilding my marriage. When I finally felt strong enough to face the world again, I ended up confronting the women from the Junior League who had belittled me so mercilessly when I was vulnerable. Some of them thanked me. A few of them got angry and never spoke to me again. One of them ended up apologizing and registering her child in Bright Beginning. In the end, it wasn't their apologies that mattered. It was the fact that I could forgive myself.

I was done with glory-hounding. I was done with the applause and laudation. I was done living a lie behind my masks of perfection and accomplishments, and I was done neglecting the areas in my life that needed my careful attention. The work wasn't easy, and it certainly wasn't fun. But little by little, I found the power to change my own narrative.

I was going to build myself back up, step after wobbly step. This wasn't fun or glamorous work, but I knew who my true friends were. I'd seen the kind of woman I wanted to be—the same type of quiet hero as the women who stood by me through the worst of times.

In a strange, macabre way, the shattering was one of the most beautiful parts of my life. It took a full breakdown to face what I'd been hiding for so many years. That's the funny thing about living a lie. You spend so much time building your defenses, you lose sight of what you were trying to protect in the first place.

In case you're wondering, I still pick up my plants once in a while and give them a good shake. There's a genuine part of me that wants them to be strong and healthy, but another, less-benevolent part that reasons a bit of adversity is only fair. These coddled, privileged house plants need a good rattle every once in a while.

I want them to feel the chaos. I want them to learn to grow.

CHAPTER 8: THE ITSY-BITSY TRIUMPH

Most people assume triumph is loud.

By no means is this assumption a fault. It's just what we're used to. At the climax of an action movie fight scene, the hero gets a trumpeting fanfare or maybe even a gritty reboot of her theme song. When life goes our way, the first thing we do is snap a photo and post it for the world to see, gleefully checking in as the hearts, thumbs up, and other points of social gamification start piling up. If you've triumphed in your business venture, you're probably going to tell someone about it—maybe even pop a bottle of something celebratory. If your child receives an award at school, there's usually some kind of ceremony to publicly honor their accomplishment.

And there's absolutely nothing wrong with sharing these special moments. We live in a communal society. Unless you spent your days in an isolated cave eating squirrels and farming pinecones (again, I would like to point out that if this were so, you probably wouldn't be reading this book), I'm sure you share the celebratory parts of your life with your community in one way or another.

I'm by no means against public validation. I appreciate sincere compliments just as much as the next person. If someone takes the time to thank me, acknowledge my work, or even point out how cute my shoes are, it brightens my day. Loud moments of celebration make our hearts swell. It feels good when other people see the value of the goals we've met and the obstacles we've overcome. But while these small, treasured moments may be social media-worthy, the hard truth is no amount of celebration can ever encapsulate the real victory.

Triumph is glorious, but it's also complicated. The real stuff—the deep-down, transformative, heroic character arc—doesn't happen in any singular moment, and unless you have a videographer following you around through every stage of your journey, you're not going to be able to capture the true magnitude of your metamorphosis. Everyone sees where you are now. Unless they're close to you, they have no idea where you've been or how you finally arrived at your present triumph.

That's why it's so hard for women to see just how much progress they're actually making. Far too often, we look for the *signals* of success rather than the quiet evidence of real transformation. We want to see awards and accomplishments. We look for familiar, easy-to-spot material features we can grasp within our own experiences. We want parades, action scenes, and the melodramatic kiss at the end of a rom-com—the brave knight to return with the head of the monster, but certainly not a full view of the monster itself.

The great irony is that the most amazing triumphs are in the places we can't see. They're not big. They're not loud. They take time and a herculean amount of grueling effort. Heroic stories mean so much to us because they symbolize the greater, immaterial truth we know in our souls. Hollywood can distill that into Rocky-esque montages and melodramatic pan-ins when the hero suddenly has her "eureka moment," but we know by virtue of being alive that two hours of screen time is a drop in the narrative ocean. Who we are, who we've been, and who we choose to become can't be illustrated in a final, show-stopping dance number. The triumph isn't the finale. It's the culmination of every small moment you choose to be different.

That's where most people get the wrong idea about triumph. It's not the snap of a second, a burst of genius, or even a tall, handsome stranger who changes your life forever.

To truly triumph—to make the decision to lead your own life—is a process.

For me, this began with a year of hiding. Not very glamorous, I know. But at that juncture, I didn't know what else to do. I was wounded. Defeated. Exhausted. I couldn't have continued the way I'd been doing things even if I'd wanted to. Watching my life crumple before my eyes forced me to stop and have a long look at who I'd been. Where was that person going, and did I really want to follow her?

Was this what I *wanted* my life to look like?

Did I really *want* to continue living this way?

What if maybe—just maybe—things could be different?

Einstein is often credited for coining this gem of a maxim, but it actually traces back to mystery novelist Rita Mae Brown: "the definition of insanity is doing the same thing over and over again and expecting different results." If my very public fall had taught me one thing, it was that what I'd been doing wasn't working. At this point, the stupidest thing would have been to try and keep limping along with a broken leg. This period of my life knocked me flat on my back, but that gave me a good opportunity to sit down, shut up, and take a good look around.

I didn't know it at the time, but I was finally stepping back to take inventory of my life. If I was going to rebuild my identity from the bottom up, I needed to be sure that I was building it on what truly mattered—the things *I* loved, cherished, and valued. When I sat down and asked myself what those values were, it took a little time and reflection to tease out the list of my top five: safety, love, connection, growth, and autonomy.

Getting down to the root of your values isn't an easy task. I dare you to ask three people what their top five values are and pay close attention to their responses. When I pose this as a casual question to my clients, most of them are surprised to find that their list doesn't come to them as easily as they might have thought.

"Well, family," I often hear after a bit of floundering. "I value my family."

After listening to that knee-jerk answer, I'll smile and nod. "That's a good start. But do you really?"

That's the point where my client usually gasps indignantly, shocked I would even *insinuate* her family wasn't her number one priority. In her mind, that makes her a bad wife and mother, two pieces of identity she's come to cling to when she isn't feeling particularly beautiful or empowered. But "family" isn't a simple concept either. It's a broad, symbolic term that means something different to every individual. It's the top layer of peaty soil in a diamond mine. You know there's value somewhere down there, but you've got to dig deeper to find it.

Family sounds good. Being a wife and a mother, I know putting family on the list feels right. You probably love your family more than anything else in the world, and your bond with your spouse and your children is nothing short of magical. But what about your slightly racist, stockbroker second cousin from Delaware? Do you have a meaningful connection to your great-aunt? *Her* second cousin? Would you do anything for a blood relative based solely on the idea that you share the same ancestry?

In this case, "family" isn't descriptive enough. When we boil the symbolic word down to the deeper meaning, we might find it's the *connection* that truly matters to this woman, which is much more useful to know. If you truly value the close relationship you have with your family, we can start looking at how much quality time you're spending with the people in that circle. Is your spouse your best friend? Do your kids feel comfortable coming to you with anything, and are you as active in their lives as they are in yours?

Questions like these run deep, which is why I call this exercise "value mining." Having done this many times in my own life, I can confidently say I've gotten pretty darned good at it. Being a professional coach has definitely honed my methods, and I've taken to breaking the process into five steps.

Firstly, I ask the individual to make a list of character traits they aspire to have. It helps to envision someone you consider to be a role model then write down what it is that you admire and respect about that person. For example: *She's a learner. She isn't defined by others. She values people, forgives, and is successful in her business endeavors. She shows gratitude, always encourages others…*

This list might end up looking something like this: *lifelong learner, independent, values others, forgiving, successful in business, grateful, encouraging.*

With the first list complete, I then ask the value miner to list the character traits they loathe. That doesn't mean coming up with a burn book of people they hate. We're looking for specific personality traits.

I loathe when people are self-pitying, cruel, and disrespectful. I can't stand when people manipulate and bully others, and I can't stand dishonesty.

The third step is to make a list of the opposite traits from list two. Self-pity hits list three as empowerment, cruelty is foiled by kindness, and manipulation can be countered by autonomy and respect.

Then comes the final list: *what brings you ultimate joy?*

I'm not asking you to Marie Kondo your life. I don't want to know how much you love deep-fried Oreos, trips to Disney World, or even a well-organized shoe closet. "Ultimate joy" goes back to the idea of character traits. When you're genuinely, purely happy, what sorts of values are present? Balance? Gratitude? Maybe even awe, intentionality, or validation? We're not talking about other people giving you something. We're talking about what makes you *feel* joy.

From there, it's on to the final step. Once you have between eight and fifteen items on each list, it's time to start looking for connections. Does the same word come up in multiple places? What about the same themes or associations? If you have "love of learning" on list one, "stagnation" on list two, "curiosity" on list three, and "awe" on list four, you probably value discovery—the never-ending exploration into new ideas and phenomena—or maybe even awe itself. If you loathe self-pity and appreciate a woman of grace, gratitude might be one of your leading values.

By the end of this exercise, most people end up between three and five "big" words that represent deeper, intrinsic concepts. *Why* you value something is just as important as *what* you value, and when you take the time to dig through the layers of expectations and habits to distill those values, it's like a breath of fresh air.

Maybe you're not spending long hours at the office because you're a horrible mom who doesn't care about her children. Maybe you value *quality* in everything you do, and knowing that, you need to rehash your schedule to give you the time to meet that high standard. Maybe you're not a helicopter mom, but you value safety for yourself and those around you. Now that you know safety is one of your values, you can acknowledge it and honor that drive for all the good things it does in your life.

Safety is one of my values, but it doesn't have to make me a stifling person. It means I have a keen insight other people might not share. However, it also means that I need to budget time, talents, and treasures toward reasonable measures and solutions. I need to listen to the people I love just as hard as I work to protect them. Safety, just like everything else, is a balancing act.

When I took the time to get my values in order, I was finally able to determine my own direction. There would be no more scrambling to meet other peoples' expectations, competing to be the best, and desperately trying to glean self-worth from others' approval. I wasn't going to live that way anymore. I *couldn't* live that way anymore.

Just because I'd made mistakes didn't mean that I had to let them take me down. I refused to let my story end this way. When I finally got a grip on these concepts, I was able to see that I wasn't actually defeated. I just needed to change.

Sure, I was at rock bottom, but the view had never looked so good.

The funny thing was, when I started doing the work to get myself back on track, everyone around me benefited from it. Between 2011 and 2012, I was rebuilding everything—my marriage, my business, and myself. This was when I finally went from running a preschool to being a *business owner*, and the difference made all the difference. Now that I was finally taking the lead in my own life, everything else fell into place.

"Lead yourself; the rest will follow," isn't a tagline. It's a lifestyle. My confidence was no longer a mask to hide behind. The bare, naked truth of my life had been dragged into the open for all to see, so what was the point of living another lie?

I could step forward as my real self—my *best* self. And when I was finally living my life as the person I wanted to be, I started attracting people and opportunities that aligned with that best self.

Values are like magnets. The choices you make will open up opportunities. If you're living life as a victim, you're going to attract other victims. If you're living in gratitude, you're going to step out each and every day into a beautiful, bountiful world. Other people who see you living this way will either be drawn or repulsed depending on their own worldview. If they're living in victim mentality, they could be inspired or ashamed. If they're seeking the very best out of life, their path will inevitably intersect with yours.

When I started engaging in life as the person I wanted to be, everything changed. The way I showed up in my marriage changed. The way I interacted with my kids changed. The way I engaged with my Bright Beginning team changed.

After the 2008 crash, I had to sit down with my books and figure out how to restructure my business. I'd always loved working with kids, but the crisis taught me something I hadn't known about myself: *I also love business management.* As I tweaked, tinkered, and toggled with the mechanics of my preschool, it became crystal clear why and how we needed to evolve. *I* was changing, and my business needed to change right along with me.

Meanwhile, other people were starting to notice.

At the time, many childcare centers were struggling in the wake of the financial turmoil. Administrators and other industry professionals began reaching out to me, wondering how Bright Beginning was thriving when so many other preschools were struggling. They wanted to know how they could change—how to find the right people to hire, how to organize their staff, and what sorts of new protocols to adopt to survive through the craziness. Having been through all of this myself, I was able to guide others through the process. I couldn't fix their businesses, but I could certainly show them how to clean things up.

Then the other calls started coming. More often than not, they started with, "Hey, so I know you're a local business owner…"

Women from all industries began reaching out—salon owners, boutique stylists, restaurant managers, private consultants… At first, I was completely taken aback. I didn't know anything about these businesses. They weren't even in my industry. But I quickly learned it didn't matter whether I could do highlights, hem a dress, or toast a crème brûlée. These women were looking for help in their businesses, and business was something I was good at.

I started going into these shops, stores, and businesses. I would conduct audits and review employee handbooks—ask about policies and how these business owners protected themselves. I loved the work and took to it naturally, but two lingering issues weighed heavy on the back of my mind.

Firstly, I didn't feel qualified. It wasn't that I couldn't do the work or wasn't getting results. I just don't like doing things without credentials. Secondly, I realized I wasn't just interested in management and administration. There was a whole other factor to the equation— the same factor I'd stumbled into while rebuilding my own business. Here were these smart, savvy, professional women building empires left and right. They didn't lack knowledge. It wasn't that they weren't working hard enough. I soon began to realize most of these women's struggles were tied to some sort of gremlin. The problem wasn't that they were bad business owners or didn't have the skills they needed to run a successful business. More often than not, they were facing down the exact same issue I was—they needed to take the lead in their own lives.

The solution to both of these issues actually came to me in the most unlikely of places. While I was attending a conference for educational administration, one of the speakers introduced herself as a professional coach. To be honest, I wasn't terribly impressed by what she had to say, and I was more than iffy about more than a few of her philosophies. But still, she was a *coach*.

As she was talking, I frantically began a string of Google searches. What, exactly, was a professional coach? How did one become a coach, and what did that journey entail? What sorts of training did someone need to get qualified? What did being a coach even look like?

I'm already doing all of this, I thought as I scrolled through the job description. *And I'm not even getting paid.*

At the time, I wasn't heavily involved with Bright Beginning. I'd laid a good foundation, and my amazing staff was doing what they did best without micromanaging or khaki pants. Meanwhile, I was also working to put my body back together. I wanted to be as healthy as I'd once been, so I started a few Facebook Groups for women trying to get back into shape. Of course, I wasn't a "health coach," but I didn't even see myself as a coach at that time. I would post workouts, document recoveries, and check in with other women who joined me for different fitness challenges.

I lost sixty pounds. I entered a professional bodybuilding competition. I was starting to build a name for myself as someone who was motivating, inspiring, and completely transparent about the struggles of being fit. The realms of childcare and fitness may seem completely disparate, but people were watching, and they started recognizing me from both realms. This wasn't about childcare or fitness; it was about building a supportive community.

However, the fitness world burned me out pretty quickly. I love teaching, and I wholeheartedly believe a good instructor can teach anything. But health and fitness just aren't my passion. I enjoy working out, and I even went back to get certified both as a personal trainer and a nutritionist. But living at the gym didn't light my soul on fire. At the end, some of it even began to get a little unhealthy. Everyone wants to lose a little weight now and then, but the *why* behind that weight loss can be just as dangerous as the weight itself. Was I really staying true to the best version of myself? Or was I once again trying to box myself into the stifling mold of who I thought I *should* be?

For me, fitness coaching wasn't sustainable, but that didn't mean it wasn't a great place to start. The experience taught me that I did want to be a coach. I was in the right field, just the wrong niche. The conversations that really filled my heart were when I talked to other women about their businesses.

I decided to enroll in coaching school. Believe it or not, there are no regulations or requirements for calling yourself a coach. You don't, technically, have to be trained, and the industry leaves it to the consumer as a "buyer beware" situation. But if I was going to make a career out of helping people, I wanted to be as qualified as possible.

I settled on iPEC, the Institute for Professional Excellence in Coaching. The program wasn't cheap, but even if I'd never earned any money from coaching, the school would have been worth every penny. Going through coaching school changed my life. Of course, I knew I had my own personal development work to do (I'd been doing it on my own for years), but I was finally able to learn methods and tools to make the process less mystical.

In order to get through coaching school, you have to learn how to coach yourself—and that includes getting to the root of your gremlins. iPEC is where I first made my "cape of accomplishments." I acknowledged my demons, gave them a name, and invited them to sit down for tea. As I was learning to coach, I was also *being* coached by my instructors and my peers.

I was doing it. Bright Beginning was my brainchild, but this was my calling.

On my first day of coaching school, I posted an announcement to Facebook and promptly forgot all about it. That weekend as I was driving home, I received a call from a local private school. They were having a staff meeting where they needed consultation from an executive coach, and a woman who worked there—a woman who had also participated in my fitness Facebook Group—saw that I was in the process of becoming a professional coach. According to the director, this woman claimed I was one of the most motivating and inspirational people she'd ever met. They wanted to hire me on the spot. I pointedly reminded them I'd only attended three official coaching classes, but they responded by offering me a hefty sum of money.

These people didn't know me. They'd never experienced any of my career coaching. But this woman knew how I had shown up in my health and wellness programs, and that had been good enough for her.

As I sat in my car, shaking my head at the awe and irony of it all, the pieces of my calamitous journey began to come together. Nothing in my life had ever been a waste. There were no random stops on the journey. Everything I'd faced—the challenges, endeavors, and failures—had brought me to this unthinkably serendipitous moment.

How you show up matters. Everywhere. All the time. Your path may not be a straight one, and you may have to circumnavigate seasons that seem to have no point at all. But somehow, someway, you'll reach your destination.

I never set out to be a coach. I never even set out to be a Leading Lady. But when you engage in life according to your values, you're always going to end up right where you need to be.

I contacted my coaching community to ask what to do about my first offer. I had no idea what to charge, what my contract should look like, or even what to call myself. Since iPEC requires their students to have a certain number of coaching hours before they graduate, my instructors encouraged me to take the job.

It was an absolute disaster.

I showed up to my first session bright and chipper, totally ready to instruct, encourage, and inspire. What I didn't know was that my class consisted of thirty employees who had recently been terminated. The school had hired me to coach them as part of their severance package.

Needless to say, that job didn't go very well. These people were angry and scared. They were the farthest thing from uplifted, motivated, or empowered. The last thing they wanted was a rip-roaring pick-me-up by some lady who'd been hired by the company that had just fired them.

I showed up, got paid, then got the heck out of Dodge with a crucial lesson under my belt: these were *not* the kind of clients I wanted to work with. I didn't leave that job feeling good. It didn't satisfy or energize me. As disappointing as the experience was, my peers and mentors coached me around it. Had I not been in my coaching program, I might have given up then and there.

But my instructors insisted that this bombed assignment was a good thing. It wasn't a failure; it was a moment of clarity.

I quickly discovered they were right. As I mentioned before, most coaches end up working with a younger version of themselves. If you come across a divorce coach, it's likely that person went through a horrible divorce sometime in their past and wants to help their clients achieve a better outcome. You wouldn't want a basketball coach who has never played basketball, and you wouldn't learn to pack a parachute from someone who's skydiving for the first time.

In rapid fire, I went through about thirty coaching clients I couldn't wait to be rid of. Every session was a learning experience. By the time I graduated from iPEC, I was unwaveringly clear on who my clients were going to be.

I wanted to work with high-achieving women. I know what it's like to suffer burnout. I know what it's like to live in the fog of pressures and expectations. Finally, I had clarity and direction. I just needed to figure out what that looked like pragmatically.

For a woman who specialized in administrative structure, this was a lot harder than I'd anticipated. All coaches build their programs differently, and no one model was going to fit my life perfectly. I still had two young kids at home. I had a flagship business to run, and Bright Beginning had since opened a second location in Glen Burnie.

How many hours did I want to work? How could I use the skills I was learning to the best of my abilities? And why in the heck would people ever want to come to me?

If there was one thing I learned through my coaching program experience, it was how to gain exposure. I started offering live workshops in Annapolis—luxury, pampering events with good hors d'oeuvres, high-quality wine, and enriching content. I wanted a beautiful, welcoming place where women could show up as their best. We were going to talk about the things that women wanted to talk about. We were going to have a girls' night out that encouraged women to take the lead.

But how were women going to learn about these events? It took some trial and error to figure out how to spread the word. I tried several different social media platforms, but none of them felt right. I didn't want these talks to be just another sleazy networking event where women felt like they had to show up and impress everyone else. My clients' time is valuable; I needed to offer her something that was worth her while. I wanted to build a safe place—an authentic place.

The best way to get the word out seemed to be a Facebook Group. In a group, I could do so much more than just promote my events. I could start discussions, foster connections, and truly build up a community. You want to learn about time management? Share your thoughts on being a woman in a male-dominated industry? Get advice about scheduling your day according to value-driven priorities? This was going to be the place.

Hey, lady, I wanted to say. *Let's hang out in this beautiful place. Let's have fun!*

The best part was throwing open the doors after the events and seeing these accomplished, beautiful women walking out, their heads thrown back in laughter. I knew they were going home after a long day of work knowing their power, and I treasured that. They'd just learned some nugget of truth that was going to make tomorrow better for them.

This was what I wanted Leading Ladies to look like.

I launched the online group in 2017 then really bolstered my live leadership series in 2018. It quickly became a chicken and egg dilemma. Was the group thriving because of the events, or were the events thriving because of the group? In the beginning, this was a pressing question. How could I take those elegant, empowering live events and translate the magic to an online platform? How could I ever capture the power and solidarity of women walking out of those seminars, laughing arm in arm?

The answer to my questions ended up being much closer than I thought. The Leading Lady evening events were based on solid, shared values. The Facebook Group was going to have to be the same way. This was more than a platform. This was a movement.

Women have always been in the lead. We're just not being quiet about it anymore.

•••

A lot of women ask me if they have to be a business owner to be a Leading Lady. I have women who message me all the time, unsure of whether or not they're supposed to be part of the group because they're not entrepreneurs.

Here's the truth of the matter: About one percent of the women in the Leading Lady Facebook Group actually fall into my coaching niche as prospective clients. Even fewer than one percent will end up hiring me as a coach. Whoever is going to work with me will end up finding me one way or another, and I'm certainly not the right person for everyone.

But Leading Ladies isn't about coaching. It's about community. I'm certainly not the woman for every job, but our group will help you find the woman who is. If you need a leadership coach, I'm your gal. But what about a landscaper? A photographer? A lawyer? A nutritionist? A plumber?

We've got them all.

I wanted a community where women could lift each other up, where female professionals could find each other, connect, and show up in their power. The best analogy I have is a sprawling, ever-growing table, constantly stretching longer and longer as more women pull up their seats and share the dishes they've brought. Someone may show up with a casserole. Another may bring in a turkey. Maybe two separate people walk in with a veggie tray. Even if multiple people show up with the same dish, there's no issue. Each woman's take on Jell-O salad or green bean casserole is going to look just a little different.

At this bountiful, infinite table, there's always enough to go around. There's no such thing as scarcity, and as women share the amazing things they've brought, others may be surprised as their tastes and palates broaden. It's an open table of ideas, stories, talents, and treasures, and there will *always* be room for another woman to pull up a seat.

The scope of this vision both frightens and thrills me. In three short years, the group went international—six thousand women and counting. The community is young, and that may be why I guard the core values so carefully. When something like this grows and takes on a life of its own, it's easy to lose sight of what that community really stands for.

Every woman is different. Every single person comes to the group with individual perspectives and needs. I get many women come to me miffed because they're not allowed to promote themselves or refer male-owned businesses. But the Leading Ladies isn't a phone book or a space to spam other women. In short, it's not a good fit for everyone. I don't get angry or sad when a woman writes to me and explains the group isn't for her. I want to hold space for the woman who *wants* a seat.

On an online platform, there's physical space (events, corporate ambassadors, live sessions, etc.), but there's also energetic space. There needs to be space for women to show up as their best, and that can't happen if they're constantly rifling through junk that doesn't pertain to them. I've been accused of censorship many times, and maybe that's fair. Leading Ladies isn't a networking platform. It's not a gossip hub or a place to critique one another's efforts. It's been challenging to maintain the values and integrity of the group as it grows, but that keeps bringing me back, time and time again, to authenticity. My purpose and the purpose of my brand is to keep pulling up seats for other leading ladies.

These days, it's easy to mistake being authentic for being loud. But being an authentic person doesn't mean that you bare all for the world without any boundaries. Being authentic means committing to your true self, leading with your values and staying dedicated to them.

I'm not an inauthentic person because I don't share every single detail of my homelife. I don't have my Facebook administrators take down unsolicited promotional posts because I hate or am against other women promoting themselves. I'm authentic by staying true to my value of safety—for protecting my family's privacy and giving my kids space to grow up and make mistakes without an entire community hearing about it. I'm authentic by reminding the unsolicited posters that there are other groups and pages where they can promote themselves, that it would be inauthentic for me *not* to remove those posts if I'm staying true to my vision of a "no-peacocking" zone. My referral days are for other women. My ambassadors who do post about their businesses have been carefully curated and vetted.

My vision is to keep pulling chairs up to the table, and I'm going to continue doing that the best way I know how. It's the small decisions—every tiny, inch-by-inch baby step—that's built this program into what it is today.

When all of these seemingly small, value-driven actions start stacking up on top of each other, you'll end up building something greater than you could have ever imagined.

.•.

My life fell apart. I don't hide that from anyone. It's something that happened and, honestly, something I'm not particularly proud of. That time in my life wasn't "highlight reel-worthy."

I broke. It hurt.

But that's the other unspoken truth about triumph. It doesn't happen if you don't face opposition. You don't triumph over anything unless you have something to triumph over. A story isn't a story if the protagonist doesn't face a challenge. No one wants to read about the happy-go-lucky woman who has it all. We want the story of the happy-go-lucky woman who loses it all, joins the circus, and then finds her life's calling as a trapeze artist.

Victory isn't a moment. It's not seconds, minutes, or even days. For most of us, our triumph is a lifetime of dips, diversions, and still, small moments where we discover what we're truly made of. Not everything makes sense at the time, and you're probably not going to see anything in full clarity until its far behind you.

I didn't start putting myself back together in order to found the Leading Ladies. I put myself back together to *become* a leading lady. When I was finally able to look my authentic self in the eye, I was able to dig down deep into what I valued. Only then could I begin rebuilding. Preschools, fitness coaching, and small business audits seemed like completely separate parts of me—until they all came together to reveal my life's true calling.

I'm not my best self all the time. As the Leading Lady program grows, I often wake up in a cold sweat, feeling like a slimy impostor. I remember where I've been and who I've been. I reflect on my day and all the stupid little mistakes I wish I hadn't made. A small, secret part of me is terrified the women at the table are going to find out I'm not actually a leading lady.

But that's when I stop thinking and start listening. I remember my own acronym, the hard-earned values that make up every single gold crack of my broken cup life. *Kintsugi*, that beautiful art of scarring, is even more vivid and beautiful in these moments. When I question what the heck I'm doing with my life, I go back to each and every one of those cracks.

I get to choose how I engage. I get to choose to keep my

authenticity in alignment with those values. I literally go through my own L.E.A.D.E.R. acronym again and again because even I recognize that just because you know something in your head doesn't mean you feel it in your heart. There's a whole market out there trying to convince us we're not who we're supposed to be. They tell us we're not the right size, we're not smart enough, fast enough... Just *not enough*.

I've spent so much time and effort on my quest to be a perfect woman, only to find at each and every phase, I always fall short. That's the dirty little secret of the game, and it's about time we tell those *not enoughs* the jig is up. There's no such thing as "enough." It's a moving target, an unfixed metric that's both cruel and arbitrary on any given day.

There's only one solution for that.

When I say, "lead yourself; the rest will follow," that's precisely what I mean. When you take the time to discover your values—to discover your true, best self—you don't have to let the *not enoughs* rule your life. You take control. You pull up a seat at the table. You empower yourself to build your life on a foundation that's going to last.

Triumph is a great big thing made up of deceptively small, unassuming things. It's built in the quiet places, composed of every laugh, tear, and decision that brought you to where you are today. In the midst of the chaos, falling apart can look a lot like coming together.

We all have a story, but none of us can reach our big, heroic moments without the culmination of every single small one. In the end, finding myself looked nothing like it does in the movies. It wasn't loud. It wasn't a singular, decisive moment. To be honest, I don't even think the process *has* a definite end.

And for some strange reason, I'm completely okay with that.

D is for dedication.

CHAPTER 9: UNLUCKY

When I grow up, I want to be just like my daughter.

Seriously. She shines. As a parent, I often find myself torn. I know it's my responsibility to teach her about the world, but it's a little hard to stay focused on that when she's constantly teaching me so much about myself. Through her, I've learned more about my values than I'd ever thought possible—things I didn't even know I valued until I had a little person walking beside me.

It can be hard to watch her navigate her way through life. This girl is pure sunshine; she's joy incarnate. As she blazes her path through her teens and off to college, I wonder what her defining moment is going to be. Of course, she's been through hardship. Everyone, in some form or another, has faced adversity in their lives. No matter what the scale, the process of struggle and overcoming comes with real, vivid feelings. If you ask her, she'll tell you that she's been through some hard stuff already.

That only makes me wonder if it will get harder. Half of me stands tall and placid, beaming with pride at this beautiful young woman while the other half is itching to throw my hands over my face the moment life starts swinging at her. God knows how much I want to dive in front of her and take the hit myself. I'm her mother. That's just what we do. To be completely honest, I don't know if I'm emotionally prepared to see her get knocked down in her adult life. But as I watch my daughter prepare to venture out into the world without me, the deeper, sadder part of my heart knows there's nothing I can do to stop that defining moment. The challenges that lie ahead of her are going to be her transformational moments. The breaking points will end up being her beautiful golden scars.

As a mother, I'm helpless. I can only sit back and watch.

It's a parent's responsibility to equip their children, and I've tried my best to stay dedicated to my own authenticity. I strive to be honest with my daughter. I tell her about my feelings, and I intentionally create space to share as much of my own happiness as I can. She's a light in my life, and I want her to know that. I want to treat her with respect and dignity.

But while all of that sounds lovely, I'm by no means a perfect parent. My daughter is very different from me. She's a free spirit—a bona fide flower child who makes sweatpants look great in any social situation. Part of me envies that, while the other part struggles to understand it. While my default is to grasp for control, she seems to let go. When I try to burrow deeper into blame and rationality, she seems to walk away with complete freedom.

It took me a long time to reconcile this. "Carefree" doesn't mean you don't care. It just means your priorities are different. I have to remind myself the goal isn't to manufacture children who look and act exactly like me. The world doesn't need another me—it needs a *her*. When I see something in her that challenges me, I actively have to stop myself from judging it.

I find myself backtracking a lot. Circling back to my values is a great place to start, but even that can get muddied. If I see her walking around the house in something that raises my eyebrows, what am I valuing more—my perception of safety or the fact that I value autonomy and self-expression? I don't want to be controlling, but I also want to be clear about how much I care. Do I really have to understand to make space for growth and respect?

Believe it or not, I don't just pull out one of my personal values from my emotional rolodex, slap it on the situation, and watch everything magically resolve itself. Life isn't that simple. *People* aren't that simple. And you aren't that simple either. While knowing your values is crucial, there's another factor of self-discovery that accounts for the dynamic parts of life that don't fit nicely on a neat little note card: *dedication.*

Life gets easier when you know what you stand for. It's like wandering through a dense forest then suddenly discovering you had a compass in your pocket the whole time. But while that compass may give you a relative direction, it's not going to clear the obstacles in your path. You're going to have to do that yourself, jumping over logs, wading through thick underbrush, and maybe even battling a rabid raccoon or two. And if you're anything like me, "roughing it" isn't the fun part.

But that's the funny thing about values. They're directional, not magical. Just because you know where you stand doesn't mean you'll never face uncertainty or challenges. You still have to navigate the path ahead, and that still requires courage, effort, and reflection. Knowing your values is one thing, but staying *dedicated* to them through uncharted territory is something else entirely. Values aren't rules to be followed; they're parts of yourself to honor. As you lead with your best self, you're going to discover even more about what that best self looks like.

That's the fun, frustrating part about raising kids. They challenge you in ways you could have never imagined. They force you to see that dedication doesn't require you to run a dictatorship. I may be the kind of person who dresses up to get on an airplane, but my daughter is going to wear whatever makes her comfortable, even if that means flying in pastel sweatpants. When I start getting nervous about what the future holds for her, I have to remind myself what real dedication looks like.

I'm not dedicated to making my daughter a miniature version of myself. I'm dedicated to love, connection, and growth—giving her the space she needs to engage as *her* best self.

Real dedication involves a surprising amount of flexibility. When I finally re-emerged after the Junior League of Annapolis debacle and hit the world with front-facing values, I had a lot to figure out. Sure, I knew what I stood for. But what did that look like in my everyday life? How did that change how I interacted with my husband? My kids? My employees?

The pragmatic answer to these questions wasn't even an answer at all. As life unfolded, it began to look more like a mindset. It was time to reconnect with people, with life—even with the Junior League. Part of me flinched at the thought of stepping back into the place I'd felt so humiliated and betrayed, but another part of me knew there was value to be found there. As I was finally facing my true self and learning what that looked like outside my coaching bubble, I had to decide what to do with the grief, anger, and betrayal. I couldn't just pack up and move away like I'd always done in the past. I couldn't hide in my house forever.

Tea seemed like a good place to start. The Junior League of Annapolis hosts gorgeous downtown tea parties on the regular, and it seemed like a place I could dip my toe back into the metaphorical pool of society without too much expectation. Of course, there were whispers and pointed glances when I showed up to the venue, but I forced myself through the door, one foot after another, my heart pounding thickly in my throat as I searched for a non-threatening place to sit.

Maybe there was a stubborn part of me that wanted to make a statement by walking in with my head held high. Maybe there was still a fierceness in my soul that demanded I show up in order to prove I wasn't a total failure. If we peel back the layers of our own egos, very few of our base motivations are *completely* pure, but to be honest, I was lonely. Aside from my work acquaintances, I didn't really have friends or social outlets, and this seemed like as good a time as any to get myself back out there. After all, I'd always enjoyed joining the ladies for tea. There's just something about dressing up, putting on a fun hat, and nibbling away at finger sandwiches in a room of floral prints. It was familiar. It felt *safe*. Even after my last experience, I figured there was no way a tea party could be uncomfortable.

I was wrong. Dead wrong. As I nervously scanned the crowd, trying to pretend I didn't notice the mutters and side-eyes, I couldn't help but wonder if I'd made a horrible mistake by showing my face in public.

But then a woman beckoned me, waved me over to the empty seat beside her. I didn't know this woman personally. I had no idea why she reached out to me. I only knew her by name, and we'd only ever spoken in passing. But she must have seen something—maybe the lingering loneliness I couldn't hide behind makeup and a colorful hat—that prompted her to invite me over. We ended up talking through the whole tea then meeting each other the next day for a run, which would have been perfect had it not been the first six-mile run I'd ever attempted in my life.

Yes. I was *that* lonely.

Despite my aching calves, this woman and I ended up becoming lifelong friends. In fact, most of my closest friends, in some way or another, trace back to the Junior League. Even though specific women had been unkind, that didn't mean the organization didn't have value. I'd been hurt by past relationships, but I still wanted to be part of a group that gave back to the community.

And therein lies the difference. When I initially joined the Junior League, there was an aspect of "saviorism" to it. I felt bad about myself, so I saw volunteering as a way to feel better. If I worked hard enough, if I was enough of a public do-gooder, then I couldn't possibly see myself as a horrible person.

Right?

But the whole thing was just another mask. It led me to the wrong mindset and a toxic group of friends who abandoned me the moment I stumbled.

When I re-entered the Junior League, I did so as a different woman. I wasn't connecting with others in hopes they would praise me and make me feel worthy; I was connecting to make a change within my community. I walked into that tea party beaten and broken, but my value was still *connection*—the small, life-giving chance to be part of something bigger than my own little world.

The League hadn't changed. *I* had changed, and because of that, my story changed. Another woman saw my loneliness, and we connected with each other in a candid, authentic way. We talked about sadness. We talked about being lonely. I'd been so focused on holding my head high and appearing strong, I didn't realize how much I needed a friend.

I remember walking out of that tea feeling like I could finally exhale, like my life was truly going to be okay. I could mend the brokenness. I didn't have to dye my hair, change my name, and move to a new city. Now that I knew my values, I could show up differently. That authenticity attracted the right kind of people, and it just so happened that those new friendships contributed to my healing.

In every part of life, triumph or tragedy, we're either winning or learning. Loss is hard, real, and fundamentally painful, but in order to make room for new growth, we have to let go of the old things we've been clinging so desperately to.

Sometimes, being dedicated means making room for change.

I never did end up reconnecting with my original group of friends, but that's not to say our friendship didn't have value. It's easy to see people's flaws, and when you've been hurt, it's even easier to take the jaded mindset that people are inherently bad. But that's a bleak way to look at life—and you lose so much when you do.

Instead of being bitter, I decided to get curious. As a coach, I'm fascinated with why people are the way they are. Ultimately, I'm a business coach for high-achieving women, but that always leads me to investigate why the female entrepreneurs I work with make the decisions they make—*why* they default to certain protocols and patterns. To see those patterns, you have to be invested in getting to know that person. How is their humanity different from your humanity? What's the story behind those worldviews and beliefs?

Chances are, my original circle of friends didn't wake up one day and suddenly decide they needed to abandon a woman in need. That's too simple—too victimizing. It took a broader perspective to think about how unhealthy our friendship was and the role I played by feeding into the negativity. When I finally identified those patterns, I was able to work on breaking them. I saw things about myself I didn't like, which gave me the unique opportunity to change. Because I learned something from that experience, I was able to foster positive, meaningful friendships in the future.

That's why it pays to be a learner rather than a judger. If you're stuck in victim mentality, everything is happening *to* you. You have to judge every experience; if you don't, how can you protect yourself? After being betrayed by my friend circle, it would have been easy to pass judgment. There were so many conclusions to draw from that place of bitter hurt: *Women are horrible. I'm just not cut out for female friendships. Life would be better if I just stayed in my house…*

But when you choose to thrive, you trade your victim mentality for a learner's mentality. Instead of wallowing in grim judgments, you begin to see what you can glean from the experience. Instead of broad, monochromatic statements, you begin to ask productive questions: *What did that experience mean? How can I apply that lesson to another situation in my life? What resources did this misfortune give me?*

I see myself sort of like Ms. Pac-Man, forever chomping my way through the labyrinth of life. I know which icons to set my sights on and which ones to avoid. I have confidence I can gather everything I need to get to the next level. While I don't purposefully try to seek out the bad, I also accept there are times when I'm cornered. No matter which way I turn, I'm eventually going to run into one of those pixelated neon ghosts. Play the game long enough, and that's inevitable.

I have yet to meet anyone who has walked through this world unscathed. Not even a winking, dot-munching videogame heroine.

•••

There's an old Taoist story about a farmer with a horse and a son.

The elderly farmer was getting up in years. He'd worked his crops diligently, and he'd made a respectable living doing what he did best.

One day, the old farmer awoke to find his paddock smashed. His horse was nowhere to be found.

"Oh," his neighbors cried, shaking their heads at the tragedy as they tried to reconcile how such a horrible thing could happen to such a good man. "How unlucky."

The farmer didn't cry. He didn't curse. "Unlucky?" He shrugged and returned to his daily duties. "Maybe."

A few months passed, and the farmer and his son awoke to the sound of whinnying in the paddock. The lost horse had returned, accompanied by a small herd of wild horses, one of which was pregnant with the runaway's foal. Overcome with glee, the farmer's son swung himself up on one of the wild animals. The horse immediately bucked him, throwing him to the ground and snapping his leg.

"Oh," the neighbors cried, shaking their heads at such a cruel twist of fate. "How unlucky."

Again, the farmer didn't cry. He didn't curse. He didn't even cast an angry glance toward the guilty horse.

"Unlucky?" He shrugged then padded over to schlep his groaning son back into the house. "Maybe."

The next day, the national army marched through the village, conscripting young men into service to fight an enemy horde in a far-off land. Women wailed, and old men pleaded with the officers, begging them not to take their sons, but every able-bodied young man was taken away. There was only one man the imperious officers ignored—the farmer's son. There was no way the boy could march with a broken leg.

As the long file of the army plodded into the distance, tearful parents gathered around the farmer's house.

"Oh," they said, their heads lolling with the weight of their grief. "Your son was spared. How lucky."

The farmer simply shrugged. "Maybe."

I absolutely love this story. There are infinite interpretations, but if you were to ask the old farmer whether there's a concrete lesson, he would probably just shrug and say, "Maybe."

Perhaps this tale struck me so hard because it turns my love of assessments on its head. If I can assess a situation, I feel safe. I'm a strong empath; it's only natural. I'll look around, get a feel for my environment, and then draw conclusions based on what I perceive. These skills served me well throughout my childhood, and they still serve me now. Where I run into trouble is where I start drawing expectations from my own limited perspective.

Oh, yes—those pesky expectations are back to haunt us again. It's good to have opinions. It's good to draw conclusions from the wide world around you. It's good to be able to tell the difference between cotton candy and poison ivy, just as it's in your best interests not to cross paths with a trenchcoated figure holding a bloody knife.

But even then, is crossing paths with a deranged serial killer… *bad?*

Okay—there are things in life that are objectively bad. Being in the presence of a vicious killer, for example, or when the farmer's son broke his leg. Without any context, most sane individuals would tell you that walking past a bloodthirsty murderer probably isn't a good idea. But would your perspective change if you were part of an elaborate sting operation to lure the madman into a SWAT team's trap? Does the boy's broken leg look different in light of the fact that being injured saved him from the gruesome battle ahead?

Horsemanship and serial killers aside, there's a lot to be gained by this shift in mentality. Of course, there will be horrible, awful things that happen in our lives, and we have every right to validate the emotions that follow. But what if we could see the bad things from a broader perspective—that while these horrible, awful things are bad in the moment, they might be putting us on a wonderful new path? Instead of being consumed by the things you can't control, can you take a moment to think about what those things taught you?

To do this, you have to be both open and willing to learn from your experiences as well as the people you meet. If I can't find the good in someone, I try looking for the lesson they taught me. This brings me back to the group of friends I had ten years ago, that squawking flock of victims that convened at Bertucci's. When those friends dumped me, the betrayal hurt. It knocked me back for a while. I felt abandoned, confused, and lost. I was unsure of how to continue fostering real, healthy friendships. Why would I even try to connect with other women if things always ended like this? If I did pick myself up and try to make new friends, how would my efforts look different?

But that experience had value. It paved the way for something better. I had new lessons and a new perspective; I started asking deeper, more empowered questions. *Why* had those friendships fallen apart? *What* was my role in all of it? *What* were the characteristics and attributes I wanted in future friends, and *how* could I exhibit those same traits while identifying them in other women?

I was able to be more discerning as I moved forward. I was more mindful of my relationships, even those that felt good in the short term. There are lots of fun, colorful people in my life, but I have to keep looking at the bigger picture. Does this person bring out the best in me? Do they support me? Do I bring out the best in them? We have to evaluate our relationships and interactions with authenticity, even when we'd rather fall into what feels comfortable and familiar. Ultimately, it took a bad friendship experience (and me accepting my contribution to that wholeheartedly) to teach me how to be a good friend.

But authenticity isn't enough. You have to be constantly dedicated to your purpose, always learning and reflecting as you navigate your way through the situations that challenge you. You can't just pick and choose when you're going to be authentic. Your dedication to your core values matters most when no one's looking.

And trust me when I say being inauthentic does catch up to you. You have to be dedicated to your values because those values *will* be challenged. We can all agree that most everyone would consider pretty, nondescript words like "gratitude" and "love" to be good things, but more often than not, the situation just isn't that black and white.

Take the value of connection, for instance. That's a broad, often misinterpreted word. I run a program called Leading Lady Ambassadors that highlights vetted, women-owned businesses. In one group of entrepreneurs, I had several business owners representing health and wellness. One was a non-diet dietician who guides her clients through intuitive eating and body love, while another is a hormone and weight loss coach who helps her clients through diet plans and supplements. It was only a matter of time before the inevitable question reared its ugly head: *if you're truly authentic in supporting these women, how can you endorse both?*

I remember taking a deep breath at that comment as I paused to evaluate the situation. Had I compromised my own values? Was it authentic to support two women with different beliefs and approaches toward health?

I claimed to be dedicated to my purpose. But what was that purpose?

It took a while to tease out the answer. In the end, I came to the conclusion that both my purpose and the authenticity of the Leading Lady brand is to provide resources to other leading ladies. When I looked at the situation again, I realized it didn't matter which program I endorsed. As long as I'd vetted both businesses as quality professionals and truly believed in the work each woman did, I was staying true to my values.

I could move forward with confidence. I *could* support both businesses, and one nutrition strategy didn't have to undermine the other. There are women in my group who want to work through intuitive eating programs; others want to achieve their goals through more measurable, concrete methods. Both companies provide a valuable, quality service, and both programs serve vastly different needs.

Just because one program works for one woman doesn't mean the next woman needs to take up that same program. Just because someone does something differently doesn't mean your methods are lesser or devalued. Being dedicated doesn't mean you have to yuck someone else's yum.

Nothing illustrates this concept better than David Shannon's children's book, *A Bad Case of Stripes*. In the story, a girl named Camilla Cream loves lima beans but stops eating them because her friends think they're gross—and she *very much* cares what her friends think. But poor Camilla starts breaking out in fantastic colors and patterns, and (spoiler alert) the only thing that can turn her back to normal is a good, hefty dose of lima beans. This book is widely interpreted as a cautionary tale about losing yourself to fit in, but I see it as a girl who's lost her identity all because the other children yucked her yum.

Yum-yuckers are the people who make others feel bad about being who they are, having the interests they have, and deriving joy from something unconventional. These individuals' golden opinions act as their shield; they can hide their own insecurities so long as they're highlighting someone else's. But having convictions doesn't have to make you a yum-yucker. Staying true to your own values doesn't mean you have to trounce on someone else's.

When I was a little girl, we had lots of yum-yuckers cycle through our house. Playmates would come over for meals or a snack, only to pucker and groan at the sight of my grandparents' food. These Filipino dishes, the cuisine I'd grown to know and love, repulsed them before they even took a bite.

"Ew," they would say. "That's so gross. You actually *eat* that?"

Yeah, I "ate that." And guess what—I *adored* it. It was chock-full of love and tradition, and it saddened me when our picky guests couldn't see that. Of course, I couldn't *make* them like my family's food. But even if they'd tried the food and hated it, they didn't have to mock me for liking it.

I see this a lot, especially between women, and it pains me on a deeply personal level. Never mind that other kids came over and made fun of my family's food. I was misunderstood because they didn't even *try* to understand me. Those comments weren't warranted, and even if they were, what good would that critique have done?

Maybe this is the teacher in me, but I keep going back to the T.H.I.N.K. acronym I use with my classes. Before a comment or critique slips from my lips, I have to ask myself:

Is this true?

Is this helpful?

Is this inspiring?

Is this necessary?

And, most importantly, *is this kind?*

If there's one thing I hate more than yum-yucking, it's crown-correcting, the need to make superficial commentary on another woman's successes. What if someone reached up to correct a queen's crown in the middle of a speech to her subjects? Can you imagine if one of the runner-up contestants walked up to smooth out Miss America's ball gown as she was accepting her trophy? These images are absolutely ridiculous. So why are we constantly doing these things to other women?

When I make a typo in a newsletter and get an email explaining my mistake, that's not helpful. When a ballerina takes her final bow to a roaring audience, only to have someone in the front row make a snide comment about the snag in her tights, that's not helpful either. Detracting from someone else's success—pointing out their flaws in a shallow, self-gratifying manner—never adds to your own glory. Again, life isn't and has never been a pie. Highlighting other women's blemishes only makes us look that much uglier.

Whether it's through yum-yucking or crown-correcting, dedication to our values isn't meant to be weaponized. Dedication empowers us to be our best selves, the kind of women who build one another up. If someone's values look different from yours, you don't have to shoot them down in order to validate your own dedication. When you're standing strong in your own authenticity, you aren't threatened by opposing viewpoints. You see differences for what they really are—learning opportunities.

•••

In a perfect world, carrying around a laminated list of your values would be enough. In a perfect world, you could clean your house one time, and it would forever remain spotless. In a perfect world, you could explain calmly and rationally to your teenager the thought-process behind your decision-making, and they would graciously defer to your mature advice. If the world were perfect, the simple effort of making it to the gym would be enough to ensure you could fit into your pre-baby jeans.

But that's the thing about perfection. It is and will always remain a very big *if*.

You and I both know that life gets a little more complicated. Your dogs are bound to track in spring mud the moment you've mopped your floor. As soon as you've presented a reasonable, thought-out argument, your teen will shoot back a snarky question. And as you start to build muscle after those long, painstaking workouts at the gym, you're bound to scuttle home only to find your rock-hard booty is too big for those jeans.

Life is never static, which is why knowing your values isn't enough. Balance, after all, isn't just a noun; it's a constantly shifting, ever-changing verb.

As soon as you've found your footing in an authentic, value-driven life, life is going to start challenging those values. While knowing where you stand allows you to take the lead, it also means you have to *keep standing* when circumstances begin to push back. Your spouse is going to challenge you. Your kids are going to challenge you. Your friends, your coworkers, and even random circumstances will end up challenging you, and that's not necessarily a bad thing.

Knowing your values isn't the be-all and end-all of an easy, actualized life. Our hard-earned values are the tools we use to engage as our best selves, no matter what the circumstance.

That's why a leading lady can't just be value driven. She also has to be dedicated. But much like authenticity, I've found that dedication isn't necessarily loud or didactic. Dedication isn't a weapon to wield against those who disagree with you. Committing to your values doesn't mean using them to take revenge, bring someone else down, or yuck their yums.

Ironically enough, being dedicated to my values has taught me to be a better listener. I truly believe there's something to be gleaned from every circumstance in our lives and every person we meet. We just have to take the time and space to look for the win or the lesson. Being dedicated means you can afford to get a little curious, to truly open your mind and heart to learn about someone else's humanity. Being dedicated also means being flexible, eager, and willing to determine how your authenticity can shine through any and every situation.

My value of connection looks very different toward my daughter than it does toward my clients, and that's completely okay. That doesn't make me an inauthentic person. As a human being, I have every right to grow, learn, and evolve in my relationships. Who knows? My core values might even shift.

Being a mom has taught me more in the realm of dedication than I ever thought possible. My daughter isn't my hero because she's a carbon-copy version of the person I think she should be. She's heroic because she's stepping into her power as a beautiful, dynamic human being. She challenges me on the daily, and it takes dedication to see that those challenges aren't threats. If I'm firmly anchored in my authentic self, I don't have to be afraid to look at things from a different angle. I can question my own worldviews, explore the possibilities that both joy and pain have to offer. Are sweatpants really appropriate airplane attire? Is that setback, disappointment, or misfortune truly unlucky?

An old Taoist farmer might just shrug and say, "Maybe."

Dedication has allowed me to get a lot more comfortable with that answer.

E is for emotional intelligence.

CHAPTER 10: THE SUPERPOWER THAT WASN'T

Ask someone how to measure intelligence. Go ahead. I dare you. If you really feel like shaking up some chaos, start the debate at a dinner party. When you start asking humans to assess one another's fitness in any capacity, be it physical, mental, or otherwise (I think about all the times nondescript, beer-sodden conversations have devolved into arm-wrestling matches), people tend to dig in fast—especially if they feel like they're on the defense.

But in order to have an articulate answer to our quandary, we need to be able to define intelligence in the first place. We could cite metrics like educational degrees and standardized tests, or we could even throw out numbers like intelligence quotients. Certain schools of thought claim there are eight different types of intelligence; others will tell you that there are actually nine different categories.

I hold that none of these metrics matter nearly as much as we've been led to believe. Quantifying intelligence says nothing about how useful that intelligence may actually be. You can own the fastest, most beautiful car in the world, but if you don't know how to drive, you're still not getting anywhere. Knowing the tools at your disposal—your gifts, talents, resources, and values—gives perspective, but what good is any sort of tool if you don't know how to use it?

If you're familiar with the idea of an intelligence quotient (IQ), you might have also heard of the emotional intelligence quotient (EQ).

Like IQ, EQ can be a tricky thing to measure. Is someone emotionally intelligent based on kindness? Their ability to get along with other people? What about agreeableness, likability, or charisma? The ability to read a room or empathize with someone in pain? The answer isn't simple to begin with, and adding a metric only makes things hazier.

Not long ago, I took an enneagram test that labeled me as a "challenger" and an "achiever." That didn't surprise me; I've lived with myself long enough to know that these are the motivations that light my fire. What surprised me was that this test came back saying my "superpower" was emotional intelligence. For the record, I *hate* defining anything as a superpower. The implication that any winsome trait is a superpower also implies you're not super if you don't shine with one of the stellar attributes on a narrow, prefabricated list. That triggers my cape mentality, and it's a cold, dark day when we have to go there.

But as bogus as the superpower idea might be, it got me thinking. Have I always been emotionally intelligent? Is this intentional, or did it come to me naturally? What does it look like to be emotionally intelligent? How can you even begin to quantify that? A "superpower" has the inherent connotation of being fated or accidental. Spider-Man was bit by a radioactive spider; Superman and Wonder Woman were just born awesome. The Hulk and Captain America were victims of freak science experiments…

I'm sure you get the picture.

The idea of "super emotional intelligence" didn't sit well with me. While I can recognize emotional intelligence in others and take the time to see it in myself, it doesn't feel *natural*. It feels intentional—deliberate. More like a diligent practice than stumbling into an atomic reactor or volunteering as a test subject in a top-secret government lab.

There are days I wish I could just roll out of bed with super emotional intelligence. I wish I could read, interpret, and address other people's complexities the way Spider-Man sees bullets whiz by in slow motion. Life would be so much easier if these things came instinctively—if we could chalk it up to "emotional giftedness" and called it a day.

But that's both the good and the bad news. Emotional intelligence may *feel* easier to certain individuals, but that doesn't change the fact that it's a deliberate practice. Emotional intelligence isn't something you are. It's something you actively *do*.

For those of you who feel naturally in sync with all the energies of the universe, this is good news. You've got incredible strength, and you can use your powers for all sorts of wonderful things. For those of you who feel like you can only take a hint when someone's spelling out their feelings in plain text, this is good news for you too. Just because you're not as attuned to subtle clues and psychological shifts doesn't make you a cold, uncaring, or inept person. Emotional intelligence may come more easily to some than others, but that by no means makes it a superpower.

That's the inherent problem with trying to measure intelligence. When we spend our time sticking labels on people—smart or dumb, empathetic, cold, or socially awkward—we're missing the point of *why* we want to be intelligent in the first place. What good is being the smartest woman alive if you spend your days in seclusion, learning nothing and teaching nothing to others? If you're not touching other lives to make the world a better place, does your level of emotional intelligence really matter?

Intelligence isn't a superpower. It's a tool. Tools can be misused; they can build something up just as handily as they can destroy that very same structure. Tools also come in various makes and degrees of quality, and certain individuals might take more of a shine to craftsmanship than others. But using a tool to build something beautiful is so much more than a talent. It's a learned skill.

I'm an empath, which leads most people to believe I was born emotionally intelligent. Nothing could be further from the truth. Being empathetic isn't the same thing as being emotionally intelligent, and one doesn't necessarily beget the other.

This was difficult for me to learn, especially after becoming so skilled at reading others throughout my childhood. I was a prodigy at picking up the subtle behavioral clues that other people missed. In order to keep myself safe, I *had* to be better. But this wasn't a practice; it was just a reaction. As deft as I'd become in reading other people, that didn't protect me from my feelings about those feelings—guilt, crushing grief, fear, vulnerability...

Reacting from a place of victimhood has consequences.

By definition, empathy is relative emotional observation, the ability to notice and classify other people's feelings based on your own understanding. But even the most sensitive empath in the world is going to run into issues trying to navigate by empathy alone. What if you misread the emotion? What if you interpret the signs correctly but classify the feeling incorrectly? What if an emotional cue means one thing for one person but something completely different for another? Or (Heaven help us) what if the person you're observing puts up a mask and hides their true emotion with *another,* more palatable emotion?

Start to follow any one of these rabbit trails, and you'll see where raw empathy gets complicated. Recognizing emotions is important, but it's only one step in a much bigger process. When I coach my clients through emotional intelligence, I break it down into four steps. And, as is with most healthy processes, the first step is always the hardest. Before you can even begin to try to assess others, you have to take emotional inventory for yourself. What are *you* feeling? And why might you be feeling that way?

This first step is simple on paper but much more difficult in practice. Most people never check in with their own emotions because they simply don't want to or honestly don't know how. Facing the truth of your ego is uncomfortable; it makes you vulnerable. Recognizing, labeling, and validating your feelings requires you to look in the mirror and acknowledge parts of yourself you might not be terribly proud of. No one wants to be jealous, sad, or hurt. No one *wants* to be the kind of person who's easily wounded.

Even after you've admitted the truth about your emotions, you're still facing a whole other can of worms. If you're feeling something uncomfortable, who made you feel that way? Are your emotions someone else's fault? Are you *wrong* for feeling that way, and if so, can you shame your way into feeling differently? Can you bury those emotions deep down in the dungeons of your psyche? Rise above them? And even after you acknowledge all those nasty feelings, what are you supposed to *do* with them?

That's why it's important to approach this first step as a learner, not a judger. There are no *right* or *wrong* feelings. Emotions are exactly what they are without justification. Instead of trying to determine whether or not you have a right to feel happy, sad, or anxious, why not just call that emotion what it is? Validate it. Address it by its proper name. That feeling is there whether you like it or not, and if you want to find out why, you're going to have to get a little friendly with it.

At Bright Beginning, we start teaching these practices at the age of two. We put mirrors at eye level in the toddler room so the kids can see their own faces throughout their day, and we often do exercises with handheld mirrors for a more deliberate approach. We tell the kids to make their "happy face," their "angry face," or their "sad face," then have the toddlers observe what those expressions look like. They learn to identify and give a name to their own emotions. They learn to match physiological reactions with emotional stimuli.

All too often, our first instinct is to hush a temperamental child by telling them to "calm down" or "stop doing this or that." The problem with this method is that it doesn't address the actual problem. If a child is upset, there's a *reason* they're upset. Maybe another kid took their favorite toy. Maybe they're tired, sick, or hungry for attention. No matter whether that reason seems valid to you or not, there *is* a reason. Trying to correct the behavior without getting to the bottom of the trigger is like trying to get rid of a weed without plucking out the roots.

When a child is misbehaving or upset, the first thing we do is ask them what they're feeling. A lot of times, kids don't have the vocabulary or self-awareness to identify those feelings, and this is often why they get frustrated over small or menial things. When a red-faced toddler, fists balled in anger, little lips quivering, looks up at me through wet eyelashes, I'll ask him to show me *where* he's feeling the discomfort.

"My tummy's grumbling," he might say.

I'll nod. His answer is sensible. It's a valid reaction to the stress he's feeling. "Are you hungry?"

"No," he'll cry with an indignant stomp of his foot. "I'm *mad.*"

Why this boy is mad, who caused the anger, and what's to be done about it are completely separate issues. At this moment, we've completed step one of our emotional intelligence check. He's mad, and now that he's identified that, we can start to identify and advocate for his needs. Ignoring the hurt, lashing out in rage, or crying in the corner isn't going to solve anything. We have to get down to *what* he's feeling in order to figure out *why* he's feeling that way.

When framing emotional intelligence from a toddler's point of view, the first step sounds stupidly simple. All you have to do is put a name to what you're feeling. How hard can that be? But there's a darker reason most people don't get past this part of the process—women especially.

I want you to stop and think for a moment about how women's emotions are portrayed in everyday life. Have you ever heard a woman described as "hysterical" (literally, from the Greek word *hystera* meaning "womb" with hysteria translating as "of the womb" or "suffering from the womb"), "emotional," or "sensitive"? If a woman displays uncomfortable responses of displeasure, anger, or even frustration, how often do we blame her period or other hormonal factors? Even in horror movies where the heroine's premonitions about haunted houses and cursed objects prove to be true, their "funny feelings" are laughed off or dismissed by their male counterparts, only to end in both characters' gruesome deaths. It may be a corny trope, but tropes exist for a reason.

Our culture loves nothing more than to bury, belittle, and invalidate emotions, *especially* women's emotions. While there's obvious social pressure on men to keep stoic and emotionless, there's also the strange, paradoxical effect of women not wanting to appear "too emotional" in order to be taken seriously. When you picture a strong, powerful, and confident CEO, do images of puffy eyes and runny mascara come to mind? What about boisterous laughter and big smiles? No, we want to see calm, cool, and collected. Stoic. Strong. *Unflappable.*

But that's the root of the paradox.

Being emotionally intelligent—the kind of person who *can be* calm, cool, and collected—doesn't mean you have some sort of supernatural ability to shut off your emotions on a whim. It means you control your feelings instead of letting them control you. And that's the dirty little secret of confident, well-adjusted people. They *are* emotional, and they've spent a significant amount of time and effort learning how to use their emotional powers for good.

Imagine a woman riding an elephant. Between the beast and the rider, who's the one in charge?

It's a trick question. The answer depends on the rider's skill—the diligent practice she's put in learning how to ride and how well she's trained that particular elephant. If the rider hasn't invested the proper time and attention, that elephant is going to trample around any way it pleases. It has the potential to be destructive and maybe even injure her in the process.

The first step to emotional intelligence is no different. If you're not the one directing your emotions, they're going to carry you wherever they please. And you probably know just as well as I do that a human's emotional headspace is a wild beast. As a hotheaded Filipino Scorpio, my elephant has the potential to tear down entire villages, but that also means it has the strength to build something magnificent.

I once had a client who took a job as an administrator. The company was temporarily short-staffed, so she worked multiple positions at the same time while only being paid for one of them. For the amount she was working, she wasn't feeling fairly compensated.

She was exhausted, flustered, anxious, and even physically achy. But this woman also suffered from misdirected agreeability—in other words, what *looked* to be kindness. "Going the extra mile," "not making a fuss," and "being a good worker" were actually poisoning her from the inside out.

At first, this client wasn't able to acknowledge her own emotions. She felt guilty for experiencing frustration, resentment, and unhappiness. After all, she did have a job. She was getting paid for *some* of the work. Rocking the boat is never a good thing, and conflict should be avoided by any means possible.

Right?

This is why agreeability can be so dangerous. Being emotionally intelligent does *not* mean you have to be a doormat in order to maintain what feels like a safe status quo. Because this client wasn't able to come to terms with her own emotions, she wasn't able to stand up to her boss. All that pent-up anger and dissatisfaction snowballed to the point where every single interaction between the two—every meeting, email, and even a passing word—was being misread through a lens of resentment. It got so bad that my client actually became excited about the inevitable emotional breakdown. Something far back in her psyche knew that if she kept stuffing these feelings down, packing them tighter and tighter, all that pressure was eventually going to explode, which would give her the perfect opportunity to jump ship and leave the company forever. In other words, she was actively and willingly running her own ship aground.

Holding out until your emotions take the lead is not a good option. When you can't check in with your emotions, you won't know how to advocate for your needs. When you can't express your emotions, you can't communicate those needs to other people. This leaves you stifled and silenced, barreling down a one-way road to victim mentality.

While I don't tend to ask my clients whether or not their tummy hurts, I do ask them where they carry their stress. This is something an emotionally intelligent leader pays attention to. Indigestion, acne, headaches, and weight fluctuation are all physiological symptoms related to stress—and stress is *literally* our endocrine system's response to perceived threats. Maybe no one has come after you with swords or battle axes lately, but working long hours without appropriate pay *is* threatening. It threatens your happiness. It threatens your time with your family. It threatens your bank account, your health, and even your self-respect.

Your emotions deserve shame and judgment just as much as a traffic light at a busy intersection. Sure, you may not like hitting a red light, but that light is there to keep you safe—to tell you something critical about your relationship to your environment. Squirming through uncomfortable emotions is just about as much fun as hitting every single red light on a long stretch of road, but those emotions exist for a reason. They're signals that something is wrong. They're a warning that something in your life needs to change.

As Julie, a dear friend of mine who runs a pelvic floor wellness program, often says, "Listen to your body when it whispers, or it will begin to scream."

•••

The second step in the journey to emotional intelligence is to recognize the other person's emotions. There's a reason we spend so much time identifying and naming feelings in Bright Beginning preschools. As our children get better at recognizing and articulating their own emotions, they begin to realize their feelings on the inside can match reactions on the outside. Once they can identify "angry fists," "sad tears," and "happy smiles" on their own faces, they start to develop a relative understanding of the expressions around them. This is where we start to see the real groundwork of empathy.

Hey, a kid may think. *My friend sitting in the corner has tight, pouty lips. When I'm upset, my face has tight, pouty lips. My friend must be upset about something.*

Again, this seems simple. *Elementary,* based on the example. But as we shape our emotional worldviews, we get more sophisticated in our emotional responses. Notice, I didn't say we get "better" with emotions; we just learn more complex, socially acceptable ways to cope with them. And while pounding your fists, screaming at the top of your lungs, and biting your coworkers may be inappropriate responses for adults in the workplace, many of our "mature" coping mechanisms turn out to be just as unhealthy.

Maybe you can relate to the following scenario. A man comes home from work to find his wife watching TV on the couch, sullen and listless. She doesn't get up to greet him. She doesn't even acknowledge him.

"Hey," he says. "Are you okay?"

The wife shakes her head but says nothing. The husband pauses for a moment. Opens his mouth, closes it again, then turns his eyes to the floor.

"It seems like you're mad," he finally says. "Did I do something wrong?"

His wife doesn't even look at him. "I'm not mad," she says shortly.

The husband retreats to the bedroom, perplexed, frantically revisiting memories of their recent interactions to figure out what he did wrong. Sure, she *says* she isn't angry, but in his book, the silent treatment is a sign of anger. So, the husband holes himself up in the bedroom, fully convinced his wife is punishing him for some egregious crime he can't remember committing. As he sits on the bed and stews, he gets anxious. Then *he* gets angry. He wonders how she could be so cruel. Why wouldn't she just tell him if he'd messed something up? Why is she punishing him? What right does she have to make him feel like this after a long, hard day of work? Now, she's not just mad at him—he's mad at *her* for being mad at him.

This is the issue with using empathy as a total solution. For all intents and purposes, this man could have made an honest empathic assessment of his wife's emotions. Maybe when he's angry, *he* becomes sullen and withdrawn, so it's only natural for him to conclude his wife is acting out of anger. He's so caught up in his own ego—so deep into his own feelings of hurt, rejection, and frustration—his vision becomes tunneled. Just because he recognized and related to his wife's emotions doesn't mean he got an accurate reading of what she's actually feeling.

In preschool, we teach children that you smile when you're happy, you frown when you're sad, and you laugh when something's funny. But as adults, we come to realize these expectations don't always hold true. Some of the funniest people are actually the saddest. Skillful individuals can hide hate, anger, and bitterness behind a beautiful smile. Not everyone who sheds tears is actually a victim, and the politicians who speak with the most sincerity are often the most corrupt.

Real communication goes beyond empathy. It gets much deeper than a simple reading of another person's actions, words, and expressions. If I have a friend who's a chronic canceller, I need to dig a little deeper than my own perception before I figure out what to do about it. Are the cancellations a pattern? Is there a reason she's cancelling so much? If she's just a sucky friend who doesn't care about my feelings, that's bound to hurt. I'm going to feel betrayed, vulnerable, and disappointed.

But this is where I have to put my own emotions in check—to take my ego out of it and tighten the reins on my elephant. Maybe this friend is really just flustered. Maybe she's genuinely remorseful about inconveniencing me. Maybe she's a jerk who's constantly making up excuses because she doesn't value my time. Either way, I need to *listen* to what this woman is saying, both in her actions and her words. Her responses are going to dictate the way I show up for her. I don't have to be a victim in this situation; I can make a deliberate decision to show up as my best self no matter what that looks like. This friend could need support, but she could also need space. I have to be an active listener to figure out what she's actually feeling and assess her needs from there.

If you need to brush up on your communication skills, try having a conversation with an angry teenager. As I write this chapter, I happen to have two strong-willed, hormonally charged teens living in my house. Sprinkle in some dating angst or a stressful project at school, and you have a recipe for *some* sort of showdown.

In times of great turbulence, my husband and I have our own special symbol. If we get caught up in an argument with one of our teens and the other parent tries to intervene, the first parent will subtly raise a curled fist. This means system overload—our child is not responsive. Their emotions are so explosive they literally *can't* process any higher order of reason. They just can't hear you when they're in that state of mind.

When the raised fist comes up, Marty and I switch tactics. We go from persuasive and reasonable to damage control. In that situation, our job isn't to outargue our child—it's to calm them down. We know from experience fueling that fire is only going to end up in an explosion, so the argument has to stop. At that moment, bickering isn't going to do anyone any good. There's no rational discussion to be had in that kind of headspace.

Sure, our kids may indicate that they *want* to argue. Their tone may get sassy, their words may get snippy, and their volume may creep up to dangerous decibels. What they need, however, is comfort—an invitation to take a breath, make some space, and give themselves the opportunity to change their shirt before they do something they regret. They *need* to know their parents aren't a threat so they can put away their guns and come down off the offensive. They need to be acknowledged, validated, comforted, and supported. They need to know they have time and space to make better choices and come back to this discussion with a more effective attitude.

This is why you never tell anyone to "just calm down." No one likes being upset. No one likes feeling vulnerable. Very few people wake up in a frenzy because they genuinely enjoy emotional chaos, and most everyone who shows up defensive, angry, and irrational is probably doing so to protect themselves from a perceived threat. Meaningful discussion, conflict resolution, and rational problem-solving require a high order of headspace. And according to Maslow's Hierarchy of Needs, you can't get to those higher orders if you feel like your basic needs for safety and autonomy are at risk.

Going back to our sad, angry couple, we see how being "good at empathy" can mean "bad at emotional intelligence." By assuming his wife is being cold and distant because she's angry, the husband has cut himself off from the opportunity to find out his assessment was completely wrong. He may conclude that his wife wants space because of the way she treated him, but what his wife really needs might be comfort, closeness, and connection.

Unwittingly, both husband and wife have stepped into a dangerous cycle of pain and misunderstanding. And once a pattern like that begins, it takes intentional effort and healing to break free from it.

•••

Once you've identified your emotions and made a clear, communicative effort to identify the other person's emotions, you take things to the next level of complexity—determining how those two sets of emotions interact with each other.

The husband who goes back to his room, angry and confused because he doesn't understand why his wife is mad, is going to interact with her based on his own assumptions. If you know someone is angry, you tend to give them a wide berth and approach them with caution. You put your guard up; you go on the defensive so you don't get hurt.

But again, this couple has missed each other completely. Maybe this woman isn't mad. Maybe she's disconnected because she's *sad*. We can assume a sad wife needs comfort, and a guarded, distant husband isn't about to fulfill any part of that need. These emotions of sadness, anger, confusion, and abandonment are going to fester. The cycle will turn, around and around again, until these small misunderstandings grow to be real and dangerous rifts in the relationship.

There are truly evil people in the world, but I've come to believe those are few and far between. Most of the time, it's not evil people who hurt other people—it's *hurt* people responding in default to what they perceive as a threat. In the 2008 edition of the *NeuroLeadership*

Journal, Dr. David Rock identified five social factors with the potential to trigger our default responses, the fight-or-flight reactions we use to defend ourselves. Dr. Rock's study organized these triggers into what he called the SCARF model: status, certainty, autonomy, relatedness, and fairness. When our emotions collide with someone else's, we have to be keenly aware of both the positive and negative feelings that come up in response to these categories. Feeling trusted, seen, and certain may be an incredible motivator, but feeling misunderstood, ignored, and powerless can be enough to make someone shut down completely.

The S in SCARF stands for status, but status isn't just about hierarchy at the office or whether or not you can get a table at your favorite restaurant. Status has to do with any social relationship with another human being. In our example with the husband and the wife, the man might feel his status as a husband—a partner, confidant, and best friend—is threatened when he concludes his wife is angry about something he's unaware of. Similarly, the woman can feel like her status in the marriage is shaky when her husband withholds love and connection from her.

C stands for certainty, the need for clarity in order to navigate the future, which is another major factor in relationships. When we get married, choose to have children, or take a job with a company, we have certain expectations of what our future will look like because of those decisions. But what if you suddenly lose your job? What if you and your spouse separate? The relatively predictable vision you had of your future goes right out the window. If the couple's argument makes either one question the certainty of their marriage, they run a high risk of plunging into stress, anxiety, or maybe even full-on panic. None of those results bode for calm, levelheaded decision-making in the future.

The A in SCARF stands for autonomy. Like status, autonomy has very little to do with the kind of job you work or where you perceive yourself on any sort of social ladder. Autonomy has to do with a person's inherent sense of agency. It's your ability to make your own choices and be the master of your own fate. When your autonomy is threatened, you're worried someone is going to take away your power of choice. The husband in our example may feel like his wife has taken away his opportunity to peacefully unwind after a long, hard day at work. Conversely, his wife may feel like her husband is being too demanding—that he's forcing her to explain herself instead of providing the comfort she needs.

R stands for relatedness, your sense of feeling seen and understood by the people you interact with. All of us have some inherent desire to need and belong. When we experience rejection, isolation, or judgment, we act out of defensiveness. The poor husband may feel rejected and wronged, while his wife feels isolated and unacknowledged.

And, finally, the F stands for fairness, the idea that our world operates by predictable cause-and-effect relationships that follow clear, established rules. If the husband feels rebuffed after genuinely asking if his wife is angry, there could be a sense of unfairness. He may feel like he didn't deserve to be treated so brusquely by his wife, while she may feel it was unfair of him to be so dismissive in her time of need.

On and on it goes, hurt upon hurt upon more, horrible hurt. Two people acting out of emotional pain is like trying to bring together the same polarities of two different magnets—north to north, south to south. Those magnets won't stick. They're only going to repel one another further.

This is why it's so important to constantly return to the SCARF model. When we know what triggers us—the seemingly inconsequential, sometimes even unintentional things that send us back into our default mode—we can learn how to step out of those cycles of pain. We need to start seeing our emotions as symptoms rather than sicknesses. When we start casting judgments based on how we think we're "supposed" to feel, we have trouble reconciling our feelings with the real issue at hand. None of us ever handle our relationships perfectly, which is why it's critical for leaders not only to understand this process but also give themselves the space they need to back out of destructive patterns.

The hurt in this couple's interaction is the indication that something is wrong. With a degree of emotional intelligence, the husband could pause, take a look at that cycle of pain, and see where he could break it. If he really reflected, maybe he would see it was dangerous for him to draw conclusions about his wife's feelings. Even after years of marriage, he's not a mind reader, and it would be unfair of her to expect him to be. He could go back to his wife and level with her about what she's really feeling—maybe even be honest with her about how *he's* reacting to those feelings.

"Hey," he could say. "Are you upset with me? I want to comfort you, but I feel guarded right now because I'm not sure if you're angry or not."

Ideally, this tears down the walls of resentment and creates a loving space for the couple to reconcile. However, things get much more difficult when you have one person with strong emotional intelligence and another who is adapting or changing. Let's say the woman responds in anger. Could her husband honestly tell her that her words are coming off angry? Could he ask her to explain why she's sad without attacking him? With any degree of emotional intelligence, could he communicate to her how her own emotional responses are wounding him?

As you begin to actualize your emotions—to level with yourself and the other person about what you're feeling, what they're feeling, and how that sloppy stew of interactions is making you both feel—you begin to see authenticity. Instead of working against each other, you begin to work as a team. When the wife acknowledges she's sad, she also acknowledges she needs comfort. She can actively choose how she wants to engage with her husband. She can *make space* for him to comfort her. Of course, there's a million different places where this conversation could go wrong, but there's also a million different places where it could go *right*.

Instead of emotions tearing this relationship apart, these same destructive feelings can make the marriage even stronger than before.

•••

I've often heard women say they wished they didn't feel a certain way. In times of crisis, some of us have wished we didn't feel anything at all. Emotions are complicated. They can often be painful and difficult. But our emotions also evolved with us over millions of years for a reason. Fear taught us to avoid predators hiding in the underbrush. Love taught us how to sacrifice the immediate gratification of devouring all the food in order to bring something back to our families.

Emotions are valuable. It's up to us to determine *how* valuable.

No matter what you're feeling, your emotional intelligence is going to have an impact on the people around you, for better or for worse. That brings us to our fourth and final step of breaking down emotional intelligence—assessing how those emotions affect our relationships.

After angrily stomping to the bedroom, the husband may sit down, cool off, and think about what just happened. He's sitting behind a wall while his wife is in pain. Is that really what he wants their marriage to look like? Sure, he could be feeling attacked, put out, and frustrated, but are those feelings *really* worth a happy, communicative marriage? Is it even worth a night of cold shoulders, a silent dinner table, and sleeping on opposite sides of the bed?

When difficult emotions arise, it's our responsibility to figure out how they're impacting the relationship and whether or not that impact is valuable. There are times when what we feel can show us sides of our relationships we've been blind to; certain emotions serve as symptoms of a deeper, more insidious problem.

If I'm feeling frustrated by my friend who keeps cancelling on me, I need to carefully look at that relationship. Is my frustration with her good for our friendship? Is this unspoken resentment making us better friends, and is this really what I want our relationship to look like in the first place? Just because I'm angry at my friend being flaky doesn't mean I have to cut ties with her altogether. It may mean I need to set boundaries, maybe stop asking her to meet me for random outings and events because I know I'll be hurt and disappointed when she doesn't show up. When we don't look at the impact and leave these deep, emotional wounds to fester, our relationships start decaying from the inside out.

There are certain times when I take emotional inventory and realize the work of recalibrating the relationship just isn't worth it. Sometimes, I get angry over petty things. Sometimes, I just don't have enough value invested in that relationship to make that conversation worth having. Not every fight has to be picked; not everything that triggers you deserves your time and attention. When a driver zips by me on the highway, threatening my sense of fairness (the speed limit is a *law*, not a suggestion) and security (I'd like to arrive at my destination in one piece, thank you), I don't have to follow that person home and give them a good talking-to about safe driving. I can just as easily chalk the value of that little interaction up as a lesson learned: don't be a reckless jerk on the highway.

But in most everyday relationships, our emotional interactions have the ability to make our connections richer, deeper, and even more wonderful. An emotionally intelligent person has the ability to see uncomfortable feelings as an opportunity.

Of course, bad feelings feel bad. Hurt *hurts*. Rejection, resentment, and rage don't feel good. That's why we have to validate our emotions in step one of the emotional intelligence process. You have every right to feel the way you feel, and you have to validate those feelings in order to even get to these higher assessments. But if something is broken, that means you can fix it. You have a unique chance to make things *better*. Every time you have a difficult conversation, confront someone about an issue, or acknowledge that something in the relationship just isn't working, you create an opportunity for a solution. You take the time and the space you need to show up as your best, authentic self, and you invite the other person to do the same. You establish a precedent of honesty, compassion, and limitless potential. You know conflict is inevitable. When it rears its ugly head, it doesn't have to be such a frightening monster.

Emotional intelligence isn't about censoring your feelings or always being rational. It's about having self-awareness of those feelings and giving others the space they need to do the same. When you take the time to assess your emotional interactions, you take the lead in fostering strong, healthy relationships. You don't have to dread conflict. You can choose to see it as a way forward.

Saying you wish you didn't feel certain things is like wishing you didn't see certain parts of the color spectrum. You can't perceive white unless you're able to see the full intensity of the primary colors. You can't have purple without blue and red. The most beautiful sunsets in the world are dancing palettes of light and darkness, and you can't have depth without shadow.

At this point in my life, I welcome all the colors—all the emotions and feelings for better or for worse. Emotions are the difference between being alive and just living. They teach us how to see in bold, beautiful colors.

I wish I could say I'm a natural artist and my ability to recognize, work through, and appreciate the value of emotions is an inherent superpower. But saying emotional intelligence is a superpower is like saying every person who walks into a paint shop is automatically a world-class artist. We all own paint in myriads of different colors. We all have rainbows of emotions, uncomfortable and comfortable, simple and challenging. In order to make something beautiful, we need to be intentional about how we use our paint. It requires skill, diligence, and practice to turn random blotches of color into works of art.

Feeling what you feel isn't a problem. Being "too emotional" isn't a problem either. Emotions in themselves aren't what matters; it's the choices we make with them.

I'm not a skilled emotional painter because I woke up that way. I may have been a deft empath from a young age, but being able to recognize a vast array of colors doesn't necessarily make you a skilled artist. The four-step process of emotional intelligence was something I had to learn—something I'm still learning to this very day.

I call 2021 "The Year of Pause." I'm the first one to confess that emotional intelligence was something I had to learn the hard way. I let my emotional elephant rampage for far too long, and people I loved got hurt. Villages were trampled. Relationships were stampeded into rubble.

To say that emotional intelligence is a superpower has a cruel sense of irony to it. I don't see many superheroes *pausing* before dodging a bullet or punching a bad guy in the face. I don't see them taking a timeout in the heat of battle to hash out a four-step process. Emotional intelligence isn't a power—it's a *practice*. And in order to practice, you have to pause.

You *pause* to identify and validate your feelings.

You *pause* to authentically inquire and assess the other person's feelings.

You *pause* to consider how your dueling emotions might be complicating the issue.

Then, you *pause* to determine what sort of impact that interaction is having on your relationship.

I wish I would have been born knowing this. I wish I could have learned it before I hurt people I loved.

But this isn't a book about wishes and regrets. This is a book about taking the lead.

CHAPTER 11: THE PIVOT

You would think there would be a definitive pivot. After bending, breaking, and coming back from the void, you would assume the story has come to a happy end. When we read a book or watch a movie, we enjoy what's called a narrative arc—the comfortable, maybe even predictable idea that our hero is going to go after something, mess up, get stronger, and ultimately triumph through the lessons she learned. We want that neat, tidy bow on the end of it. Our hero *learned* something. She *won*. Cue the music, turn up the lights, and fish your car keys out of your purse. No more to see here, folks.

That's what's frustrating about the real world. That's what's *beautiful* about the real world. There's no straight line through life where we learn things, level up, then go on our merry ways. Lessons aren't checks in a box. They're not updates or achievement badges. The values we learn—our beautiful, golden scars—are constantly shifting and stretching as we mature into new perspectives.

When I finally came to grips with my own emotional intelligence, I had already fallen, metamorphosed, and returned with one heck of a comeback. I'd started the Leading Ladies and proclaimed myself a leader in my own life. My whole brand revolved around supporting other women. For all intents and purposes, that *should* have been my happy ending. I'd grown. I'd learned. I'd overcome. End of story, curtains close.

Right?

But that's the tricky thing about real life. Just because I'd *learned* these lessons didn't mean I was done learning. Just because I'd unmasked my own pain and hurt didn't mean I was done hurting other people.

Emotional intelligence is a complicated thing, more of a living, breathing process than any singular definitive action. In my own life, coming to grips with emotional intelligence has been kind of like watching a four-way car wreck in slow motion. I can see each moment play out before my eyes frame by frame, and though I know all too well how this story ends, I cringe every time I hear the crunch of wheezing metal.

It's never easy to watch. It's never easy to look back at that kind of destruction without some sort of residual ache for the damage it caused. But these horrible, painful situations are the reason we have four-way stops in the first place. The mere idea of a T-bone collision is enough for most of us to take a pause at the crossroads to run over the four key pillars of emotional intelligence.

What am I feeling?

What is the other person feeling?

How are our emotions impacting one another?

How is this emotional smorgasbord affecting our relationship?

But emotional intelligence doesn't protect you. Simply knowing these four steps will never be enough. No matter how long you have your driver's license, you're always in danger of getting in an accident. No matter how skilled you may be when you're driving that car, you still have a responsibility to hit the brakes before a stop sign. And no matter how careful and reactive you may be, if you drive long enough, you're inevitably bound for *some* sort of casualty, whether it be a flat tire, a door ding, or even a flattened woodland creature on the highway.

Life is a dangerous road. Someone, somewhere, is going to get hurt. And it's often in the good times of life—when we're barreling down the highway at full-speed, belting out ABBA in the sunshine—

that we least expect the crash.

•••

"You don't know what you don't know," someone once told me. The adage makes sense, but it doesn't give me the warm and fuzzies. At this point in my life, I know I can get through anything. I've survived everything up until this moment, and after all I've experienced, I'm pretty confident just about everything is "figureoutable." Even so, there's something daunting about facing the gaps in your own knowledge. It's the worst kind of betrayal because there's no one else to blame. There was no way I could have seen the pitfalls in my own perspective until it was far too late.

At the time, everything was going so well. The preschools were booming. I'd spent much-needed time and effort picking up the broken pieces of the 2008 fallout, and I was finally feeling like a leader rather than an achiever. I was getting comfortable with my values. I was charging forward with authenticity. I was a hashtag boss mom with two successful businesses—the kind of woman *other women* came to when they needed advice or direction. It was 2014. I had lived, I had learned, and now, I was finally winning.

Bright Beginning was thriving, and a large part of that momentum was fueled by my amazing administrative team. We now had two locations, and one of my directors just so happened to also be my best friend. I put a lot of power into her hands. I was very deliberate about giving her space so she could grow into the role. It was a promising amount of responsibility for someone so young, but I'd been young when I'd started my business. In a weird, reflective way, trusting her was like trusting a younger version of myself.

In my mind, everything was working out perfectly. She was winning. I was winning. I was giving her what she needed to win, and if that wasn't the definition of leadership, I couldn't have given you the right one. My business was healthy. My marriage was back on track. It finally felt like things were coming together.

The last thing I expected was a knock on my door, and when this woman slipped into my office, hangdog and teary-eyed, the words that came out of her mouth were not the words I wanted to hear. She told me she was at a pivot point of her own. She couldn't keep working as a director; she was falling apart at the seams. She had no idea what she was doing now and no idea what she wanted to be doing in the future. She was caught in the middle of an existential tailspin, and everything I'd invested in her career was going straight down with her.

At the time, I can honestly say I was in tune with my emotions. I'd been a skilled empath for over three decades, and if we're counting the practice hours it takes to master a skill, I was a bona fide expert. But reading other people's emotions is where my own emotional intelligence started and ended. Sure, I was empathetic—but only to protect myself from perceived threats.

The first time I'd ever experienced unconditional love was when I was twenty-seven years old. I'd learned not to trust positive emotions; they always came with some sort of catch. As a child, I'd spent most of my time avoiding *any* kind of emotional attention—positive or negative—so I could slip under the radar or hide behind the mask of all my shiny accomplishments. I'd been in survivor mode for so long, I'd come to believe the only time the jungle ever went quiet was when danger came slinking up from behind.

When this woman bared the most vulnerable parts of her soul to me, I only heard threats. I wasn't thinking about her needs or how I could help her. I was thinking about how much hurt *she* was poised to cause *me*. I'd given her an entire preschool; I'd trusted her completely. We'd worked so hard to build the business up, and she was willing to throw it away based on what I could only see as a knee-jerk whim.

I tensed. I bristled. What I didn't realize at the time was that my reaction was more about my *perception* of a threat than the actual reality of one. I'd built a place where I felt safe, and she was ready to bring the whole thing crashing down on top of me. Her emotions were fear, confusion, guilt, shame, and sadness, but all I could see was selfishness. To me, this wasn't just about the job. This was about loyalty, gratitude, and wasted potential.

That day in the office, I responded the only way I knew how. I let my emotional elephant rampage. If she was going to hit, then I would hit back harder. If she was going to hurt me, I would do everything in my power to make sure she could never do it again.

I fired my director that day. In my mind, that was the only way to keep myself safe. This wasn't just business. *This* was personal.

I wish I could say that was the end of the cheap shots, but things got nasty. In any tight-knit community, "he-said-she-said" has horrible staying power. Our spouses reeled. Our families, their friends, and *their* families felt the shocks of the conflict echo down. There's no point in going into the full details of the cutting remarks and vicious phone calls, but the consequences didn't end at the office—the poison of that conflict followed us straight home. This woman ended up taking a job in another state, and she and her family moved away not long after.

I was angry. I felt attacked, victimized, and misunderstood by those who should have been my most trusted allies. And when all those emotions finally boiled away, I realized I was *in pain*—real, raw, heart-wrenching pain. Here I was, thinking the real crux of the issue would be finding a new director, but the damage was so much greater.

I spent hours sitting in that pain, ping-ponging from fury to loss and then back to fury again. I remember calling another close friend and coworker months after the fallout. I was a complete and utter wreck—angry beyond words. It felt like I was being eaten alive from the inside out.

My friend, one of the only women who stuck with me through my own crisis, listened to me for weeks. She gave me time. She gave me space. She let me cry.

"You're not mad," she finally told me after one of my rambling, sob-ridden calls. "You're hurt."

The difference made all the difference. This woman was the first person who honestly helped me see the truth of my emotions before I even knew they were there.

Not mad. Hurt.

Having that one person who was able to help me connect with my emotions—a friend who gave me the grace and patience to acknowledge and validate those feelings—showed me both the first and second step of real emotional intelligence. And for the first time in my life, it finally clicked that empathy *wasn't* the same thing.

Low and behold, I'd hit another pivot point. Just when I thought I'd done all of this work to build myself back up as a leader who supported and even mentored other women, what I'd always considered to be my greatest strength had done me in. I'd been working so hard to be the captain of my fate and the master of my soul, but in the end, I'd become a victim of my own devices.

The realization was humbling. It was *visceral.* I've never felt so vulnerable. It wasn't the first time in my life I'd been a victim, but it was the first time I had no one to blame but myself.

This is a hard-learned lesson for any leader. No matter how much you grow and learn—no matter how much work you put into reshaping and redefining yourself—if you miss how you impact others, all your work means nothing. It doesn't matter how much you give or how grand your gesture may be. If you miss the impact, you miss everything.

The last thing I wanted to do was hurt this woman. She was like a sister to me. I wanted to give her the world. By setting her up with that preschool, I thought I was doing what was best for her. I was so wrapped up in my own expectations, so fixated on how perfectly everything was working together, I couldn't see the true need. By coming into my office, she wasn't trying to threaten me. She was asking for a listening ear, *a moment of pause* to try to work things out.

I play that terrible conversation over and over again in my head. There are so many ways it could have gone—so many better ways things could have turned out. We could have slowed down. We could have hit the brakes on the pain train, taken a moment to assess the emotional factors involved, and then worked together to find a real solution instead of simply reacting to this maelstrom of horrible feelings. We could have found a compromise. We could have made an exit strategy. We could have helped one another. We could have made things better. Deep down, I did everything for this woman because I loved her. If I'd only taken a pause to see that, to remind myself what I valued and how my emotions were impacting that relationship, things would have gone so differently.

It's harrowing to work so long and hard for change only to find yourself back in the same default patterns.

Taking the lead is a lot like peeling an onion. You think your life's pivot point will be a eureka moment. The clouds will part, a divine light will shine down, and your eyes will be opened to a fresh new start. But once you start learning these lessons—exploring your authenticity, breaking down your values, and peeling back the layers of destructive habits and patterns—you find that there are levels. When you finally see the patterns, you have to work your way down to the pain. When you finally reach that pain, you've got to find where it fits into your story. And when you finally catch a glimpse of where those destructive cycles are leading you, you have to decide to be different.

When I fired my director, a few of my confidants praised me for being authentic. In their eyes, I'd been completely in the right. I'd worked hard to build my business, and I had every right to defend my program from any sort of threat. But saying I'd been authentic just because I'd reacted from a place of genuine fear wasn't the whole truth of the matter. If I'd been acting like a real leader, I would have responded with both authenticity *and* emotional intelligence. I would have known enough about myself and my director to ask whether or not my feelings reflected how I wanted to show up for the people around me. Instead of lashing out, I could have checked in with the SCARF model to see that I was *scared*—that my sense of security and certainty were being threatened. If I'd been more thoughtful and intentional, I could have checked back in to make sure I was staying dedicated to my purpose. Yes, I was being authentic in the way I was reacting to my feelings, but feelings are fleeting sensations, snapshots of time that don't necessarily represent the whole picture.

Had I stepped back, I could have seen that my real purpose in hiring this woman was to bring out the best in her—to give her the space and resources she needed to take the lead as *her* best self.

When we think about the people in our lives, we tend to frame them as characters in our own narrative. Our days are a collection of mini sagas, and other people move in and out, playing a variety of roles. It takes a degree of separation to set our own egos aside and ask what role we play in someone else's story. When we talk about our life's purpose, we're not talking about our ambitions. We're talking about how we affect others.

When people look back on my life, I want them to say that I was thoughtful—that I could remove my ego to be fair and honest in everything I did. This isn't because I care about what others think of me. It's because I'm honestly dedicated to the way I show up. I've seen who I want to be, and that person exhibits all the traits I listed above. If I were watching myself react to a situation through someone else's eyes, what would I want to see?

Your life's purpose is directly tied to your values, and if you're leading by those values, you can be intentional rather than reactive. If I had paused for a half a second and taken a moment for some inner dialogue, I could have considered how I *wanted* to show up—what being an authentic leader would look like in this unprecedented situation.

But that brings us back to our elephant rider analogy. If your emotions are a giant, multi-ton beast, you have a responsibility to learn how to tame and control them. Feelings are autonomic; there's no right or wrong, good or bad when it comes to emotions. But in order to be authentic, you have to actualize those feelings. If you judge them, stuff them down, or even downright ignore them, you're reacting, not leading. Your crazy, destructive elephant will break free and take complete control of your life.

That's why it's so important to acknowledge and validate your feelings. If you don't, you can never be authentic with others or yourself. Yes, I *reacted* to my feelings, but I didn't stop to think about where they actually came from and what they truly meant. Of course, I was mad, scared, and upset. Those feelings weren't right or wrong. They just were. When something or someone presents a threat to your dreams and visions, it's completely normal to feel the way I felt. It took me a long time to stop judging myself for that. I had to come to grips with the fact that my feelings didn't make me a bad person; any business owner in my shoes probably would have felt a similar way. To truly find my authenticity, I had to stop judging and start learning. Only then would I have the space to learn—to understand myself just a bit better and figure out what I needed to do to stay true to my purpose.

As much as it stings, you've got to peel back the layers of that stinky onion. You have to get down to the real problem instead of band-aiding the symptoms with cop-outs. I hear them all the time, and I recognize them because I've used so many of them myself.

Oh, I was just overemotional.

He made me so mad I couldn't think straight.

I just can't stand it when people act like that.

He's such an idiot. He makes me so mad…

But dismissive platitudes aren't good enough. They're useless because they don't address the real problem. When a woman comes to me and tells me she's mad because her coworker is an idiot, we have to keep digging. It's not the external situation—it's the *internal* reaction. So your coworker is an idiot. Why do you react the way you do? What about that person's reckless actions makes you feel annoyed, threatened, or appalled? What letters of the SCARF model do these offenses trigger?

When we start getting down to the core of the issue, we start getting workable insights into the actual problem. It's like solving a mystery, following a trail of sneaky clues until you rip the mask off the real villain. As I work through these layers with my coaching clients, the dialogue usually goes something like this:

"I'm frustrated because my coworker is an idiot," my client might say.

But why is your coworker an idiot?

"My coworker is an idiot because he always turns in his half of the report late."

Why is that frustrating?

"Because he knows better! I've spoken to him about it before, but I'm afraid to go to my boss because I don't want anyone else to think I'm a snitch."

Where are you carrying this frustration? Can you feel it anywhere?

"In my stomach and my head. I get these killer headaches. It's like no matter what I do, I can't get this coworker to shape up."

So, is there something besides frustration there?

"Well… Anxiety, I guess."

And why would you feel anxious?

"I feel anxious because these late reports threaten the certainty of my promotion. I fear for my autonomy because his laziness could make or break my opportunity, and that also triggers my sense of fairness. I've worked so hard for this promotion! I value excellence, and that's how I want to show up at work."

And—*bingo*. You're not frustrated with your coworker because he's an idiot. You're anxious because your hard work is being taken advantage of. You can't just band-aid the symptoms of this issue. If you really value excellence in your work, you'll have to find a solution. Your coworker isn't the problem, and your reaction to your coworker isn't the problem. The problem to solve is keeping the integrity of the product, and that's a solid starting point to finding a resolution.

Learning your emotional triggers gives you real power. When you can identify what bothers you and *why* it bothers you, you can skip over the destructive, energy-sapping patterns that rip relationships apart. You don't have to be passive-aggressive. You don't have to hide behind a mask of what you "should" be feeling. You don't have to play the blame game, and you don't have to keep feeding into pain cycles. If you don't know why you're hurting, you're not going to be able to make that pain stop. Even if you go to a doctor and tell them you're in pain, that physician can't do anything unless you know *where* the hurt is coming from. They can scan your body from head to toe, but the whole process is so much easier if you already have an idea of where that pain might be coming from.

When I'm feeling one of my own SCARF triggers, I intentionally have to stop and make time for a few emotional scans of my own. I call these primers—planned, intentional "space holders" where I can run through the four steps of emotional intelligence. When something sets me off or I feel an uncomfortable emotion, I'll go for a walk or hop in the shower. To be perfectly honest, some of my best fights happen in the shower. A lot of times, I don't even have to have a full conversation afterwards because I've worked out everything myself.

Hey, you're reacting this way because this is important to you. Anyone would feel this way. You don't need this person's excuses. You've already got all the validation you need, girl. Do you really need to hinge your happiness on this person's half-hearted apology?

And then, when the half-hearted apology comes (because, let's be honest, most people are horrible at apologizing), I'm able to brush it right off. I've got tight control of my emotional reins, and my elephant and I are able to lumber off to do something constructive—build a city, have an adventure, or whatever else elephants do.

Needless to say, I didn't have all this figured out back in 2014. When the unforeseen consequences of firing my director started piling up—when people *who weren't even involved* started calling me, berating me and screaming about what a horrible person I was—I did the only thing I knew how.

I put on my monster face.

You've seen it all before. Dogs raise their hackles. Flamingos fluff their feathers. I'm sure you've even seen drunk men at a dive bar flexing their chests if they feel their status is threatened. "Puffing up" was my default. If life was threatening me, I just had to look more threatening. It took a long time to see the truth of that. I wasn't acting out of strength or authenticity. I was *scared*.

Seeing that monster face changed me. There was so much collateral damage—so much pain—and I felt fully responsible for it. I knew my values. I knew what kind of person I wanted to be. I knew that, at my best, I could show up with love and compassion, but I'd limped out of that situation as my cold, broken self. This experience made me so cautious about how I interact with other people. I don't want to be who I was. I don't want to wear that monster face again.

It took six long years to even start gathering the pieces of the broken friendship with my former director. I had to forgive myself before I could even approach her. We were both so young (me in my early thirties, her in her early twenties), and neither of us were proud of the way we responded. We were both vulnerable. We both reacted out of hurt.

There were never any apologies. When we peeled back the layers and finally found the truth, there was no need to apologize. She showed up in her pain, and I showed up in mine. Finally, we could give each other space to admit that. What we truly needed was *understanding*—an agreement to stop the cycle of hurt and blame that had engulfed our friendship and our families.

Yes, there's a scar, but at least we've closed the wound. I've taken the time to think about the value of our relationship, and I can confidently say this woman's friendship means more to me than pride or regret. Now that we both have control of our elephants, we can rebuild. We don't have to let the emotions of the past define the potential of the future. We may not be as close as we once were, but this golden scar is still precious beyond words. This was another pivotal leadership lesson. Intentions, no matter how pure or good, mean nothing if we're not paying attention to the *impacts* of our decisions.

••

In 2020, I opened a course called *Confronting Confrontation: Finding a Diamond in the Rough Conversations.* Confrontation, in one form or another, inevitably comes up both in my coaching sessions and in my masterclasses. If you're an entrepreneur, a wife, a mother—a *human being*—you'll eventually have to have a rough, uncomfortable, or just plain awkward conversation somewhere down the line.

Personally, I love working through this topic. It's one of my favorite things to teach. I've seen so much freedom and growth in my own life that I don't see confrontation as a negative. Of course, when my emotions flare up, I get anxious, angry, and defensive, but those are just emotions—signals that need to be validated and honored because something, somewhere, went wrong. Those emotions aren't a bad thing either. Triggers are triggering for a reason. If my uncomfortable feelings are a red light, I know I'm going to need to hit the brakes and work through some good ol' emotional intelligence.

Confrontation isn't a bad thing. It's a chance to make the world *better.* If two people disagree on something (as two people certainly will), conflict gives you a unique opportunity to find a solution that meets everyone's needs. And if you think "compromise" is a dirty or shameful word, you're living in a prison of your own expectations. If you come to the table fully convinced that your way is the *only* way, you're already in victim mentality. There could be a better way for both you and the other party, but you've already blinded yourself to the very possibility.

Leaders aren't tyrants. Leaders are learners. If you're dedicated to being the best version of yourself, you're dedicated to a lifetime of growth. Some of the most difficult conversations of my life have been the most valuable. After releasing my *Diamond* course, I finally had the clarity to call up my estranged ex-director and start making things right.

Like everything else, it all comes back to emotional intelligence. These lessons have made me a better wife. They've made me a better mom, a better coach, and a better leader in my businesses. Being able to show up as my best self despite emotional turmoil—to use my feelings as useful tools rather than weapons to tear another woman down—was a definitive pivot, and now that I've found my freedom, nothing pleases me more than empowering other women to do the same.

I still own two preschool centers, and I still have an incredible team of women on staff. Believe it or not, these women don't always get along. There have been times when I've had to call both my directors and my teachers to the table in order to work through the emotional intelligence steps. One of these meetings happened just the other day. Me and my *incredibly pregnant* executive director showed up to the conference room to make space for two other staff members who had serious bones to pick.

As owner and CEO, I started that conversation right where I needed to. I laid out *my* feelings on the issue. I was annoyed. I was frustrated. I didn't understand the complexities of the situation, and the steadily growing conflicts were really beginning to grate on me. I came forward with my feelings on the issue, and I invited the others to do the same. If I didn't know how they felt, I wouldn't know how to appropriately respond. In order to get to the bottom of the real problem, we had to identify and validate those emotions.

Each person got the opportunity to speak. One by one, every woman at the table set down the emotional burden she'd been carrying—kind of like cowboys hanging up their guns before walking into a bar. There would be no sharpshooting, cheap shots, or sniping. From the very outset of the conversation, I made it clear these emotions were tools and not weapons.

After each woman spoke her piece, we took a step back and looked at the whole tableful of feelings. Now that all the chips were down, we could see how these emotions were playing off each other— the "emotional soup," so to speak. One woman was pouring her emotions on top of another's, and now the whole thing had started bubbling over.

How was that nasty soup affecting the relationship? It was

affecting Bright Beginning. The rest of the staff could feel the tension. Even the kids could pick up on the strife. When teachers are unhappy and don't feel comfortable at work, it's the students who ultimately suffer. At Bright Beginning, we're dedicated to our students. First and foremost, our purpose is to provide a safe and loving place for them to learn.

Even though these two staff members didn't agree on everything, they could both agree on staying dedicated to the preschool's purpose. From there, we knew we had to come up with a plan. There was never a moment where we suggested anyone should or shouldn't feel one way or another; we'd already hashed out how everyone felt. Now, it was time to figure out what we could do to address the needs these negative emotions elucidated.

The problem with most conflict-resolution methods is that they're focused on judgment. You present your argument, I present my argument, and an arbitrary mediator decides who makes the better argument. This is how our legal system works. One party wins, and another loses. But while "you versus me" judgment may work in traffic court, it can be *disastrous* in leadership situations. At the end of the day, you're not going to change how someone feels. If you're not willing to communicate about those feelings, you've already lost. When the emotional dust finally settles, do you really want a winner and a loser? As a leader, I'd much rather have two empowered winners. That's best for my staff. It's best for my business. It's best for my preschoolers.

When sitting down for a difficult conversation, you have to make space. Never again will I simply assume I know what's best for another person. I would have given my prior director the moon if she'd asked for it; I would have given her the moon if I thought she needed it. But she didn't want the moon. She only wanted the stars. If I'd paused and taken the time to learn that, our relationship would have looked very different.

It took that great loss to teach me to listen for a need before I make an assumption. Every time I have issues at Bright Beginning or within the Leading Ladies, I immediately snap to my *new* default: *This is how I feel. I want to know how you feel. Let's see how those feelings work together, and let's make an agreement before we slap down expectations.*

You have to come to an understanding before you come to an agreement. You have to talk to one another about why you're showing up the way you are, monster face and all, in order to show up *better*.

As leading ladies, let's start recognizing that. Let's give other women the chance to change their shirt—to ask if there's another way they would *rather* engage than their default stress responses. You can tuck in your trauma. You can change that soiled shirt. You can come back to the table, and when you do, there's going to be a chair waiting for you.

That chair is the space. That chair is the *pause*.

•••

You have to learn to relish the uncomfortable. Every lesson you learn, every scar you lace in gold, is something to be proud of.

For a while there, I thought I had things figured out. After all I'd learned from my 2008 meltdown, I truly believed I'd done the work to be the best version of myself I could be. My lessons in emotional intelligence (or lack thereof) were humbling. They were harrowing. They were *painful*. Once again, I found myself wandering down those old, haunted corridors, wondering how I'd returned to those wretched default patterns. I'm not proud of the way I showed up to learn those lessons, but I'm proud that I learned them. I'm grateful for the scars of that broken friendship and the beauty we've both found in making something new.

Thinking back on what happened in 2014 *is* a bit like replaying a car wreck frame by frame. You see two vehicles barreling down the road in separate directions. You see the pain when they hit. You flinch at the sound of pulverized metal. You see how easy it would have been for one of them to have just slowed down—to have swerved, to have done *anything* differently—and you mourn what could have been.

But you also see both drivers in that car wreck are survivors. They got out of those old, busted cars. They're back on the highway, and now, they drive a little differently. They're more careful, more mindful, and more deliberate about stopping at red lights.

Emotional intelligence goes so much deeper than what we feel. Being able to take the lead in this area of our lives—to fully embrace ourselves and others for who we are, right here, right now—is freedom. It's the freedom to forgive ourselves. It's the freedom to forgive other people. It's the freedom to pause, check back in with the person we want to be, and return to the table with our best shirts on.

R is for resilience.

CHAPTER 12: FAST CARS AND WAFFLES

It's hard to know where to start. Or where to end, for that matter.

Over the last forty years, I've put on more personas and cycled through too many versions of myself to count. The fact that I'm still here, able to tell these stories with all my limbs intact, has to be some sort of testament to the last letter in the L.E.A.D.E.R. acronym.

The textbook definition of resiliency is the ability to recover from an illness, adversity, or change. Based on that description, resiliency is my middle name. I was born halfway across the world into a military family. I spent the first five years of my life as an only child, then suddenly became a middle child after my baby brother was born and my parents adopted my teenage uncle. Add a transpacific relocation, seventeen moves, my little brother's deadly medical condition, and...

Well, let's just say we all had a lot of adapting to do.

It's interesting to look at my family and see how each of us coped with the bizarre circumstances of my childhood. When I look at my brothers, I'm reminded how different humans can be. Each of us wrestled ourselves through those circumstances in our own unique ways. Each of us has manifested the lessons of our childhood experiences very personally. If you ask either one of my brothers what happened, why it happened, and what the ultimate consequences ended up being, you're going to get two separate accounts vastly different from my own. Our childhood was in constant flux, a never-ending flow of new schools and alien dynamics where the only certainty was that nothing, in the end, was certain.

Full disclosure: I had to look up the definition of resiliency before breaking down this final chapter. Seeing resiliency as the *ability* to recover from something works well enough for a web search or a dusty page in a dictionary, but as I think about myself and my brothers— what we went through and how we came out the other side—I can't help but think that ability to adapt and overcome is the *result* of being resilient rather than resiliency itself.

Let me explain.

Saying resiliency is the ability to adapt is like saying fitness is the ability to have washboard abs. We can all acknowledge the effects of both fitness and resiliency are pretty darned awesome, but we also know a sculpted six-pack involves so much more than simply being a fit person. If you want abdominals you can scrub your laundry on, you'll probably have to do specific exercises to get that kind of definition—maybe even kiss sugar goodbye completely (which, alas, is one of the many reasons I won't be doing laundry on my own tummy anytime soon). Being fit is certainly an enjoyable byproduct of that kind of lifestyle, but fitness is a state of being. "Fitness" doesn't encompass what you have to *do* to reach your ab-tastic goal.

The same goes for resiliency. If we can acknowledge that fitness is a process that *leads* to a result rather than the raw result itself, why do we assume resilience is as simple as rebounding after a mishap? Sure, we know resilient people get back up. But what *is* resiliency, really?

While the textbook definition is fairly easy to grasp, the real significance of the word is much harder to pin down. There are lots of survivors in this world, and no two stories will ever look the same. A bullied high schooler is resilient by definition, but their perspective on the subject is going to look much different from someone who has survived cancer or spent time in prison. To say one person is more resilient than the other implies a dangerous metric. When we start framing our worthiness in terms of other people, we might begin to wonder if our struggles even matter.

When I moved to America at five years old, my world was absolute chaos. It was like being hauled off to a completely different planet. My traditional, tight-knit family had always doted over me, but in the States, what had once made me enviable and precious in the Philippines isolated me from both worlds. Here I was, too dark to be "normal" but still too white to be Filipino. I was no longer the baby, the joy-bringer, or the little Miss Asia America doll. I was just *there*.

Meanwhile, my brothers were living completely different experiences. The eldest, Charles, was a teenager. On top of the language barrier, he'd been born with damaged eardrums and had to deal with hearing loss. As a baby, my younger brother, Michael, was sick and fragile after his SIDS episode which (by no fault of his own) demanded constant care and attention. I can't speak to those experiences, only the empirical evidence of struggle I saw as a little girl. Even then, I knew things were hard for my brothers in ways I couldn't understand. I could see it in my dad's temper or the haggard lines on my mom's face. We were all resilient, but none of us coped the same way. For Michael, resiliency was playing outside with the neighbor kids. For my mom, it could be as powerfully simple as a fresh coat of nail polish.

I'm not satisfied with the idea of resiliency as a result because the results of our lives haven't been the same. My brothers and I adapted very differently. We weren't all bitter. We didn't end up defined by the trauma, anger, and fear. Maybe we cycled through those feelings as we processed individually, but to this day, we've never seen eye to eye on what all this calamity meant. How can we claim that resiliency means adapting and overcoming if we can't define what adapting and overcoming looks like?

Comparing our emotional journeys has brought me closer to a puzzling truth. We want to think of resilience as a boxer struggling back to her feet after taking a brutal hit or a widow raising her children in the aftermath of her husband's tragic death. But when we take this narrow, dramatized view, we miss the point of defining resilience in the first place.

We can't define resiliency by the trauma, but we can't define it by the aftermath either.

Discussions like these make me wary of the comparison game— the "my trauma is bigger than yours" attitude. Oftentimes, this mentality surfaces in the realm of parenting and childcare, and it scares me beyond words.

On the surface, the logic seems sound enough: If a child never experiences any hardship, can that child actually learn resilience? Are children who experience heart-wrenching traumas (I'm thinking of spunky survivors like Little Orphan Annie or Tiny Tim) actually *better people?*

Therein lies the danger—"better or worse," "weaker or stronger." Judging resiliency on a metric of trauma is still judging. Of course, people who overcome extraordinary hardships have learned and adapted in extreme ways. Of course, you have to honor the human beings who have survived impossible circumstances. But if you truly believe you need everything you have and have everything you need, you realize there's value in overcoming *any* hardship.

A toddler learning to walk is going to think their first tumble is the worst thing in the world. Can you really blame the kid? At that tender age, a painful fall probably *is* the worst thing that baby has ever experienced. To older, wiser adults who have fallen in bigger, more painful ways, the tiny tumble is nothing. We coo, chuckle, and shake our heads as the toddler bursts into tears. We gently inform them everything will, in fact, be okay. We know this is no big deal. We've been walking for years.

But the frightened toddler doesn't know that yet. When that kid stands up, they do so as a defiant act of resilience—a deep, instinctual motivation that they can and *will* learn to walk upright. What may seem small to us is a critical juncture in that toddler's emotional development. This may be the first time they realize they *can,* by sheer force of willpower, get back up and try again.

Can we honestly say those triumphant moments don't matter simply because they're mundane or low risk from our adult perspectives?

When I look at my kids and wonder if I've done them a disservice by actively valuing their safety, I have to remember to stay dedicated to my authenticity. I know full-well I can't shelter my kids from pain and struggle, but I'm not dedicated to being harsh or unfeeling in order to impart some sort of karmic lesson. I'm not about to destabilize their lives by moving them halfway across the world for the sake of "toughening them up." I don't have to weigh and measure my kids' inner turmoil to justify their levels of resiliency. If I operated by that mentality, I might as well have held their heads underwater until they learned to swim.

If there's one thing I've taken from my own childhood, it's that I don't have to teach my kids that life is both cruel and challenging. The world does a fine job of that on its own, thank you very much.

I hope and pray my kids have a better sense of stability in their own childhoods than I did in mine. When they come to me about feeling isolated without the latest video game or stifled because I won't let any offspring of mine leave the house looking like *that* (moms, you know exactly what I'm talking about), it's not helpful for me to belittle their feelings. It's not my place to try to one-up them with stories of being left behind in Panama or having to hide from danger in my own house. My kids don't need exorbitant heartache to teach them the world will knock them down, nor do they need my own personal traumas to see the power and pride in fighting back.

The truth about resiliency is it's so much more than responding to trauma. You don't have to wallow in the cause. You don't have to be chained to the effect either. The real value is in what lies between.

I've always been resilient, but it's only recently that I've started to wrap my mind around what that actually means. When I've observed a resilient person in the *literal act* of resilience, I've found it's not often loud or showy. Resilience happens in the quiet. It's found in the strength you don't know you have.

I think of those stories of mothers picking up cars with sudden, herculean strength to save their children. I think of captives and political prisoners who languish for years—even decades—through inhumane conditions. Time and time again, the people who survive are the ones who find something strong enough to motivate them through every circumstance. That motivator may be external—the thought of your children being harmed or simply wanting to give them a safe, loving home—but that motivator can also come from an internal hope or idea. Wherever you find that supernatural strength, resilience is what enables you to pull it out when it's needed.

I've been aware of this strength ever since I was a little girl, but what I didn't understand was that this inherent power continually starts and returns to a place of rest. "Recovering from" or "rising in the midst" of something implies that *something* has knocked you down to begin with. By virtue of hitting the ground, you arrive at a place of mandatory pause. This period of rest lasts as long as it takes for you to start moving again.

Between 2007 and 2008, I was in that place of brokenness. I had to lie low, lick my wounds, adjust, and reprioritize before I returned to face the world. That's not to say there wasn't a time of grief. There were many days when I curled up in bed to mourn the pain and loss. But when we check in with our emotional intelligence, we can acknowledge that making space to process those feelings isn't greedy—it's necessary. We have to identify and validate those emotions if we're ever going to move past them. If I hadn't worked through all the horrible years of nearly unraveling my marriage, watching my business flounder, losing my friends, and burying my father, I would have never seen the deeper, darker wounds I'd been carrying with me.

When I finally hit rock bottom, I didn't take that time because I *wanted* to rest. I rested because I had no other choice. I was too weak to do anything else.

I'm sure you've heard plenty of pithy advice about rising after a fall. Someone probably encouraged you to get back on your childhood two-wheeler after you took your first tumble, and if I told you to get "back in the saddle," you would know exactly what I meant. As women, especially high-achieving women, we're expected to climb right back onto the horse that throws us. That makes us brave. That makes us *gritty*. If you hop back up fast enough, maybe no one will even notice you fell.

But this is where we start to develop a twisted idea of resilience. We become so eager for the comeback, maybe even a chance to prove that we should never have fallen, we scramble to get up as fast as we can without thinking about why we fell in the first place.

Believe me, I've been there. Part of it is embarrassment. Part of it is the longing for what's called a "corrective experience"—a reset, a do-over, or even the chance to make things right. Oftentimes, the shame and the consequences of our mistakes are so painful, we can't bear to face them. If we clamber back into that saddle fast enough, maybe we can continue on as if nothing ever happened.

But if you've ever fallen, you know for a fact you're going to fall again. It's just what we do. It's what makes us human. If you water down resilience as a mere reaction to the fall, you're missing the point. *Humans fall*—inevitably, publicly, and painfully. It's not climbing back up that makes us better riders. It's taking the time to figure out what went wrong.

I used to be petrified of failure. Sin of any kind (sin, by definition, is "to come up short" or "miss the mark") disqualified me from my "good girl" persona, the only promise of safety and stability throughout the turmoil of my childhood. I became so afraid of failure I didn't want to acknowledge it. To sit with myself, even for a moment, meant I had to face the truth, and any amount of soldiering on, no matter how pitiful or pointless, was better than *that*.

That's why 2008 was such a pivotal moment. For the first time in my life, I couldn't keep going. I couldn't hop back into the saddle. I was *literally* broken. If I was ever going to get back up, I had to find a way to heal.

That healing happened, but the process was slow and deliberate. It started at home then travelled with me to work. I brought it along when I re-entered society and went to tea with the Junior League of Annapolis. It kept going when one woman took the time to smile and invite me to come over and sit with her.

I couldn't hide my vulnerability anymore. I was so broken, so burdened with loss and grief, that I couldn't find the strength to don another mask. The friendships I built *had* to be authentic because I didn't have the wherewithal to fabricate anything else. The love had to be unconditional. These women had to take me as I was, golden scars and all. I knew how I wanted to show up, and I knew I wasn't going to put energy into being anything other than myself.

There's something magical about that kind of brokenness. When you're that desperate to rediscover your inner confidence, to find those roots of value and dedication within yourself, you won't settle for anything less than authenticity. At the time, I wasn't afraid of losing friends. The ones I could lose had already left me the moment my house of cards collapsed. I wasn't afraid of grief either. I was already drowning in it.

The great thing about being completely broken is you have nothing left to lose. All that was left was to stand there, open and honest. I was finally *me,* for better or for worse, and the friends I needed—the dearest, most cherished friends I've ever had in my life— were waiting with open arms.

This was my time of rest and healing. Lying in the dirt is never fun, but sometimes, it's the best place to be. Spending time in that place of love and rejuvenation showed me the fall itself was nothing to be feared. I didn't have to live my life on pins and needles, terrified of messing *something* up for fear of shattering my perfect persona. I didn't have to outmaneuver, anticipate, or flinch at any hardship. I'd hit rock bottom, but I wasn't finished. I was broken—not defeated.

We can never be so afraid of falling that we don't take the time we need to lie in the dirt. I know it doesn't sound comfortable. I know it's not where any of us *prefer* to be. But think about it this way: If you're already down there, your shirt is probably soiled anyway. Why not take a moment to pause? Why not take a moment to rest and catch your breath? Why not see what you can learn from this new, prone perspective?

When I suddenly found myself flat on my back, I finally began to see what I'd been missing. That time of healing was also a time of discovery. After losing my superficial motivations, I had to dig *deep* to find the real ones.

This is where resiliency goes hand in hand with a learner's attitude. Instead of judging yourself for ending up on the ground, you can take a moment to consider what it's going to take to get back up. I knew I was going to have to do things differently. I needed to find my own inner strength—an unshakable center that could keep me dedicated no matter what the circumstance.

I was resting, I was healing, and most importantly, I was *learning*. When I took time to investigate my values, I discovered a source of strength that would both anchor me *and* keep driving me forward. Before, I'd been determined to balance everything on my own shoulders—my career, my family life, my friendships… I kept building up and up, hoping the sheer, splendid height of my efforts would be enough to sustain me.

But no one can hold everything forever. It wasn't that the efforts themselves were unsustainable. I was missing a solid foundation.

That's when I started building on my values. I started building on my family. I started building on my true self. And as I built, *the entire structure only got stronger*. I didn't have to hold everything up by myself anymore. My energy, my mood, and even my circumstances could change, but I could keep going with the confidence that my efforts were grounded in something greater than my own strength.

All of a sudden, there was space for learning and growth—space I'd never allowed myself because I'd been so busy trying to stand beneath the weight of my own expectations. No matter what happened, I could show up strong and confident. Sure, I wouldn't be perfect. Of course, I was going to fall again. But my life no longer hinged on an illusion of perfection. It was cemented in dedication and purpose.

No matter how broken you are or how lost you feel, when you're anchored in your values, you know you'll always have that solid foundation. Even if your whole world crumbles, you're never going to have to start from ground zero. When I reconstructed my life, I could feel the change from the inside out.

Resiliency isn't measured by how quickly you pop back up after the fall. It's measured by how much you learn while you're down.

Rest. Heal. Learn. Return. It's a cycle. A looping narrative. An ethos.

A leader recognizes you can't just have the "R" of the L.E.A.D.E.R. acronym. You have to listen for the lesson, learn from it, choose how to engage differently, make sure you're authentically aligned, stay dedicated to your purpose, and be emotionally intelligent enough to understand what you need to do to heal. Then and only then are you ready to return with resilience. It's no coincidence the steps to a triumphant comeback mirror the L.E.A.D.E.R. acronym so closely.

We often describe people as resilient, and it's true that certain personalities are more adaptable or agreeable than others. But the truth behind resiliency is the same as emotional intelligence. It's a process, not a trait, and when we start identifying those patterns, we begin to see failure in a different light.

The dirty truth is there's really no such thing as failure. Only lessons to be learned. Before you dismiss this as some sort of high-minded, psychobabble *Star Wars* quote, think about the actual purpose and reasoning behind a fall. We fall because something is wrong with ourselves or our environment. We fall because we're off balance, uncentered, or trying to run too fast over uncertain ground. We fall because there's something, be it internal or external, telling us we need to change.

When you begin to look at the mechanics, you see a fall isn't necessarily a failure. It's simply an indicator that there's a way to do things better.

If you fall and don't learn, that fall is just a fall. Getting up without having learned anything is the very definition of insanity. Like a broken bone, those wounds will heal crookedly. Sure, you can keep moving forward, but at what cost? If you keep hobbling on that broken leg, how much greater is the damage going to be?

Of course, there's a time for grit. Sometimes, you just have to clench your teeth, put your head down, and suck it up, buttercup. There's value in being able to persevere when you're battered and hurting. There are seasons of life when you truly have to hustle.

However, resilience and grit are *not* the same thing. Grit is continuing on, even when things get difficult. Resilience is when you break—when you collapse, utterly incapacitated—until you find a way to start moving again. Prefabricated expectations (oh, yes, there's that #hustlelife again) would love for you to believe that grit and resilience are identical, that if you're not limping through the door at the end of the day with a baby strapped to your back, a cure for cancer in your Coach bag, and the Next Great American Novel tucked under your arm, you don't deserve to rest. But there's a huge difference between limping the last quarter mile of a marathon and trying to push through appendicitis at mile thirteen. One can be managed; the other will literally poison you.

Like every other virtue, there's a place for grit and a place for resilience. I see so many women terrified to build space for resilience because they believe a moment of rest will mean missing their goals. Nothing could be further from the truth! Goals aren't linear; the path to success is never a straight line. Even in the flattest marathon on earth, you're going to have slight dips and elevation changes somewhere in those twenty-six miles. Extend that over a lifetime, and you're looking at some veritably varied topography.

If grit and drive are the momentum that keep you moving forward over hills and across long stretches, resiliency is what bounces you back from those sudden, sharp falls. Death, loss, grief, disappointment— they're all inevitable. There's absolutely nothing we can do to avoid sharp drops and jagged canyons in our lives. We can, however, count on the fact that those moments will come. Learning from those experiences and becoming empowered by *every season* in our lives, both high and low, is what turns falls into bounces and bounces into comebacks.

I wish I could say knowing all this makes life simple. I wish I could say identifying cycles of resilience means you'll never have anything horrible to bounce back from.

But you and I both know that would be a big, fat lie.

•••

Writing this book through the COVID pandemic has been... interesting. While I've spent a lot of time revisiting my past, when I started the project, I had no idea I would be preaching to the choir. Of course, I use the L.E.A.D.E.R. acronym in every facet of my life (things are so much easier when you're making an active effort to show up as your best self), but there's something much more visceral about watching your own lessons being put to the test *while* you're writing about them.

As you can probably imagine, a global pandemic is a nightmare for preschools. Between writing and rewriting this chapter, I've been knuckling down to try and figure out what Bright Beginning's bounce back is going to look like. If a fall is a prerequisite for resilience, this pandemic has been a metaphorical knockout.

Thinking about resilience from a leadership position of any kind involves breaking the situation down in layers. At the deepest, most personal level, I know I have to keep careful tabs on my own mental health and emotional intelligence. This kind of crisis is the thing that shakes me to my core. It's completely, utterly, and helplessly out of my control. That's going to whip up a maelstrom of default responses, and I have to be cognizant about what my own resiliency is going to look like.

These ripples travel straight upward and outward. I have to

consider my teachers, staff, and administrators, each in their own personal situation with their own personal fears. I have to consider my students and what their parents are going to need during an unprecedented time like this. Then, I have to zoom out even further and consider what this means for Bright Beginning as a business. Our classes were reduced to bare-bones capacity, but that doesn't mean the bills stopped. There's still overhead, Payback Protection Program loans, salaries, ever-changing sanitation directives…

Figuring this out has taken (and currently *is taking*) some good, quality rest time, flat on my back in the dirt.

The first thing to do was recognize the preschools are in the healing and learning stages of the resiliency process. It's fair to say that we, just like everyone else, are suffering some serious blows. We need energy for damage control and sustainability, and that means we've had to cut things that are hard or downright impossible to do. This also means we've had to go back to the core values of our schools to make sure the cutbacks are aligned with our purpose of providing children a secure, loving learning environment. In the world of the "new normal," this translated to getting teachers and students through the school day as safely as we could. And if that level of safety required cutting things like our healthy meal services and requiring our kids to bring sack lunches from home, so be it.

Yes, lunch provisions are nice. Yes, it's comforting to know your kid can show up to a school where a balanced, nutritious meal is included. But for me and my team, providing food was a *want,* not a need.

When the human body is faced with extreme circumstances like deathly cold, the brain will autonomically restrict blood flow to the body's core in order to take care of the vital organs. A huge part of our resilience lesson was learning that we had to protect our core in order to survive, and that meant our day-to-day operations were going to look very different. Once we realized the scope of the pandemic and how long we were going to have to subsist in this "shrunken" state, we moved our mentality from rest to healing. We sent our staff to positive mindset training, each in rotation to learn how to implement self-care, shift into resilient mental practices, and help their coworkers do the same.

Every investment I make in my staff is an investment I make in my business. I'd learned painfully from my own breakdown that I couldn't hold everything up, so I had to change my strategy. If I took the focus off *me* being strong and instead used my resources to strengthen my *people*, Bright Beginning would be strong by default. Instead of one woman trying to heft the world on her shoulders, we would have a whole team of dedicated professionals sharing the load.

No one likes to think about teaching as a scary job, but this has been one of those seasons where the reality is downright terrifying. All the unknowns—the discoveries, the "what-ifs," the incessant news chatter—takes a toll on the spirit, and that's why I wanted to open a space to listen to my teachers' needs. We built in time to talk about their struggles, check in on their home lives, and honestly ask how they were feeling. This wasn't for accountability. It was for support. With so many things out of our control, we needed our teachers at their best. And high performance isn't about expectations—it's about *empowerment*.

We've had to be honest with each other about our fears and energy levels. We've had to be authentic about where our headspace might be drifting on any given day. If we're all holding this colossal enterprise up, we need to know who can stand in for a shift and who needs a breather. No single one of us could ever keep these schools afloat by themselves. Everyone is bound to have bad days in the pressure cooker of the pandemic, and I knew we were all eventually going to have some sort of breakdown. As long as we weren't falling apart at the *same time*, we could find a way to manage.

The world is changing fast—so fast we have to be especially deliberate about staying dedicated to our authentic purpose. Emotional intelligence has been crucial in maintaining that authenticity. Once again, a central part of my life is in turmoil, but this time, I'm checking in with myself before I hide my real emotions behind my stoic,

#kickassbosslady mask.

Yes, there's a need for grit. Yes, there's a need for stability. But I've never been so honest with my staff about feeling so, *so* scared. I didn't know where the money would come from. I didn't know when the schools were going to be back at full capacity. My people were feeling vulnerable about the situation, so I had to be completely transparent about my own vulnerability. If I was going to ask them to stay on staff through all this uncertainty, they needed to know what they were signing up for and the truth about the situation. There was no way I could keep this business running by myself. I didn't have all the answers. I needed my team behind me.

Some of my staff were able to commit to that. Others weren't. In the moment, it hurt when employees chose to leave Bright Beginning, but there was no shame in it. Not everyone was comfortable working in our circumstances, and not everyone has the same amount of emotional investment I do. I can't expect that from them. Bright Beginning, after all, is *my* business. What I needed to do as a leader in that business was provide a genuinely open place for my staff to engage if they chose to. Thanks to my past experiences, I have enough emotional intelligence to recognize this situation is far beyond my control. Each one of my staff is on their own emotional rollercoaster, and it's my job to honor that.

To be completely honest, it has been refreshing to be able to let things go without taking them personally. There's a lot of power in being able to change. In a strange, subtle way, it's evidence of healing. If I can step back and observe the cycle of resilience—the *learning* during the rest, heal, learn, return process—I don't have to be afraid.

Of course, my team and I will still be adapting as the terrain continues to shift. We will get through this pandemic, and I can rest a little easier knowing I don't have to have every single detail of our comeback worked out right at this moment. My whole staff knows we're going to come out of this celebrating. We're going to be stronger. We're going to be even more dedicated. It takes impossible circumstances to build an unbreakable team.

Resiliency is working. I recently snapped a picture of two of my teachers laughing in the breakroom and posted it on my staff page. Sure, these women are wearing masks. Sure, they're not going to hug each other. But you can still see genuine joy beneath those swatches of fabric. Their smiles shine straight through. When I look at that picture, I know for a fact these teachers show up every day because they're dedicated to their purpose. Instead of clamping down on demands, we empowered them with choices.

Never underestimate the leadership power of four simple words: *what do you need?*

This has been my go-to. *Do you need to step back? Do you need to pause? Do you need rest? Do you really have to be strong right now?*

If you make real, transparent space to learn from your people, they're going to tell you everything you need to know.

I can't tell you what lies ahead for Bright Beginning, but I trust the process of resiliency. I'm seeing it play out in real time both in and out of my business. My staff is bouncing back, and they're stronger than ever before.

On March 1st, 2020, we had one-hundred percent enrollment. One of my teachers returned from earning her master's degree, and we recently promoted a new director. Through all the anxiety, confusion, and exhaustion, I'm beginning to see that Bright Beginning is actually *better* than we were before the pandemic. Our roots run deeper. Our staff has done the growth work, and because of that, our preschools are thriving. I would never say COVID has been a fun, easy, or particularly enjoyable period in Bright Beginning's history, but I *will* say my staff can honestly look at one another and know they can weather any challenge in the future.

My team has shown remarkable resilience, and I'm committed to modeling those steps in my own life. Since 2020 was the "Year of the Dumpster Fire," I decided to make 2021 the "Year of Pause." I dedicated myself to resting. I penciled in intentional space to heal and reflect. Part of that might be my age. Part of it might just be where I happen to be in my own journey. Truth be told, I spend less time thinking about where this need comes from and more time marveling at the shift in my mentality.

Resting isn't shameful anymore. Falling isn't something to fear; it's just something that happens. I know I'm going to need space to work through these processes, but that's not because I'm weak. It's because I'm resilient.

Proactive rest is the name of the game. If I can take a moment to check in with myself and acknowledge my own needs, I'm already setting my comeback in motion.

I'm by no means a NASCAR fan, but the collective strategy of completing a five-hundred-mile race is a pretty good illustration. If you've ever watched something like the Daytona 500, you'll see the cars pulling in for pit stops throughout the race. The driver's pit crew will hustle out, refuel the car, refresh the driver, and change all four tires in *eleven and a half seconds*.

Yes. You read that right. In less than twenty seconds, that car is back on the road.

These pit crews are professionals. They're hired specifically because they're the best at their jobs. You see them bustle around throughout the race, but you don't see the hours upon hours of practice—the deliberate, synchronous teamwork orchestrated behind the scenes—that go into running these stops like clockwork.

NASCAR teams have industrialized the art of resiliency. Those drivers know when they have to pull in for a pit stop, and they don't hesitate to do so. There's no guilt about running out of gas. There's no shame in the fact that they need a moment to change piping hot tires before barreling around the track at 190 miles per hour. NASCAR drivers know this brief period of rest is critical to winning the race. They've built those stops directly into their strategy.

There are times when drivers will stretch their stops thin, especially as they near the end of the race. However, the *single most dangerous thing* a driver can do is run out of fuel or blow a tire on the track. If your car stops in the middle of the raceway, not only are your competitors zooming by at deathly speeds—you're going to have one heck of a time getting your car *off* that murderous tarmac. If you don't take time to rest and fail to space your stops out properly, there's a greater chance of losing your life than there is of crossing the finish line.

Let's have another example, maybe something a little closer to home. If you've ever run a marathon or participated in any sort of endurance sport, you know you have to keep fueling throughout the event. Sure, you may drag yourself across twenty-six miles, enervated and dehydrated, but studies have shown that marathoners who stop to eat and drink at aid stations actually record faster times than those who run straight through the checkpoints.

When I was marathon training, I knew from miserable, spaghetti-legged experience that I had to eat my power waffle at mile six. If I didn't, I would feel like complete garbage by mile eight. Power waffles (as I'm sure I've mentioned) are delicious, but the sweet, sticky goodness wasn't enough. I needed to know myself well enough to know *when* to take proactive power waffle breaks. I needed to build those breaks into my race plan and honor the fact that my body requires energy intake in order to produce output.

I'm not running marathons anymore, but the power waffle strategy has stuck with me. These days, I build little "trampolines" into my schedule—tiny pockets of time where I know I can rest, heal, learn, and recover. It's not a question of what's going to burn me out. It's knowing burnout *will* happen.

Everything in life is an exchange of energies. Work production, running marathons, cars that go fast… If I want to put effort into the world—to truly engage with authenticity according to my values—I need deliberate, routine rest. I know I'm never going to squeeze that time into my schedule, so I hardwire it in instead. There's no honor in running myself ragged trying to keep up with the hustle culture. That lifestyle isn't good for me. It's not good for my teachers and *certainly* not good for my preschools.

I work with high-achieving women, which means I work with a lot of women suffering from burnout. It's no mystery why this happens. The cruel, calloused mechanisms of the hustle gods wreak havoc in every facet of life. The solution isn't apparent, and more than often, it's not what my coaching clients want to hear.

Feeling out of control? *Let go, just for a moment.*

Running too fast? Pause. *Sit down.*

Overwhelmed and exasperated? *Listen to what those feelings are trying to tell you.*

Feeling broken, beatdown, and defeated? *Hang out in the dirt for a while. You'll be surprised by what you learn.*

We have to let go of the shame surrounding rest. We have to stop assuming that stepping back means defeat, realignment is akin to failure, and pause is the same as laziness. If you can't make space for the pause, there is no resilience—just failure after pointless, backbreaking failure.

Knowing how to rest is a powerful thing. When you learn how to rest, you learn how to heal yourself. And when you know how to heal yourself, there's no way to lose.

We know we need to put gas in our cars in order to make them go. We have specific times where we plug in our phones in order to use them efficiently throughout the day. If we can acknowledge these facts as basic principles of the natural universe, why do we judge ourselves so harshly for having the same needs?

NASCAR, power waffles, and personal power have one theme in common—the deliberate practice of *refueling.*

Resilience may be easy to see, but the cycle of resting, healing, learning, and returning goes far beyond any singular outcome. I'm a survivor by nature, but I'm resilient by choice. I'm not just going to survive the harrowing, unexpected, and even horrible things that lie ahead. I'm going to actively choose to *thrive* within them.

Resiliency takes our falls and makes them lessons. It turns our struggles into strategies and our failures into strengths. It's coming up to a brick wall and recognizing it as an opportunity rather than a barrier. When you begin to see resiliency as a lifestyle rather than a momentary reaction, you might even realize there's no such thing as barriers at all. When you're able to bounce back from anything, *there is no wall.*

The next time you fall, I highly encourage you to spend some time lying in the dirt. If you need to wallow, make space for that. If you need a moment to rededicate yourself to your values, carve out that place in time. Trust me when I say you'll be better for it. Your spouse, your family, and your team will be better for it. As leaders, we have to be intentional about the cycles we perpetuate, and if we see resiliency as a reaction rather than an intentional process, our entire community misses out on any real value.

It may be hard to know where to start when it comes to resiliency, but it's clear to me that there is no ending—just layered cycles of growth, learning, and rejuvenation. I see it in my business. I see it in myself.

Part of taking the lead is taking time to rest.

EPILOGUE

If you're driving down River Road in Crownsville, Maryland, I can't, in good faith, encourage you to divert your attention to anything besides that stretch of winding asphalt.

Seriously. Pay attention. Don't go running off the road or flattening tiny woodland creatures.

But if you do end up taking that drive, I hope you find a moment to look out the window, if only just for a glance. Depending on which season you visit, you'll be stepping into a brand-new world. Some mornings, I wake up to scintillating sheets of ice that bead the blackened tree branches like a thousand liquid diamonds. Other times, I find myself in a maelstrom of colored leaves—burning reds, golden yellows, and vivid, pumpkin oranges. There are days I open my door to a sea of rolling green. There are days when I pull out of my driveway through scraggly forest copses and pockets of pale mist.

Everything is living. Everything is dying. It's all the same and yet horribly, beautifully chaotic.

As much as I enjoy my drives down River Road, there are times when I have to walk it. Once in a while, I'll even step out of my car. When you look a little closer, you start to see how all these changing scenes are so closely interconnected. Beneath their little winter ice hats, you can spot the nubby beginnings of new, springtime buds. You notice how the mottled carpet of last autumn's leaves nourishes the springtime sprouts. You watch the animals skittering around with their summer bounties to prepare for the winter, and you witness the early spring ice melt down to water, nourishing the plants and packing down that nutrient-rich layer of last autumn's leaves.

It's all the same. It's all different. It's an eternal, linear ribbon of snapshots and snippets—mere moments of time that flow into a never-ending reel. There's life. There's death. There's growth. There's destruction. Writers have spent thousands of years trying to articulate the mechanics, but we've all come back from that endeavor emptyhanded. The closest we can get is symbolism and stories.

I would go so far as to say this is why we need stories. We have to have a way to articulate ideas beyond the scope of words, to take what we know in our hearts and somehow feed it to our heads. When I tell you that you have the inherent power to take the lead of your life and your world, there's so much more to be said. Saying you're a Leading Lady is like saying "winter is cold" or "spring is a beautiful season."

Yes, it's true on a mundane, surface level. You can look out a window during a frosty winter and empirically observe that snow gathers in white clumps.

But that's only a glimpse of the truth.

When people ask me what it takes to be a Leading Lady, my simple answer is to live at the cause of your life rather than the effects. In my humble opinion, it's a pretty good answer, but as far as taglines go, it's not particularly empowering.

This is why I love the L.E.A.D.E.R. acronym. Of course, it can be superficially misinterpreted. Of course, it's not as poetic as an ode to nature or some sobering fable. What I love about this acronym is that it's a start.

Clear as mud, right?

I look at the acronym the way I look at nature. There's no definite place to start. There's no *real* end to one season signaling the beginning of the next, and that same season is going to vary from year to year. There is no checklist. There are no rules. We can sit there kvetching about how unseasonably hot it is or how rain isn't "supposed" to come here or there, but anyone who has ever tried to foist their own expectations on the natural world is destined to be bitterly disappointed.

When I tell women they have the power to take the lead in their lives, I'm not talking about rules, checklists, and requirements. Truly stepping up as a leader is going to look different in every season of your life. It's not a single action; it's a collection of greater, outpouring cycles that ripple into every facet of your life. Your listening, learning, engagement, authenticity, dedication, emotional intelligence, and resilience aren't separate actions or even a linear ethos. They feed off of and bleed into each other like the seasons on River Road.

As I've said many times in this book, no one magically wakes up as a Leading Lady. A leader isn't something you are or aren't. It's every conscious choice you make—the amalgamation of thousands of tiny decisions, actions, and beliefs. A leader, by nature, is constantly changing and growing. A listener and learner is constantly reassessing the wider world around her, seeking how to engage with dedication according to her values. She's thriving through change and adaptation, relishing the cycles of resilience as she falls, rises up, and then returns stronger than before.

On and on the cycle goes, as winter to spring to summer to fall, each stage beautiful and different in its own right. There are easy seasons and difficult ones, scorching summers and gentle springs. When we look for the lesson wherever we're at, we see the value in that season, despite the circumstances. No matter where you find yourself, you're either winning or learning—surviving or thriving.

Taking the lead isn't an action. It's a never-ending journey.

Since there's no way I could possibly capture the real heart of the Leading Ladies, my sincere hope is that this book helps paint an outline. There's so much more to these stories than I could ever put down on paper. The people, the places, the lessons, the losses… Not all of it belongs in the pages of this book, and there are many parts of the story that just aren't my tale to tell.

But this isn't a book about my life. This is a book about the lessons I've learned—the beautiful, golden scars that have shown me what it means to take the lead in my own life. I didn't wake up with a divine epiphany. It's not some perfect, fairytale formula you can pick up and put down when you please. Being a leader is real, it's raw, and it makes all the difference in the universe.

I've seen the change in my marriage. I've seen it in my family. I've seen it in *me*.

That's why the last word in this book is by no means an ending. To be a Leading Lady is to undertake a lifelong adventure, and just like the seasons on River Road, I never want that adventure to end. I will constantly be growing and changing, and so will the world around me. When you take the time to know yourself and your values, the ups and downs in life aren't threats—they're opportunities.

When I look down at my hands, I can hardly believe what I see. These clean, manicured fingernails belong to the same hands that were grubby after playing with my cousins in our Filipino village, bunched into fists when lashing back at the world, shaking on the side of the highway when I realized my life had no purpose, and perfectly poised as I stood up on pageant stages, trying to hide my pain.

These strange, scarred hands can do beautiful things. They've shown me I don't have to live in my default—that it's a good and honorable thing to be a different person than I was yesterday. My hands remind me I can give myself space when I need it and I don't have to hold on to everything myself. They're a testament that I can choose to live for my life's cause rather than at the mercy of my circumstances. When I look down at my hands, I see the same endless potential I see in every Leading Lady.

You have the power to take the lead. You have the choice to live a dedicated life of purpose. Be a learner and a listener. Dig deep for your values, whatever they may be, and don't settle for anything less. Engage as the person you want to be—the very best version of yourself—knowing that you can always take a moment to change your shirt.

Stay dedicated to your purpose. Let that dedication shine when everything else in your world has gone dark. Be brave enough to face yourself in your deepest of hearts, even when those feelings are complicated and uncomfortable. Use your emotions as tools and not weapons. Make the time and space to see how your decisions impact others. Embrace the pause. Treasure peace. Build cycles of resilience into your world so there is no more failure, only learning, healing, and opportunity.

No matter where you come from or what that journey looks like, we need you. We need your strength. We need your wisdom. We need your time, treasures, and talents. We need your light. We need your stories.

We need you to take the lead.

If you're already a Leading Lady, know that our world needs *you*. Women have always been in the lead; we're just not being quiet about it anymore. And if you're just now joining us at the leadership table, let me be the first to welcome you. It doesn't matter where you are. It doesn't matter where you've been or what your hands look like.

Please, pull up a chair. We've been saving you a seat.

REFERENCES

Below, you'll find attributions for the literature, speeches, and publications mentioned in this book. Though these words and ideas were not my own, they played a formative role in my own journey, and I highly recommend further reading.

Page 3, "Don't be fooled."

Charles C Finn, "Please Hear What I'm Not Saying," in *For the Mystically Inclined* (Bloomington: 1stbooks, 2002), page 3, lines 1-8.

Page 63, "The pain body."

Eckhart Tolle, *The Power of Now: A Guide to Spiritual Enlightenment* (Novato and Vancouver: New World Library and Namaste Publishing, 2004).

Page 212, "The SCARF model."

David Rock, "SCARF: A Brain-Based Model for Collaborating with and Influencing Others," *The NeuroLeadership Journal*, (2008).

ABOUT THE AUTHOR

AliceAnne Loftus was born in the Philippines. Having moved over a dozen times as a child with her military family, she loves being able to call Annapolis, Maryland, her home. While her educational background is rooted in early childhood education, she has been an entrepreneur and business owner for nearly two decades and uses her experience to coach high-achieving women. "Empowered women empower women," and the strength of community and connection have inspired her to live this motto.

Like many women juggling a myriad of responsibilities, AliceAnne balances her roles as a wife, mother, friend, businesswoman, and community leader dedicated to living, loving, and leading as her best authentic self. Her beloved English Setter, Millie, certainly helps her along that journey.

ACKNOWLEDGEMENTS

Thank you to Hannah Kates, the most talented writer I've ever had the privilege of working with. She is a word wizard and has the remarkable ability to take my thoughts and words and translate them beautifully so I could share my story.

My husband, Marty. My greatest support and the foundation of our family. Thank you for always being my champion and believing in me even when I had trouble believing in myself.

My children, Marissa and Christian, for letting me share their stories and the lessons I've learned about myself as I've navigated this amazing (and terrifying) road called parenting. You're my inspiration.

My mother, Consuelo, reminds me of the Zen proverb: "Only when you can be extremely pliable and soft can you be extremely hard and strong." Thank you for teaching me when to stand strong and connected to my roots as well as when to bend with the winds of life so as not to break.

To the women I've had the honor to share my journey with over the last forty years. I've learned so much and have been inspired by so many. I truly believe that empowered women empower women. When we live in a world where we're not only lifting each other up but also celebrating one another, we all win.

To all who have loved me, cheered me on, and championed me when I moved towards my goals, discovered myself, and evolved. Your encouragement has kept me going with focus and determination.

Finally, to all who doubted me, tried to tell me I was "too much," or chose not to love and accept me for who I am. You have been an invaluable part of my journey. Thank you for reminding me I was not meant to live and lead small. Thank you for helping me set the boundaries for what I will not settle for. Thank you for the lessons that could only come from pain.

A quick note from the author.

If you purchased this book, thank you.

If you read this book, thank you.

If you didn't read or buy this book but still picked it up and flipped to this page, thank you.

I'm honored to play even the smallest part in your day, and if you have three minutes, I would like to ask you a huge favor.

Please consider leaving a review on Amazon, Goodreads, or Google Books. An online review is one of the best ways you can support authors—aside from recommending their book to a fellow leading lady.

Thank you in advance. Your love and support empower me.

Scan the QR code to learn more about the Leading Lady community.

Facebook Group
Collective and Ambassador Programs
Group Masterclass
Private Coaching
Workshops and Events
Podcast

CPSIA information can be obtained
at www.ICGtesting.com
Printed in the USA
BVHW041125161122
651143BV00006B/74/J

9 798985 136005